중학 영문법

클리어.

Grammar clear

Level 1

문법 개념과 내신을 한번에 끝내는
중학 영문법 클리어

문장 구조 시각화로 **핵심 문법 개념 CLEAR!**
시험포인트 및 비교포인트로 **헷갈리는 문법 CLEAR!**
더 확대된 실전테스트로 **학교 시험 대비 CLEAR!**

학습자의 마음을 읽는 **동아영어콘텐츠연구팀**
동아영어콘텐츠연구팀은 동아출판의 영어 개발 연구원, 현장 선생님, 그리고 전문 원고 집필자들이
공동연구를 통해 최적의 콘텐츠를 개발하는 연구조직입니다.

원고 개발에 참여하신 분들
강남숙 신영주 이유진 최현진 홍미정 홍석현

교재 검토에 도움을 주신 분들
강군필 강은주 고미선 김민성 김은영 김우경 김호성 백명숙 신영주 이상훈
이지혜 임남주 정나래 정은주 정혜승 조수진 조은혜 최재천 최현진 한지영

중학 영문법 클리어.

Level 1

STRUCTURES 구성과 특징

1 | 문장 시각화로 핵심 문법을 한 눈에 이해!

---

unit 01 be동사의 현재형과 과거형

1

1 be동사

be동사는 '~이다', '(~에) 있다'로 해석하며, be동사 뒤에는 명사나 형용사, 장소의 부사(구)가 온다.

He	is	a student.	그는 학생이다. (be동사+명사)
		happy.	그는 행복하다. (be동사+형용사)
		in the classroom.	그는 교실에 있다. (be동사+장소의 부사(구))

'be동사+명사 / 형용사」: ~이다, 'be동사+장소의 부사(구)」: (~에) 있다

2 be동사의 현재형

be동사의 현재형은 주어의 인칭과 수(단수, 복수)에 따라 형태가 달라지며, 주어와 be동사는 줄임말로 쓸 수 있다.

	단수		줄임말	복수		줄임말
1인칭	I	am	I'm	Minsu and I [We]	are	We're
2인칭	You	are	You're	Jimin and you [You]	are	You're
3인칭	Kevin [He] Jenny [She] The car [It]	is	He's She's It's	Kevin and Jenny [They]	are	They're

I am hungry now. = **I'm** hungry now.
You are very smart. = **You're** very smart.
She is a famous writer. = **She's** a famous writer.
They are at the park. = **They're** at the park.

3 be동사의 과거형

be동사의 과거형은 주어가 단수일 때는 was, 복수일 때는 were를 쓰며 '~이었다', '(~에) 있었다'로 해석한다.

I	was	13 years old last year.	작년에 13살이었다
Mark		in Beijing two weeks ago.	2주 전에 베이징에 있었다
The boys	were	late for school yesterday.	어제 학교에 늦었다

Ms. Baker **was** very busy last weekend.
We **were** in the same class two years ago.

2

시험 point 주어의 인칭과 수 파악하기

주어의 인칭과 수를 잘 파악해서 be동사를 사용해야 한다.

1 Your book (is / are) on your desk.
2 Mina and Jake (is / are) my friends.

012 중학영문법 클리어 LEVEL 1

3

Answers p. 2

개념 우선 확인 1 밑줄 친 be동사의 옳은 뜻에 고르기

1 Leo is my brother.	2 Leo is happy now.	3 Leo is in Seoul.
☐ ~이다	☐ ~이다	☐ ~이다
☐ ~에 있다	☐ ~에 있다	☐ ~에 있다

A 괄호 안에서 알맞은 것을 고르시오.

1 This game (is / are) very popular.
2 He and I (am / are) in the same class.
3 Jim (was / were) the school president last year.
4 Kelly and Luke (are / were) at school yesterday.

B 밑줄 친 부분을 줄임말 형태로 바꿔 쓰시오.

1 He is from Japan.
2 They are twins.
3 I am ready for school.
4 We are at the market now.

C 우리말과 일치하도록 알맞은 be동사를 써서 문장을 완성하시오.

1 오늘 날씨가 좋다.
→ The weather _____ nice today.
2 그녀는 10년 전에 부자였다.
→ She _____ rich 10 years ago.
3 그의 열쇠들이 탁자 위에 있다.
→ His keys _____ on the table.
4 내 사촌들은 지난 토요일에 그 콘서트에 있었다.
→ My cousins _____ at the concert last Saturday.

4

30초 완성 map

be동사	현재형	I (am / are) a doctor.	나는 _____.
		She (is / am) in the room.	그녀는 _____.
		You (is / are) tall.	너는 키가 크다.
	과거형	He (is / was) tired yesterday.	그는 어제 _____.
		They (was / were) in London last week.	그들은 지난주에 _____.

Chapter 01 be동사 013

---

① 핵심 문법 개념 확인

문장 구조를 시각화하여 꼭 알아야 할 핵심 기본 문법들을 이해하기 쉽게 설명

③ 개념 우선 확인

본격적인 문제로 넘어가기 전 문법 개념 이해를 다시 한번 확인하는 단계

② 시험 POINT & 비교 POINT

시험에 자주 나오거나 혼동되는 문법 개념들을 다시 한번 짚어주고 복습하는 장치

④ 30초 완성 MAP

다음 Unit으로 넘어가기 전에 map을 완성하며 해당 Unit의 문법 개념을 잘 이해했는지 확인하는 코너

2 | 서술형 집중 훈련 & 시험 출제 포인트 확인

서술형 대비 문장 쓰기

- 서술형 쓰기에 많이 나오는 4가지 유형(문장 완성, 오류 수정, 문장 전환, 영작 완성)을 집중 훈련

시험에 꼭 나오는 출제 포인트

- 시험에 꼭 나오는 중요한 문법 출제 포인트를 한번 더 확인
- 고득점 Point로 내신 고난도 문제 대비

3 | 실전 TEST로 학교 시험 완벽 대비

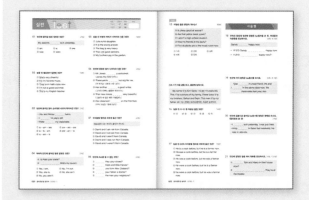

실전 TEST

- 어려워진 내신 시험에 대비하기 위한 최신 기출 유형과 고난도 유형 반영
- 서술형 문항 추가로 학교 시험 완벽 대비

+ WORKBOOK

본책 학습 뒤 Unit마다 2쪽으로 구성된 연습문제를 풀며 부족한 부분을 추가로 학습할 수 있도록 구성

- 개념 확인, 어법 선택, 어법 수정, 문장 전환, 영작 등 학습 유형별 문제 제시로 자학자습 효과 향상

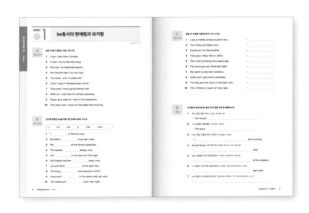

 CONTENTS 차례

품사는 각각의 **단어를 쓰임새와 역할에 따라 나눈 것**으로, 영어에는 다음과 같이 8개의 품사가 있다.

명사 사람이나 사물, 장소 등의 이름을 나타내는 말
예 girl, apple, ball, cat, school, Seoul 등

a **hat**

형용사 사람이나 사물의 모습이나 색깔, 성질 등을 나타내는 말
예 big, tall, pretty, colorful, cute 등

an **empty** hat

대명사 명사를 대신하는 말
예 she, he, it, they, we 등

It's my hat.

동사 사람이나 사물의 움직임이나 상태를 나타내는 말
예 eat, play, study, sleep, make 등

wear the hat

Quiz **1** **다음 단어들의 품사를 빈칸에 쓰시오.**

1	book		**2**	pretty	
3	she		**4**	run	
5	Tom		**6**	cute	

접속사 단어와 단어, 구와 구, 문장과 문장을 연결해주는 말
예 and, but, or, so, when, if 등

a hat **and** a stick

부사 동사, 형용사, 부사 또는 문장 전체를 꾸며주는 말
예 very, quickly, slowly, fast, soon 등

Look **carefully**!

전치사 명사나 대명사 앞에 쓰여 시간, 장소, 수단 등의 뜻을 더해주는 말
예 in, at, on, to, for, with, from 등

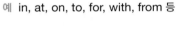

a rabbit **in** the hat

감탄사 말하는 사람의 기쁨, 놀람 등의 감정을 표현하는 말
예 Wow!, Oh!, Oops!, Ouch! 등

Oops!

Quiz ❷ **다음 단어들의 품사를 빈칸에 쓰시오.**

1	and		**2**	very
3	in		**4**	wow
5	happily		**6**	with

영어 문장을 이루는 구성 요소에는 **주어, 동사, 목적어, 보어**가 있다.

1 주어

동작이나 상태의 주체가 되는 말로, '~은/는/이/가'로 해석한다.

The baby + cries.
주어   동사

그 아기가 운다.

2 동사

주어의 동작이나 상태를 나타내는 말로, '~이다/하다'로 해석한다.

The baby + **smiles.**
주어   동사

그 아기가 **웃는다.**

3 목적어

동사의 대상이 되는 말로, '~을/를'로 해석한다. 목적어는 주로 동사 뒤에 온다.

The baby + drinks + **milk.**
주어   동사   목적어

그 아기가 **우유를** 마신다.

4 보어

주어나 목적어를 보충 설명해 주는 말로, 주격보어는 주어를 보충 설명하고, 목적격보어는 목적어를 보충 설명한다.

The baby + is + **happy.**
주어   동사   보어

그 아기는 **기쁘다.**
〈주격보어〉

The baby + makes + us + **happy.**
주어   동사   목적어   보어

그 아기는 우리를 **기쁘게** 만든다.
〈목적격보어〉

Quiz ❸   **밑줄 친 부분에 해당하는 문장의 구성 요소를 빈칸에 쓰시오.**

1 They are honest.

2 Mom made this dress.

품사와 문장 구성 요소의 관계

문장의 각 구성 요소에는 특정한 품사들만 올 수 있다.

주어 자리	동사 자리	목적어 자리	보어 자리
명사	동사	명사	명사
대명사		대명사	대명사
			형용사

	Jennie	+	**has**	+	**cookies.**	Jennie는 쿠키를 가지고 있다.
구성 요소	주어		동사		목적어	
품사	명사		동사		명사	

	She	+	**made**	+	**them.**	그녀가 그것들을 만들었다.
구성 요소	주어		동사		목적어	
품사	대명사		동사		대명사	

	They	+	**are**	+	**delicious.**	그것들은 맛있다.
구성 요소	주어		동사		보어	
품사	대명사		동사		형용사	

	Jennie	+	**is**	+	**a cook.**	Jennie는 요리사이다.
구성 요소	주어		동사		보어	
품사	명사		동사		명사	

Quiz ④ 밑줄 친 부분에 해당하는 문장의 구성 요소와 품사를 빈칸에 쓰시오.

1 The boys are tall.

구성 요소		
품사		

2 They watched a movie.

구성 요소		
품사		

Answers for Quiz

Q1 1 명사 2 형용사 3 대명사 4 동사 5 명사 6 형용사   Q2 1 접속사 2 부사 3 전치사 4 감탄사 5 부사 6 전치사
Q3 1 주어, 보어 2 동사, 목적어   Q4 1 주어 – 명사, 보어 – 형용사 2 주어 – 대명사, 목적어 – 명사

chapter

01

be동사

나 배고파.

Q. "나 배고파."를 영어로 표현하면?

☐ I hungry.　　☐ I am hungry.

be동사의 현재형과 과거형

1 be동사

be동사는 '~이다', '(~에) 있다'로 해석하며, be동사 뒤에는 명사나 형용사, 장소의 부사(구)가 온다.

He	is	a student.	그는 학생**이다**. 〈be동사+**명사**〉
		happy.	그는 행복하**다**. 〈be동사+**형용사**〉
		in the classroom.	그는 교실에 **있다**. 〈be동사+**장소의 부사(구)**〉

주의 「be동사+명사/형용사」: ~이다, 「be동사+장소의 부사(구)」: (~에) 있다

2 be동사의 현재형

be동사의 현재형은 주어의 인칭과 수(단수, 복수)에 따라 형태가 달라지며, 주어와 be동사는 줄임말로 쓸 수 있다.

	단수		줄임말	복수		줄임말
1인칭	I	am	I'm	Minsu and I [**We**]	are	We're
2인칭	You	are	You're	Jimin and you [**You**]	are	You're
3인칭	Kevin [**He**] Jenny [**She**] The car [**It**]	is	He's She's It's	Kevin and Jenny [**They**]	are	They're

I am hungry now. = **I'm** hungry now.
You are very smart. = **You're** very smart.
She is a famous writer. = **She's** a famous writer.
They are at the park. = **They're** at the park.

3 be동사의 과거형

be동사의 과거형은 주어가 단수일 때는 was, 복수일 때는 were를 쓰며 '~이었다', '(~에) 있었다'로 해석한다.

I	**was**	13 years old *last year*.	*작년에* 13살**이었다**
Mark		in Beijing *two weeks ago*.	*2주 전에* 베이징에 **있었다**
The boys	**were**	late for school *yesterday*.	*어제* 학교에 늦**었다**

Ms. Baker **was** very busy *last weekend*.
We **were** in the same class *two years ago*.

시험 point

주어의 인칭과 수 파악하기

주어의 인칭과 수를 잘 파악해서 be동사를 사용해야 한다.

1 Your book (is / are) on your desk.

2 Mina and Jake (is / are) my friends.

개념 우선 확인 | 밑줄 친 be동사의 옳은 의미 고르기

1 Leo <u>is</u> my brother.
- ☐ ~이다
- ☐ ~에 있다

2 Leo <u>is</u> happy now.
- ☐ ~이다
- ☐ ~에 있다

3 Leo <u>is</u> in Seoul.
- ☐ ~이다
- ☐ ~에 있다

A 괄호 안에서 알맞은 것을 고르시오.

1 This game (is / are) very popular.

2 He and I (am / are) in the same class.

3 Jim (was / were) the school president last year.

4 Kelly and Luke (are / were) at school yesterday.

B 밑줄 친 부분을 줄임말 형태로 바꿔 쓰시오.

1 <u>He is</u> from Japan. _____

2 <u>They are</u> twins. _____

3 <u>I am</u> ready for school. _____

4 <u>We are</u> at the market now. _____

C 우리말과 일치하도록 알맞은 be동사를 써서 문장을 완성하시오.

1 오늘 날씨가 좋다.

→ The weather _____ nice today.

2 그녀는 10년 전에 부자였다.

→ She _____ rich 10 years ago.

3 그의 열쇠들이 탁자 위에 있다.

→ His keys _____ on the table.

4 내 사촌들은 지난 토요일에 그 콘서트에 있었다.

→ My cousins _____ at the concert last Saturday.

30초 완성 map

be동사	현재형	❶ I (am / are) a doctor. She (is / am) in the room. You (is / are) tall.	나는 _____. 그녀는 _____. 너는 키가 크다.
	과거형	❷ He (is / was) tired yesterday. They (was / were) in London last week.	그는 어제 _____. 그들은 지난주에 _____.

be동사의 부정문

1 be동사 현재형의 부정문

「am/are/is+not」의 형태로 '~이 아니다', '(~에) 없다'라고 해석한다.

			줄임말
I **am**		sleepy.	**I'm not**
She **is**	not	a singer.	He/She/It **isn't**
They **are**		in the room.	We/You/They **aren't**

Mark **is not** angry.
= Mark **isn't** angry.

The girl **is not** my cousin.
= The girl **isn't** my cousin.

His friends **are not** in the stadium.
= His friends **aren't** in the stadium.

2 be동사 과거형의 부정문

「was/were+not」의 형태로 '~이 아니었다', '(~에) 없었다'라고 해석한다.

			줄임말
I **was**		busy.	I **wasn't**
He **was**	not	a soccer player.	He/She/It **wasn't**
They **were**		late for the meeting.	We/You/They **weren't**

The box **was not** heavy.
= The box **wasn't** heavy.

It **was not** your book.
= It **wasn't** your book.

Joe and Daniel **were not** in Seoul last year.
= Joe and Daniel **weren't** in Seoul last year.

시험
point

줄임말로 쓸 수 없는 경우

am not과 This is는 줄임말로 쓰지 않는다.

1 (I'm not / I amn't) a nurse.

2 (This's / This is) my new English teacher.

1 _____ a teacher.
☐ I amn't
☐ I'm not

2 _____ foolish.
☐ You aren't
☐ You isn't

3 _____ late yesterday.
☐ He isn't
☐ He wasn't

A 괄호 안에서 알맞은 것을 고르시오.

1 My parents (isn't / aren't) teachers.

2 The toys (weren't / wasn't) in the box.

3 He (is not / was not) hungry two hours ago.

4 Mark and I (am not / are not) in the library now.

B 밑줄 친 부분을 줄임말 형태로 바꿔 쓰시오.

1 The cake is not delicious. _____

2 I am not ready for the test. _____

3 The books were not difficult. _____

4 The weather was not hot yesterday. _____

C 우리말과 일치하도록 빈칸에 알맞은 말을 넣어 문장을 완성하시오.

1 내 모자가 그 가방 안에 없다.
→ My cap _____ _____ in the bag.

2 그녀는 경찰관이 아니었다.
→ She _____ _____ a police officer.

3 내 여동생은 어제 아프지 않았다.
→ My sister _____ sick yesterday.

4 우리 부모님은 지난주에 바쁘지 않으셨다.
→ My parents _____ busy last week.

5 Tom과 나는 더 이상 같은 동아리에 있지 않다.
→ Tom and I _____ _____ in the same club anymore.

30초 완성 map

be동사의 부정문	현재형	❶ I (am not / amn't) hungry.	나는 배고프지 않다.
		They (isn't / aren't) at the party.	그들은 파티에 없다.
		He (isn't / aren't) my uncle.	그는 나의 _____.
	과거형	❷ She (wasn't / weren't) busy yesterday.	그녀는 어제 바쁘지 않았다.
		We (wasn't / weren't) in Busan last night.	우리는 어젯밤에 _____.

be동사의 의문문

1 be동사 현재형의 의문문

「Am/Are/Is+주어 ~?」의 형태로 '~이니?', '(~에) 있니?'라고 해석한다.

긍정의 대답은 「Yes, 주어+am/are/is.」로 하고, 부정의 대답은 「No, 주어+am/are/is+not.」으로 한다.

		긍정의 대답	부정의 대답
Am I		Yes, you are.	No, you aren't.
Are you	on Main Street?	Yes, I am.	No, I'm not.
Is she		Yes, she is.	No, she isn't.

A **Are you** pilots? → Are you 뒤에 복수명사(pilots)가 오므로 we로 답한다.
B Yes, **we** are. / No, **we** aren't.

A Is **your brother** in the bathroom?
B Yes, **he** is. / No, **he** isn't.
→ 의문문에 대한 대답은 의문문의 주어를 대명사로 바꿔 답한다.

2 be동사 과거형의 의문문

「Was/Were+주어 ~?」의 형태로 '~이었니?', '(~에) 있었니?'라고 해석한다.

긍정의 대답은 「Yes, 주어+was/were.」로 하고, 부정의 대답은 「No, 주어+was/were+not.」으로 한다.

		긍정의 대답	부정의 대답
Was he	late for class?	Yes, he was.	No, he wasn't.
Were they		Yes, they were.	No, they weren't.

A **Was she** your English teacher last year?
B Yes, she was. / No, she wasn't.

A **Were your parents** in Paris last month?
B Yes, they were. / No, they weren't.

❯ be동사의 의문문에 대한 부정의 대답에서 am not을 제외한 「be동사+not」은 주로 줄임말로 쓴다.

비교
point

'너'와 '너희들'을 모두 나타내는 you

Are you ~?에 대한 적절한 답을 판단할 때는 Are you 뒤에 오는 명사가 단수인지 복수인지 확인해야 한다.

1 A Are you a dancer?
  B Yes, (I am / we are).

2 A Are you dancers?
  B No, (I'm not / we aren't).

개념 우선 확인 | 옳은 해석 고르기

1 Are you at school?
- ☐ 너는 학교에 있니?
- ☐ 너는 학교에 있었니?

2 Is your mom home?
- ☐ 너의 엄마는 집에 계시니?
- ☐ 너의 엄마는 집에 계셨니?

3 Were you busy?
- ☐ 너는 바쁘니?
- ☐ 너는 바빴니?

A 괄호 안에서 알맞은 것을 고르시오.

1 (Are / Is) the cookies delicious?

2 (Was / Were) the children polite?

3 (Are / Is) your aunt a teacher, too?

4 (Are / Is) Eva and Simon from Germany?

5 (Was / Were) your father in Spain last year?

B 빈칸에 알맞은 말을 넣어 의문문에 대한 답을 완성하시오.

1 A Are you from Canada? **B** Yes, _____ _____.

2 A Is this your cell phone? **B** No, _____ _____.

3 A Was he in the living room? **B** Yes, _____ _____.

4 A Were they happy at the party? **B** No, _____ _____.

C 우리말과 일치하도록 괄호 안의 말과 be동사를 이용하여 문장을 완성하시오.

1 그 영화는 재미있니? (the movie)

→ _____ _____ _____ exciting?

2 그 셔츠들은 비싸니? (the shirts)

→ _____ _____ _____ expensive?

3 그 학생들은 운동장에 있었니? (the students)

→ _____ _____ _____ on the playground?

4 너의 아빠는 2020년에 뉴욕에 계셨니? (your dad)

→ _____ _____ _____ in New York in 2020?

30초 완성 map

be동사의 의문문

현재형

A Am I in the wrong class? **B** Yes, _____ _____.

A _____ _____ a pianist? **B** No, I'm not.

A Is your sister cute? **B** Yes, _____ _____.

과거형

A _____ your grandpa busy? **B** Yes, _____ was.

A _____ they at work yesterday? **B** No, they _____.

서술형 대비 문장 쓰기

□ 빈칸 완성   괄호 안의 말과 be동사를 이용하여 빈칸 완성하기

01   Jordan과 나는 축구선수이다. (I)

→ Jordan and _____ _____ soccer players.

02   그 가게는 너의 집 근처에 있니? (the store)

→ _____ _____ _____ near your house?

03   그 아이는 어제 수업 시간에 조용하지 않았다. (the child)

→ _____ _____ _____ quiet in class yesterday.

04   그 책들이 서점에 있었니? (the books)

→ _____ _____ _____ in the bookstore?

✓ 오류 수정   어법에 맞게 문장 고쳐 쓰기

05   I amn't an actor.

→ _____ an actor.

06   The students is very diligent.

→ The students _____ .

07   Tim and Jina is not in the garden now.

→ Tim and Jina _____ now.

08   Are they at the amusement park yesterday?

→ _____ yesterday?

≡ 배열 영작   괄호 안의 말을 바르게 배열하기

09   그 마술쇼는 10대들에게 인기가 있다. (popular, the magic show, is)

→ _____ with teens.

10   내 친구들은 파자마 파티에 늦지 않았다. (weren't, my friends, late)

→ _____ for the pajama party.

11   저 놀이기구는 재미있었니? (exciting, that ride, was)

→ _____

12   그 온라인 게임들은 쉽지 않다. (not, the online games, easy, are)

→ _____

시험에 꼭 나오는 출제 포인트

Answers p. 2

출제 포인트 ❶ 주어의 인칭과 수를 파악하여 be동사를 사용하자!

빈칸에 들어갈 말이 순서대로 바르게 짝지어진 것은?

> • Sora _____ very honest.
> • The children _____ at school now.

① is – am ② is – is ③ is – are

④ are – is ⑤ are – are

고득점 POINT and로 연결된 복수 주어

우리말과 일치하도록 빈칸에 알맞은 be동사를 쓰시오.

Amy와 David는 10살이다.

→ Amy and David _____ 10 years old.

출제 포인트 ❷ 시간 표현으로 시제를 파악하자!

밑줄 친 부분을 바르게 고쳐 쓰시오.

(1) My friends <u>were</u> in Hong Kong now. → _____

(2) Her brother <u>isn't</u> busy yesterday. → _____

출제 포인트 ❸ 줄임말로 쓸 수 없는 경우를 기억하자!

밑줄 친 줄임말이 <u>잘못된</u> 것은?

① <u>You're</u> very pretty.
② <u>This's</u> a present for you.
③ <u>I'm</u> not a basketball player.
④ The museum <u>wasn't</u> open yesterday.
⑤ Ben and Jenny <u>weren't</u> in the hospital.

출제 포인트 ❹ 질문에 답할 때 주어는 대명사로 바꾸자!

알맞은 대명사와 be동사를 써서 대답을 완성하시오.

(1) **A** Is your sister a musician?

　　B Yes, _____ _____.

(2) **A** Were Jisu and Minho at the library
　　　yesterday?

　　B No, _____ _____.

고득점 POINT 주어 you가 단수인지 복수인지 파악해야 한다.

빈칸에 알맞은 말을 넣어 대화를 완성하시오.

A Are you middle school students?

B No, _____ _____.

유형	문항수	배점	점수
객관식	17	60	
서술형	10	40	

01 빈칸에 들어갈 말로 알맞은 것은? |3점|

My parents _____ sick yesterday.

① am ② is ③ are
④ was ⑤ were

02 밑줄 친 줄임말이 잘못된 것은? |3점|

① She's very cheerful.
② It's my favorite music.
③ They're in math class now.
④ I'm not a good swimmer.
⑤ This's my English teacher.

03 빈칸에 들어갈 말이 순서대로 바르게 짝지어진 것은? |3점|

• Jisu and Minsu _____ twins.
• I _____ 14 years old.
• Peter _____ my classmate.

① is – am – are ② are – am – are
③ is – is – am ④ are – am – is
⑤ is – am – is

04 대화의 빈칸에 들어갈 말로 알맞은 것은? |3점|

A Is Kate your sister?
B _____ She's my cousin.

① Yes, I am. ② No, I'm not.
③ Yes, she is. ④ No, she isn't.
⑤ No, you aren't.

05 밑줄 친 부분의 의미가 나머지와 **다른** 것은? |3점|

① Julia <u>is</u> his daughter.
② It <u>is</u> the wrong answer.
③ The bag <u>is</u> very heavy.
④ They <u>are</u> good dancers.
⑤ My brothers <u>are</u> in the garden.

06 빈칸에 알맞은 말이 나머지와 **다른** 것은? |3점|

① Mr. Jones _____ a cartoonist.
(Jones 씨는 만화가이다.)
② These pants _____ too big for me.
(이 바지는 나에게 너무 크다.)
③ Her brother _____ a good writer.
(그녀의 오빠는 훌륭한 작가이다.)
④ Their new house _____ very beautiful.
(그들의 새 집은 매우 아름답다.)
⑤ Our classroom _____ on the first floor.
(우리 교실은 1층에 있다.)

07 우리말을 영어로 바르게 옮긴 것은? |3점|

David와 나는 캐나다 출신이 아니다.

① David and I am not from Canada.
② David and I not are from Canada.
③ David and I aren't from Canada.
④ David and I was not from Canada.
⑤ David and I weren't from Canada.

08 빈칸에 **Are**를 쓸 수 **없는** 것은? |3점|

① _____ they your shoes?
② _____ Mark and Ellie friends?
③ _____ you from New Zealand?
④ _____ your father a doctor?
⑤ _____ the men your neighbors?

09 빈칸에 들어갈 말이 순서대로 바르게 짝지어진 것은? |3점|

A _____ you at the library an hour ago?
B Yes, I _____ .

① Are – am   ② Are – was
③ Was – were   ④ Were – am
⑤ Were – was

10 빈칸에 들어갈 be동사가 〈보기〉와 같은 것은? |4점|

보기 The tickets _____ not in the bag last night.

① It _____ very hot today.
② Mike _____ not happy this morning.
③ My sister _____ 20 years old last year.
④ The stores _____ not open now.
⑤ Kevin and Sam _____ in their classroom 30 minutes ago.

고난도
11 다음 중 대화가 어법상 **틀린** 것은? |5점|

① A Am I right?
   B Yes, you are.
② A Are you his fans?
   B Yes, I am.
③ A Was she a designer?
   B No, she wasn't.
④ A Were you tired then?
   B No, I wasn't.
⑤ A Were Eric and Sam kind to you?
   B Yes, they were.

12 다음 중 어법상 옳은 문장은? |4점|

① I am scared last night.
② Are your name Minho?
③ Their story was surprising.
④ The shoes was too expensive.
⑤ The movie not was interesting.

13 대화의 빈칸에 공통으로 들어갈 말로 알맞은 것은? |3점|

A Is your grandma in the living room?
B _____ She's in the kitchen.
A Is your mom with her?
B _____ She's in her room.

① Yes, she is.   ② Yes, they are.
③ No, it isn't.   ④ No, she isn't.
⑤ No, they aren't.

최신기출 고난도
14 빈칸 ⓐ~ⓔ에 들어갈 말이 **잘못** 짝지어진 것은? |5점|

A Jenny, _____ⓐ_____ pizza your favorite food?
B No, _____ⓑ_____ isn't. My favorite food _____ⓒ_____ spaghetti.
A Are you a good cook?
B No, _____ⓓ_____ not. But my dad _____ⓔ_____ a great cook. I love his spaghetti.

① ⓐ: are   ② ⓑ: it
③ ⓒ: is   ④ ⓓ: I'm
⑤ ⓔ: is

15 어법상 옳은 문장의 개수는? |5점|

> ⓐ Is Jessy good at soccer?
> ⓑ Are that yellow book yours?
> ⓒ I amn't a high school student.
> ⓓ Was his friends at the party?
> ⓔ Five students are in the music room now.

① 1개 　　② 2개 　　③ 3개
④ 4개 　　⑤ 5개

[16-17] 다음 글을 읽고, 물음에 답하시오.

> My name ⓐis Kim Sena. I ⓑam 13 years old.
> This ⓒis a picture of my family. These boys ⓓis
> my brothers, Sehun and Sejin. This man ⓔis my
> father. (A) 그는 전에는 요리사였지만, 지금은 농부이다.

16 밑줄 친 ⓐ~ⓔ 중 어법상 틀린 것은? |4점|

① ⓐ 　② ⓑ 　③ ⓒ 　④ ⓓ 　⑤ ⓔ

17 밑줄 친 (A)의 우리말을 영어로 바르게 옮긴 것은? |3점|

① He is a cook before, but he is a farmer now.
② He was a cook before, but he is a farmer now.
③ He was a cook before, but he was a farmer now.
④ He were a cook before, but he is a farmer now.
⑤ He were a cook before, but he was a farmer now.

서술형

18 주어진 문장의 빈칸에 알맞은 be동사를 쓴 후, 부정문과 의문문을 완성하시오. |3점, 각 1점|

> Sandy _____ happy now.

→ (부정문) Sandy _____ happy now.
→ (의문문) _____ happy now?

19 빈칸에 각각 알맞은 be동사를 쓰시오. |3점, 각 1점|

> Tyler _____ my best friend. He and
> I _____ in the same class now. We
> _____ classmates last year, too.

20 빈칸에 공통으로 들어갈 be동사를 알맞은 형태로 쓰시오.
(줄임말로 쓸 것) |4점|

> • I _____ sick yesterday. I was just tired.
> • Andy _____ in Seoul last weekend. He
> was in Jeju-do.

21 빈칸에 알맞은 말을 써서 대화를 완성하시오. |4점, 각 2점|

> A _____ Tom and Harry in their house now?
> B _____, _____ _____. They're at the theater.

22 괄호 안의 말과 be동사를 이용하여 우리말을 영작하시오.

|4점, 각 2점|

(1) 그들은 어젯밤에 병원에 없었다.

(in the hospital, last night)

→ _____

(2) 너의 아버지는 야구선수시니?

(your father, a baseball player)

→ _____

23 밑줄 친 ⓐ~ⓔ 중 어법상 틀린 것을 찾아 기호를 쓰고, 바르게 고쳐 쓰시오.

|4점|

Paul and I ⓐare middle school students. I ⓑam 14, and Paul ⓒis 16. Paul ⓓis a guitarist in his school band. But he ⓔis on a soccer team two years ago.

(　　　) → _____

24 그림을 보고, 〈조건〉에 맞게 글을 완성하시오.

|4점, 각 1점|

Happy   Leo

조건 1. 반드시 be동사를 사용할 것
　　　2. 부정어는 줄임말을 사용할 것

I'm Lily. I have two pets. Happy _____ a dog, and Leo _____ a cat. Happy and Leo _____ white. They are brown. Their tails _____ long.

25 우리말과 일치하도록 〈조건〉에 맞게 문장을 완성하시오.

|3점|

이틀 전에 Brad와 그의 아내는 여기에 없었다.

조건 1. 반드시 be동사를 사용할 것
　　　2. 괄호 안의 말을 모두 포함하여 쓸 것

→ Brad and his wife _____ _____ _____ two days ago. (not, here)

26 밑줄 친 ⓐ~ⓓ 중 어법상 틀린 문장을 찾아 기호를 쓰고, 바르게 고쳐 쓰시오.

|5점|

A Susan, who is that?
B That is Joe. ⓐHe's Brad's cousin.
A I see. ⓑIs he a middle school student?
B ⓒYes, he is. ⓓWe are in the same class last year.

(　　　) → _____

_____

27 표를 보고, 〈조건〉에 맞게 문장을 완성하시오.

|6점, 각 2점|

이름	Sumi	나이	25
2년 전 직업	a singer	현재 직업	a dancer

조건 1. 수미가 자신을 소개하는 내용으로 쓸 것
　　　2. 반드시 be동사를 사용할 것

My name _____ . I am 25 years old. I _____ two years ago, but now I _____ .

chapter

2

일반동사

나는 축구를 좋아해.

Q. "나는 축구를 좋아해."를 영어로 표현하면?

☐ I like soccer.   ☐ I'm like soccer.

일반동사의 현재형

1 일반동사

일반동사는 주어의 동작이나 상태를 나타내는 동사이다.

I	study	English.	나는 영어를 **공부한다.**
	live	in Seoul.	나는 서울에 **산다.**
	love	K-pop.	나는 K-pop을 **아주 좋아한다.**

2 일반동사의 현재형

주어가 I/You/We/They일 때는 동사원형을 쓰고, 3인칭 단수(He/She/It)일 때는 「동사원형＋-(e)s」의 형태로 쓴다.

I/You/We/They	**want**	some water.
He/She/It	**want**s	

We **play** baseball on Saturdays.
They **speak** Chinese very well.
He **likes** action movies.
My mom **works** at a bank.

3 일반동사의 3인칭 단수 현재형 만드는 법

대부분의 동사	동사원형＋**-s**	comes plays runs eats works
-o, -s, -x, -sh, -ch로 끝나는 동사	동사원형＋**-es**	does goes passes mixes fixes brush**es** wash**es** watch**es** teach**es**
「자음＋y」로 끝나는 동사	**y**를 **i**로 고치고＋**-es**	study → stud**ies** cry → cr**ies** fly → fl**ies**
have		**has**

My brother **eats** cereal for breakfast.
Lisa **goes** to school by subway.
Peter **brushes** his teeth after every meal.
That man **has** very short hair.

시험
point

주의해야 할 일반동사의 3인칭 단수 현재형

주어가 3인칭 단수인 경우 일반동사의 현재형은 동사원형에 -s나 -es를 붙여 쓴다.

1 He (play / plays) basketball after school.

2 My sister (studys / studies) math in the evening.

개념 우선 확인 | 옳은 형태 고르기

1 He _____ fast.
- ☐ run
- ☐ runs

2 This bird _____ high.
- ☐ flys
- ☐ flies

3 They _____ well.
- ☐ dance
- ☐ dances

A 괄호 안에서 알맞은 것을 고르시오.

1 Cathy (know / knows) your phone number.

2 All my uncles (live / lives) in Busan.

3 Paul and Kate (go / goes) to the library every day.

4 Mr. Gates (teach / teaches) science at a middle school.

B 괄호 안의 동사를 현재형으로 써서 문장을 완성하시오.

1 Time _____ quickly during vacation. (pass)

2 Jiyun _____ a piano lesson today. (have)

3 My father _____ his car every weekend. (wash)

4 Her brother _____ art history at university. (study)

C 우리말과 일치하도록 괄호 안의 말을 이용하여 문장을 완성하시오.

1 Leo와 Mark는 8시에 학교에 간다. (go)

→ Leo and Mark _____ to school at 8.

2 그들은 매주 일요일 오전에 축구를 한다. (play)

→ They _____ soccer every Sunday morning.

3 저 화가는 그림을 위해 다른 색들을 섞는다. (mix)

→ That painter _____ different colors for his paintings.

4 Karen은 만화책을 많이 가지고 있다. (have)

→ Karen _____ a lot of comic books.

5 나의 이모는 매일 패션 잡지를 읽는다. (read)

→ My aunt _____ fashion magazines every day.

30초 완성 map

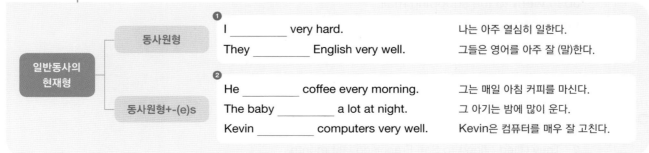

| 일반동사의 현재형 | 동사원형 | ❶ I _____ very hard. / They _____ English very well. | 나는 아주 열심히 일한다. / 그들은 영어를 아주 잘 (말)한다. |
| | 동사원형+-(e)s | ❷ He _____ coffee every morning. / The baby _____ a lot at night. / Kevin _____ computers very well. | 그는 매일 아침 커피를 마신다. / 그 아기는 밤에 많이 운다. / Kevin은 컴퓨터를 매우 잘 고친다. |

unit 2 일반동사의 과거형

1 일반동사의 과거형

일반동사의 과거형은 과거에 일어난 일을 나타낼 때 사용하며, 과거를 나타내는 표현(yesterday, last ~, ~ ago 등)과 함께 자주 쓴다.

| I | **work** | in New York | now. | 나는 지금 뉴욕에서 **일한다**. 〈현재〉 |
| | **work**ed | | two years ago. | 나는 2년 전에 뉴욕에서 **일했다**. 〈과거〉 |

Ryan **played** the violin last night.
I **watched** a baseball game yesterday.

2 일반동사의 과거형 만드는 법

일반동사의 과거형은 주어의 인칭이나 수에 관계없이 형태가 같으며, 규칙 변화(동사원형＋-(e)d)와 불규칙 변화가 있다.

🔗 부록 p. 168

	대부분의 동사	동사원형＋-ed	watch**ed** started walk**ed** play**ed** listen**ed**
규칙 변화	-e로 끝나는 동사	동사원형＋-d	lik**ed** lov**ed** liv**ed** mov**ed** danc**ed**
	「자음＋y」로 끝나는 동사	y를 i로 고치고 ＋-ed	study → stud**ied** cry → cr**ied** try → tr**ied**
	「단모음＋단자음」으로 끝나는 동사	자음을 한 번 더 쓰고＋-ed	stop**ped** drop**ped** plan**ned**
불규칙 변화	형태가 같은 동사		put → **put** cut → **cut** hit → **hit** read → **read**
	모음이 바뀌는 동사		run → **ran** sing → **sang** come → **came** write → **wrote** get → **got** give → **gave** know → **knew** drink → **drank** fall → **fell** swim → **swam** drive → **drove** begin → **began**
	형태가 완전히 달라지는 동사		feel → **felt** tell → **told** break → **broke** eat → **ate** see → **saw** make → **made** hear → **heard** leave → **left** speak → **spoke** buy → **bought** do → **did** go → **went** have → **had** stand → **stood** fly → **flew** find → **found** teach → **taught** send → **sent**

The party **started** ten minutes late.
We **moved** here two years ago.
Joan **went** to the shopping mall.
I **bought** a cake at the bakery.

시험 **point**

틀리기 쉬운 일반동사의 과거형

1 I (stoped / stopped) at the bus stop.
2 They (flied / flew) to San Francisco last month.

개념 우선 확인 | 옳은 형태 고르기

1 She _____ TV.
- [ ] watchd
- [ ] watched

2 They _____ juice.
- [ ] drank
- [ ] drinked

3 He _____ it.
- [ ] buyed
- [ ] bought

A 괄호 안에서 알맞은 것을 고르시오.

1 Julia (cried / cryed) in front of me.

2 They (heared / heard) a beautiful song.

3 She (left / leaved) Seoul last year.

4 We (planed / planned) a trip to France.

B 괄호 안의 동사를 과거형으로 써서 문장을 완성하시오.

1 The little boy _____ to his mom. (run)

2 We _____ a math test yesterday. (have)

3 Many leaves _____ from the trees last night. (fall)

4 She _____ a lot of books for children. (write)

C 우리말과 일치하도록 〈보기〉에서 알맞은 동사를 골라 과거형으로 써서 문장을 완성하시오.

보기	know	tell	feel	see

1 우리는 어젯밤에 좋은 영화 한 편을 봤다.

→ We _____ a good movie last night.

2 그는 그 질문에 대한 답을 알고 있었다.

→ He _____ the answer to the question.

3 Annie는 우리에게 재미있는 이야기를 해 주었다.

→ Annie _____ us a funny story.

4 그 선수는 경기 후에 피곤함을 느꼈다.

→ The player _____ tired after the game.

30초 완성 map

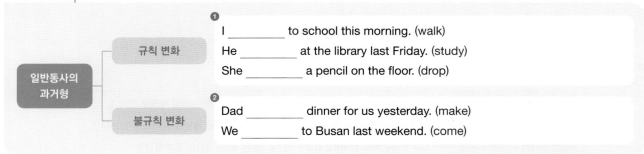

일반동사의 과거형

규칙 변화
❶
I _____ to school this morning. (walk)
He _____ at the library last Friday. (study)
She _____ a pencil on the floor. (drop)

불규칙 변화
❷
Dad _____ dinner for us yesterday. (make)
We _____ to Busan last weekend. (come)

일반동사의 부정문과 의문문

1 일반동사의 부정문

일반동사의 부정문은 「do/does/did＋not＋동사원형」의 형태로 나타낸다.

	do		
I		not	**like** Indian food.
	did		

나는 인도 음식을 **좋아하지 않는다.** 〈현재〉

나는 인도 음식을 **좋아하지 않았다.** 〈과거〉

They **do not read** comic books.
= They **don't read** comic books.
→ 일상 생활에서는 줄임말인 don't, doesn't, didn't를 많이 사용한다.

She **does not speak** Japanese.
= She **doesn't speak** Japanese.
→ 주어가 3인칭 단수(he/she/it)인 경우 does를 사용한다.

We **did not go** to the concert yesterday.
= We **didn't go** to the concert yesterday.

2 일반동사의 의문문

일반동사의 의문문은 「Do/Does/Did＋주어＋동사원형 ~?」의 형태로 나타낸다. 긍정의 대답은 「Yes, 주어＋do/does/did.」로 하고, 부정의 대답은 「No, 주어＋don't/doesn't/didn't.」로 한다.

Do		
	you	**study** in the same class?
Did		

너희들은 같은 반에서 **공부하니?** 〈현재〉

너희들은 같은 반에서 **공부했니?** 〈과거〉

A **Do** you **like** K-pop?
B Yes, I do. / No, I don't.

A **Does** he **live** near your house?
B Yes, he does. / No, he doesn't.

A **Did** they **come** to Korea last year?
B Yes, they did. / No, they didn't.

비교 point do의 여러 가지 쓰임

일반동사(~을 하다)	They **do** their homework every day. (그들은 매일 숙제를 한다.)
일반동사의 부정문에 사용	They **do**n't like board games. (그들은 보드 게임을 좋아하지 않는다.)
일반동사의 의문문에 사용	**Do** they like board games? (그들은 보드 게임을 좋아하니?)

개념 우선 확인 | 옳은 형태 고르기

1 She _____ eat onions.
☐ don't
☐ doesn't

2 They _____ it.
☐ didn't do
☐ don't did

3 Did you _____ him?
☐ call
☐ called

A 밑줄 친 동사의 부정형을 줄임말 형태로 쓰시오.

1 Sophie likes vegetables. _____

2 It rained a lot last night. _____

3 We have music class today. _____

4 They walked to school yesterday. _____

B 괄호 안에서 알맞은 것을 고르시오.

1 (Do / Does) Lucas live in Italy now?

2 Did you (invite / invited) Susan to your house?

3 Does Jim (call / calls) his parents every day?

4 (Do / Does) they take the subway every morning?

C 빈칸에 알맞은 말을 넣어 질문에 대한 답을 완성하시오.

1 A Did Sujin make this cake?
   B No, _____ _____.

2 A Does Tom wear glasses?
   B Yes, _____ _____.

3 A Does Ben have a girlfriend?
   B No, _____ _____.

4 A Do you like Mexican food?
   B No, _____ _____.

5 A Did your parents enjoy the trip?
   B Yes, _____ _____.

30초 완성 map

일반동사

부정문
❶
I _____ _____ mobile games. (play) 나는 모바일 게임을 하지 않는다.
He _____ _____ carrots. (eat) 그는 당근을 먹지 않는다.
We _____ _____ TV yesterday. (watch) 우리는 어제 TV를 보지 않았다.

의문문
❷
_____ she _____ her own blog? (have) 그녀는 자신의 블로그가 있니?
_____ you _____ well last night? (sleep) 너는 어젯밤에 잘 잤니?

서술형 대비 문장 쓰기

□ 빈칸 완성 괄호 안의 말을 이용하여 빈칸 완성하기

01 미나는 남동생 한 명과 여동생 한 명이 있다. (have)

→ Mina _____ one brother and one sister.

02 Tommy가 뉴욕에서 나에게 엽서를 보냈다. (send)

→ Tommy _____ a postcard to me from New York.

03 Lucy는 커피에 설탕을 조금 넣었다. (put)

→ Lucy _____ some sugar in her coffee.

04 나는 3년 전에 이 배낭을 샀다. (buy)

→ I _____ this backpack three years ago.

✔ 오류 수정 어법에 맞게 문장 고쳐 쓰기

05 Jina doesn't wants that yellow dress.

→ Jina _____ .

06 Did Tim wrote this message?

→ _____ this message?

07 We standed in front of a big building.

→ We _____ .

08 He reads a lot of books last week.

→ _____ last week.

≡ 배열 영작 괄호 안의 말을 바르게 배열하기

09 아빠는 매주 일요일에 등산을 하러 가신다. (hiking, goes, Dad)

→ _____ every Sunday.

10 그는 그 소녀의 이름을 모른다. (he, know, doesn't)

→ _____ the girl's name.

11 우리는 어제 수학을 공부했다. (studied, we, math)

→ _____ yesterday.

12 너는 오늘 아침을 먹었니? (you, have, did, breakfast)

→ _____ today?

시험에 꼭 나오는 출제 포인트

Answers p. 4

출제 포인트 ① 주어의 인칭과 수에 맞게 일반동사 현재형을 사용하자!

괄호 안에서 알맞은 것을 고르시오.

(1) David (play / plays) the piano every day.

(2) Mike and Jane (wash / washes) their hands before meals.

> **고득점 POINT 주의해야 할 일반동사의 3인칭 단수 현재형**
>
> 다음 문장을 주어진 주어에 맞게 바꿔 쓰시오.
>
> Many students study at the library.
>
> → My brother _____ at the library.

출제 포인트 ② 일반동사 과거형의 형태를 익혀 두자!

밑줄 친 부분이 어법상 틀린 것은?

① I wrote a letter to Yuri yesterday.
② We made a snowman last weekend.
③ Minsu read my email last night.
④ The car hitted a tree this morning.
⑤ I bought these pants two years ago.

출제 포인트 ③ 일반동사의 부정문 형태에 유의하자!

빈칸에 알맞은 말을 넣어 부정문을 완성하시오. (줄임말로 쓸 것)

(1) My father teaches math.

　→ My father _____ _____ math.

(2) His friends enjoyed the school festival.

　→ His friends _____ _____ the school festival.

출제 포인트 ④ 일반동사의 의문문 형태에 유의하자!

밑줄 친 부분을 바르게 고쳐 쓰시오.

(1) Does he plays the cello well?

　→ _____

(2) Did they went camping last Sunday?

　→ _____

> **고득점 POINT 일반동사 do가 쓰인 부정문과 의문문에서 do를 빠트리지 않도록 유의해야 한다.**
>
> 괄호 안의 말을 이용하여 문장을 완성하시오.
>
> 너는 매일 설거지를 하니? (do)
>
> → _____ the dishes every day?

[01-03] 빈칸에 들어갈 말로 알맞지 <u>않은</u> 것을 고르시오.
|9점, 각 3점|

01

_____ love Korean food.

① We
② Mr. Jones
③ The students
④ Eric and Jane
⑤ Ann's classmates

02

I _____ the book two years ago.

① find
② read
③ borrowed
④ wrote
⑤ bought

03

Did you call me _____?

① yesterday
② tomorrow
③ this morning
④ last night
⑤ 30 minutes ago

04 다음 질문에 대한 대답으로 알맞은 것을 <u>모두</u> 고르면?
|2점|

A Do your friends like the singer?
B _____

① Yes, I do.
② Yes, they do.
③ No, I don't.
④ No, you don't.
⑤ No, they don't.

[05-06] 빈칸에 들어갈 말이 순서대로 바르게 짝지어진 것을 고르시오.
|6점, 각 3점|

05

• Mark _____ breakfast every day.
• Amy doesn't _____ breakfast.

① eat – eat
② eat – ate
③ eats – eat
④ eats – eats
⑤ ate – eats

06

A Did Jackson _____ to the park last weekend?
B Yes. He _____ there with his family.

① go – go
② go – went
③ goes – goes
④ goes – went
⑤ went – goes

07 밑줄 친 부분이 어법상 틀린 것은?
|3점|

① The baby <u>cries</u> a lot.
② Mom <u>goes</u> to work by bus.
③ My sister <u>haves</u> long hair.
④ Somi <u>takes</u> good selfies.
⑤ She <u>watches</u> a movie every Friday.

08 〈보기〉의 문장을 부정문으로 바르게 바꾼 것은?
|3점|

보기	He rode his bike to school.

① He rode not his bike to school.
② He didn't rode his bike to school.
③ He didn't ride his bike to school.
④ He doesn't rode his bike to school.
⑤ He doesn't ride his bike to school.

09 빈칸에 들어갈 말로 알맞지 <u>않은</u> 것끼리 짝지어진 것은?

|3점|

_____ has a lot of shoes.

ⓐ Her parents	ⓑ Mr. Kim	ⓒ She
ⓓ The children	ⓔ The man	ⓕ They

① ⓐ, ⓒ, ⓔ　　　　② ⓐ, ⓓ, ⓕ
③ ⓑ, ⓒ, ⓔ　　　　④ ⓑ, ⓓ, ⓕ
⑤ ⓒ, ⓔ, ⓕ

10 다음 중 대화가 어법상 <u>틀린</u> 것은?

|4점|

① A Do you have a pet?
　B No, I don't.
② A Do you go shopping on Sundays?
　B Yes, we do.
③ A Does James like fishing?
　B No, he don't.
④ A Does your sister walk to school?
　B No, she doesn't.
⑤ A Did Lisa go to the museum yesterday?
　B Yes, she did.

11 (A)~(C)에 들어갈 말이 바르게 짝지어진 것은?　|4점|

• ____(A)____ your mom read the newspaper
every morning?
• Joe ____(B)____ not do his best yesterday.
• My parents ____(C)____ yoga every weekend.

	(A)	(B)	(C)
①	Do	does	do
②	Do	did	does
③	Does	did	do
④	Does	does	do
⑤	Does	did	does

12 밑줄 친 부분이 어법상 옳은 것은?　　　　|4점|

① I <u>live</u> in Busan 10 years ago.
② He <u>don't listen</u> to classical music.
③ My father <u>wash</u> his car every month.
④ Jim <u>read</u> a book with his dad last night.
⑤ Did Sumi <u>came</u> home early yesterday?

최신기출
13 다음 우리말을 영작할 때 필요하지 <u>않은</u> 단어는?　|3점|

Jenny는 숙제를 하지 않았다.

① do　　　　　　② does
③ did　　　　　　④ not
⑤ homework

14 밑줄 친 부분의 쓰임이 나머지와 <u>다른</u> 것은?　|4점|

① <u>Do</u> you love me?
② <u>Did</u> they enjoy the party?
③ <u>Does</u> Rebecca have a dog?
④ They <u>did</u> not like Italian food.
⑤ He <u>does</u> the dishes after dinner.

최신기출
15 어법상 <u>틀린</u> 부분을 찾아 바르게 고쳐 쓴 것은?　|4점|

A Did you go to the beach yesterday?
B Yes, I did. I see the sunset there.

① Did → Do　　　　② go → went
③ Yes → No　　　　④ did → do
⑤ see → saw

16 어법상 옳은 문장의 개수는? |5점|

> ⓐ Jisu didn't drew this picture.
> ⓑ Does Mina and Harry want pets?
> ⓒ I putted my key on this table.
> ⓓ We studied at the library yesterday.
> ⓔ They don't knew about the problem.

① 1개　② 2개　③ 3개　④ 4개　⑤ 5개

[17-18] 다음 대화를 읽고, 물음에 답하시오.

> A What did you do yesterday?
> B I ⓐdid my science project at home.
> A (A) 너는 그 과제를 다 끝냈니?
> B Yes, I did. What did you do yesterday?
> A I ⓑwent to the mall with my sister.
> B Did you buy anything?
> A Yes. We ⓒbuyed some nice shoes. Then we
> ⓓate pizza. We ⓔhad a great time.

17 밑줄 친 ⓐ~ⓔ 중 어법상 틀린 것은? |3점|

① ⓐ　② ⓑ　③ ⓒ　④ ⓓ　⑤ ⓔ

18 밑줄 친 (A)의 우리말을 영어로 바르게 옮긴 것은? |3점|

① Do you finish the project?
② Did you finish the project?
③ Were you finish the project?
④ Do you finished the project?
⑤ Did you finished the project?

19 그림을 보고, 주어진 질문에 대한 대답을 완성하시오. |3점|

> A Does Jane like rainy days?
> B _____, _____ _____.

20 자연스러운 대화가 되도록 대화의 빈칸에 각각 알맞은 말을 쓰시오. |3점|

> A _____ you write this letter?
> B No, I didn't. My brother _____ it.

21 괄호 안의 말을 이용하여 빈칸을 완성하시오. |3점|

> It _____ a lot yesterday, but it _____
> snowing this morning. (snow, stop)

22 괄호 안의 말을 사용하여 빈칸에 알맞은 말을 쓰시오.
|4점, 각 2점|

(1) I was not hungry, so I _____
dinner yesterday. (eat)

(2) She _____ to Korea last year.
She lives in Seoul now. (come)

23 〈보기〉에서 알맞은 말을 골라 우리말 영작을 완성하시오. (필요시 형태를 바꿀 것) |4점, 각 2점|

> Davis 선생님은 영어를 가르치신다. 그녀는 목소리가 좋다.

> 보기 a good voice   teach   have   English

→ Ms. Davis _____.

  She _____.

24 그림의 내용을 설명하는 문장을 괄호 안의 말을 이용하여 〈조건〉에 맞게 쓰시오. |4점, 각 2점|

> 조건 1. 일반동사를 사용하여 현재시제로 쓸 것
>   2. 긍정문과 부정문을 한 번씩 쓸 것

(1) He _____ in the sky. (fly)

(2) He _____. (walk)

고난도

25 〈보기〉에서 동사를 골라 알맞은 형태로 쓰시오. |6점, 각 2점|

> 보기 speak   go   have

> I _____ on a trip to France two years ago. I didn't _____ French, but I _____ a lot of fun.

26 다음 글의 'I'를 'Kate(she)'로 바꿔서 다시 쓰시오. |3점, 각 1점|

> I come from Australia. I don't speak Korean, but I have many Korean friends.

→ Kate _____.

  She _____,

  but she _____.

27 밑줄 친 부분이 어법상 틀린 문장을 찾아 기호를 쓰고, 바르게 고쳐 쓰시오. |4점|

> ⓐ My sisters don't like chocolate.
> ⓑ Do your brother speak Chinese?
> ⓒ Yuri joined our dance club last week.
> ⓓ Did he change his hairstyle?

(_____) → _____

28 다음은 두 사람의 취미 생활을 나타낸 표이다. 표를 보고 아래 대화를 완성하시오. |6점, 각 2점|

	play tennis	read books
Brad	○	○
Amy	×	○

A Does Brad play tennis?

B (1) _____, _____ _____.

A Does Amy play tennis, too?

B No. She (2) _____ tennis.

A (3) _____ _____ _____ books?

B Yes, they do.

chapter

03

명사와 관사

나는 사과를 가지고 있어.

Q. "나는 사과를 가지고 있어."를 영어로 표현하면?

☐ I have apple.　　☐ I have an apple.

1 셀 수 있는 명사

(1) 셀 수 있는 명사가 하나일 때는 명사 앞에 a/an을 붙이고, 둘 이상일 때는 뒤에 -(e)s를 붙여 복수형을 만든다.

I have	a **pen**.	단수: a/an+명사
	three **pen**s.	복수: 명사+-(e)s

(2) 셀 수 있는 명사의 복수형 만드는 방법   🔗 부록 p. 170

대부분의 명사	명사+**-s**	books balls cats pens rings
-s, -x, -sh, -ch, -o로 끝나는 명사	명사+**-es**	buses boxes dishes benches watches potatoes tomatoes
「자음+y」로 끝나는 명사	y를 i로 고치고+**-es**	baby → babies lady → ladies city → cities party → parties fly → flies puppy → puppies
-f, -fe로 끝나는 명사	f, fe를 v로 고치고+**-es**	wolf → wolves leaf → leaves knife → knives
불규칙 변화		man → **men** woman → **women** tooth → **teeth** foot → **feet** child → **children** mouse → **mice**
형태가 같은 경우		fish → **fish** deer → **deer** sheep → **sheep**

2 셀 수 없는 명사

셀 수 없는 명사 앞에는 a/an을 붙이지 않으며, 항상 단수형으로 쓰고 복수형으로 만들 수 없다.

(1) 셀 수 없는 명사의 종류

물질을 나타내는 명사	sugar, salt, water, milk, coffee, juice, paper, money, air 등
사람이나 지역 이름을 나타내는 명사	Mark, New York, France 등 주의 첫 철자는 항상 대문자로 쓴다.
추상적인 개념을 나타내는 명사	love, friendship, luck, health, happiness 등

(2) 셀 수 없는 명사를 세는 방법: 담는 용기나 모양을 나타내는 말을 단위로 사용하여 나타낸다.

a piece of	paper, cake	한 장(조각)의 ~	**a cup of**	coffee, tea	한 컵(잔)의 ~
a glass of	milk, water, juice	한 컵(잔)의 ~	**a bottle of**	milk, water, juice	한 병의 ~
a bowl of	soup, rice, cereal	한 그릇의 ~	**a slice of**	pizza, cheese, cake	한 조각의 ~

She ate **a piece of** cake.
I ate **two pieces of** cake.

시험 point

셀 수 없는 명사의 수량 표현

셀 수 없는 명사를 복수형으로 나타낼 때는 단위를 나타내는 명사만 복수형으로 쓴다.

1 I drank (two glass of waters / two glasses of water).

2 She eats (three slices of cheese / three slices of cheeses) every day.

개념 우선 확인 | 옳은 복수형 고르기

1 four _____
☐ books
☐ bookes

2 three _____
☐ dishs
☐ dishes

3 five _____
☐ citys
☐ cities

4 two _____
☐ knifes
☐ knives

A 주어진 단어의 복수형을 빈칸에 쓰시오.

1 bench → _____

2 potato → _____

3 lady → _____

4 mouse → _____

5 leaf → _____

6 man → _____

7 foot → _____

8 sheep → _____

B 우리말과 일치하도록 빈칸에 들어갈 말을 〈보기〉에서 골라 알맞은 형태로 쓰시오.

보기	glass	bottle	bowl	piece

1 우유 한 잔 → a _____ of milk

2 시리얼 한 그릇 → a _____ of cereal

3 케이크 한 조각 → a _____ of cake

4 포도주 한 병 → a _____ of wine

5 주스 네 잔 → four _____ of juice

6 수프 두 그릇 → two _____ of soup

7 종이 다섯 장 → five _____ of paper

8 물 열 병 → ten _____ of water

C 우리말과 일치하도록 빈칸에 알맞은 말을 넣어 문장을 완성하시오.

1 James는 아침으로 사과를 한 개 먹었다.

→ James ate _____ _____ for breakfast.

2 우리는 지난 일요일에 물고기 다섯 마리를 잡았다.

→ We caught _____ _____ last Sunday.

3 Sam은 매일 아침 물 한 잔을 마신다.

→ Sam drinks _____ _____ _____ _____ every morning.

4 배고파요. 피자 두 조각 주세요.

→ I'm hungry. Give me _____ _____ _____ _____, please.

30초 완성 map

명사
- 셀 수 있는 명사
  - 단수일 때 ❶ _____ dog _____ egg _____ orange
  - 복수일 때 ❷ two cat____ three box____ 주의 five _____ (여자 다섯 명)
- 셀 수 없는 명사 ❸ sugar (○ / ×) a sugar (○ / ×) sugars (○ / ×)
  주의 수 세는 방법: a bottle of milk, two _____ of milk ...

1 부정관사 a/an

부정관사 a와 an은 셀 수 있는 명사의 단수형 앞에 쓰여 '불특정한 하나'라는 의미를 나타낸다.
명사의 첫소리가 자음이면 a, 모음이면 an을 쓴다.

| **a** | **a** book, **a** pencil, **a** dog, **a** house, **a** tree, **a** man |
| **an** | **an** egg, **an** apple, **an** orange, **an** actor, **an** umbrella |

I have **a** son and **a** daughter.
She bought **an** apple and **an** orange.

> 주의 a나 an은 철자가 아니라 발음으로 구분하여 명사 앞에 쓴다.   **a** uniform / **an** hour

2 정관사 the

정관사 the는 셀 수 있는 명사의 단수형과 복수형, 셀 수 없는 명사 앞에 모두 쓸 수 있으며, '특정한 것'이라는 의미를 나타낸다.

앞에 나온 명사를 다시 언급할 때	I ate a hamburger. **The** hamburger was delicious.
가리키는 대상을 서로 알고 있을 때	Could you close **the** door? Pass me **the** salt, please.
악기 이름 앞에	Amy plays **the** piano very well. Chris played **the** guitar for me.

3 관사를 쓰지 않는 경우

식사, 운동 경기, 과목 이름 앞	We didn't have **lunch**. I played **baseball** with my friends. She likes **math** and **science**.
by+교통수단	He will go to Busan by **train**. They went to Japan by **ship**.
장소가 원래 목적으로 쓰일 때	I go to **bed** at ten every day. (잠자리에 들다) How do you go to **school** every morning? (등교하다)

비교
point **play+the+악기 vs. play+운동 경기**

play 뒤에 악기 이름이 올 때는 주로 the를 쓰고, 운동 경기 이름이 올 때는 the를 쓰지 않는다.

1 I played (a flute / the flute) on the stage.
2 They play (soccer / the soccer) every Sunday.

| 개념 우선 확인 | 옳은 부정관사 고르기 |

1 _____ ant
☐ a
☐ an

2 _____ uniform
☐ a
☐ an

3 _____ orange
☐ a
☐ an

4 _____ sandwich
☐ a
☐ an

A 괄호 안에서 알맞은 것을 고르시오.

1 They study (science / the science) every Friday.

2 We had (breakfast / the breakfast) early this morning.

3 They will go to Pyeongchang (by car / by a car).

4 She drew a picture. (A picture / The picture) was beautiful.

B 빈칸에 알맞은 말을 〈보기〉에서 골라 문장을 완성하시오. (필요 없는 곳에는 ×표 할 것)

| 보기 | a | an | the |

1 Alex plays _____ violin very well.

2 It's raining. Do you have _____ umbrella?

3 We play _____ table tennis after school.

4 A cat is on the bench. _____ cat is black and white.

C 우리말과 일치하도록 괄호 안의 말을 이용하여 문장을 완성하시오. (단, one은 쓰지 말 것)

1 그는 한 시간 동안 수학 공부를 했다. (hour)

→ He studied math for _____ _____.

2 그녀는 우리를 위해 첼로를 연주했다. (cello)

→ She played _____ _____ for us.

3 너무 덥네요. 창문 좀 열어 주시겠어요? (window)

→ It's too hot. Can you open _____ _____?

4 나의 집 근처에 공원이 하나 있다. 그 공원에는 나무가 많다. (park)

→ There is a park near my house. _____ _____ has many trees.

30초 완성 map

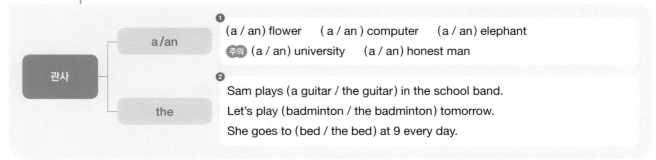

❶ (a / an) flower   (a / an) computer   (a / an) elephant
주의 (a / an) university   (a / an) honest man

❷ Sam plays (a guitar / the guitar) in the school band.
Let's play (badminton / the badminton) tomorrow.
She goes to (bed / the bed) at 9 every day.

관사 ─ a/an ─ the

서술형 대비 문장 쓰기

Answers p. 6

빈칸 완성 괄호 안의 말을 이용하여 빈칸 완성하기 (단, one은 쓰지 말 것)

01 나의 삼촌은 아이가 세 명 있다. (child)

→ My uncle has _____ _____.

02 나는 보통 아침으로 계란 한 개를 먹는다. (egg)

→ I usually eat _____ _____ for breakfast.

03 그들은 커피 두 잔을 원한다. (cup)

→ They want _____ _____ _____ coffee.

04 그의 가족은 기차를 타고 해변에 갔다. (train)

→ His family went to the beach _____ _____.

오류 수정 어법에 맞게 문장 고쳐 쓰기

05 I need three piece of paper.

→ I need three _____.

06 My baby sister has only two toothes.

→ My baby sister _____.

07 They played the badminton after school.

→ _____ after school.

08 Did you study the math last night?

→ _____ last night?

배열 영작 괄호 안의 말을 바르게 배열하기

09 벽에 사진이 한 장 있다. 그 사진은 아름답다. (picture, the, is)

→ There is a picture on the wall. _____ beautiful.

10 어젯밤에 다섯 명의 남자들이 파티에 왔다. (men, five, came)

→ _____ to the party last night.

11 그는 저녁으로 먹기 위해 감자 두 개를 삶았다. (boiled, potatoes, two, he)

→ _____ for dinner.

12 나는 수업 전에 물 두 잔을 마셨다. (water, drank, two, of, glasses, I)

→ _____ before class.

시험에 꼭 나오는 출제 포인트

Answers p. 6

출제 포인트 ① 셀 수 없는 명사 앞에는 a/an을 쓰지 않는다!

괄호 안에서 알맞은 것을 고르시오.

(1) My uncle wants (camera / a camera).

(2) Dave drinks (milk / a milk) every morning.

고득점 POINT 명사의 불규칙 변화 복수형

어법상 틀린 부분을 모두 찾아 바르게 고쳐 쓰시오.

We saw two mans and five sheeps there.

→ We saw _____ there.

출제 포인트 ② 셀 수 없는 명사의 수나 양을 나타내는 방법을 기억하자!

우리말과 일치하도록 빈칸에 들어갈 말을 〈보기〉에서 골라 알맞은 형태로 쓰시오.

보기	cup	bottle	piece

(1) a _____ of pizza (피자 한 조각)

(2) two _____ of juice (주스 두 병)

(3) five _____ of tea (차 다섯 잔)

출제 포인트 ③ a와 an의 쓰임을 구분하자!

빈칸에 a가 필요한 것을 두 개 고르면?

① I have _____ laptop.

② Did she eat _____ orange?

③ She wears _____ nice shoes.

④ Do you need _____ new phone?

⑤ We went to the bookstore by _____ bus.

고득점 POINT a와 an은 명사의 첫 철자가 아니라 첫소리로 구분한다.

빈칸에 a나 an을 쓰시오.

(1) We played the game for _____ hour.

(2) He doesn't wear _____ uniform at work.

출제 포인트 ④ 정관사 the를 쓰는 경우와 관사를 쓰지 않는 경우를 기억하자!

밑줄 친 부분을 어법에 맞게 고쳐 쓰시오.

(1) Yujin plays violin very well. → _____

(2) I don't usually eat the breakfast. → _____

(3) I played the basketball with my friends yesterday. → _____

유형	문항수	배점	점수
객관식	18	60	
서술형	10	40	

01 다음 중 명사의 복수형이 알맞지 <u>않은</u> 것은? |2점|

① box – boxes
② wolf – wolfes
③ glove – gloves
④ class – classes
⑤ party – parties

02 빈칸에 들어갈 말로 알맞은 것은? |3점|

I want a _____.

① egg
② apple
③ umbrella
④ uniform
⑤ orange

[03-04] 빈칸에 들어갈 말로 알맞지 <u>않은</u> 것을 고르시오.
|6점, 각 3점|

03

Andy has two _____.

① juice
② books
③ brothers
④ deer
⑤ caps

04

I had a slice of _____ for breakfast.

① cake
② pizza
③ rice
④ cheese
⑤ bread

[05-06] 빈칸에 들어갈 말이 순서대로 바르게 짝지어진 것을 고르시오. |6점, 각 3점|

05

• My brother studies _____ very hard.
• I found a box. _____ box was empty.

① science – A
② science – The
③ a science – A
④ the science – The
⑤ the science – A

06

I saw _____ bird in the morning.
_____ bird was white.

① a – A
② a – The
③ an – A
④ an – The
⑤ the – An

07 밑줄 친 부분이 어법상 <u>틀린</u> 것은? |3점|

① Dentists fix our <u>teeth</u>.
② Cats catch <u>mouses</u>.
③ Trees have colorful <u>leaves</u> in fall.
④ The park is full of <u>children</u>.
⑤ He has two pigs and three <u>horses</u>.

08 빈칸에 공통으로 들어갈 말로 알맞은 것은? |3점|

• Turn off _____ TV. It's too loud.
• Pass me _____ pepper, please.

① a
② an
③ the
④ any
⑤ some

09 우리말을 영어로 바르게 옮긴 것은? |3점|

> 나는 우유 두 병이 필요하다.

① I need two bottle milk.
② I need two bottle of milk.
③ I need two bottle of milks.
④ I need two bottles of milk.
⑤ I need two bottles of milks.

10 빈칸에 the(The)가 들어갈 수 <u>없는</u> 것은? |3점|

① Can you close _____ window?
② Please turn on _____ lights.
③ We had _____ dinner together.
④ I saw a tree. _____ tree was very tall.
⑤ Ben played _____ guitar for his mom.

[11-12] 밑줄 친 부분이 어법상 옳은 것을 고르시오.
|8점, 각 4점|

11 ① My brother has big <u>foot</u>.
② This is <u>a</u> interesting story.
③ The boy bought <u>a</u> water.
④ I usually read <u>book</u> after dinner.
⑤ We saw a lot of <u>sheep</u> on the hill.

12 ① Does Andy <u>play piano</u> well?
② Mom goes to work <u>by the bus</u>.
③ Let's <u>have lunch</u> at 12 o'clock.
④ Do you <u>play the basketball</u> after school?
⑤ Mr. Kim <u>teaches the music</u> at my school.

13 빈칸에 들어갈 관사가 나머지와 <u>다른</u> 것은? |4점|

① I have _____ little brother.
② I play _____ violin every day.
③ My aunt is _____ doctor.
④ She drank _____ glass of juice.
⑤ I have _____ pencil and two books in my bag.

14 (A)~(C)에 들어갈 말이 바르게 짝지어진 것은? |4점|

> • Jim has a dog. ___(A)___ dog really loves Jim.
> • ___(B)___ week has seven days.
> • My mom is ___(C)___ animal doctor.

	(A)	(B)	(C)
①	A	An	the
②	A	A	an
③	The	The	a
④	The	A	an
⑤	The	An	the

고난도

15 밑줄 친 부분이 어법상 옳은 것끼리 짝지어진 것은? |5점|

> ⓐ They stayed there for <u>a hour</u>.
> ⓑ She caught five <u>fish</u> yesterday.
> ⓒ Please put some <u>salt</u> in my soup.
> ⓓ <u>Friendship</u> is very important to me.
> ⓔ Dad drinks <u>two cups of coffees</u> every day.

① ⓐ, ⓑ, ⓔ ② ⓐ, ⓒ, ⓓ ③ ⓑ, ⓒ, ⓓ
④ ⓑ, ⓓ, ⓔ ⑤ ⓒ, ⓓ, ⓔ

A Please pass me a _____ ⓐ _____ of paper.
B Sure. Why do you need one?
A I want to make _____ ⓑ _____ airplane. It is my art homework.
B I see. Here it is.

16 빈칸 ⓐ에 들어갈 말로 알맞은 것은? |3점|

① cup   ② glass   ③ piece
④ bottle   ⑤ bowl

17 다음 우리말과 일치하도록 할 때 빈칸 ⓑ에 들어갈 말로 알맞은 것은? |3점|

저는 비행기를 하나 만들고 싶어요.

① a   ② it   ③ this
④ an   ⑤ the

최신기출
18 어법상 틀린 부분을 바르게 고친 것끼리 짝지어진 것은? |4점|

(A) The movie is about a money.
            (→ money)
(B) Those tall woman are volleyball players.
            (→ womans)
(C) We visited three citys in Europe.
            (→ cities)
(D) I had a tea and two bread for breakfast.
            (→ a cup of tea and two breads)

① (A), (B)   ② (A), (C)   ③ (B), (C)
④ (B), (D)   ⑤ (C), (D)

서 술 형

19 괄호 안의 말을 알맞은 형태로 바꿔 빈칸에 쓰시오. |2점, 각 1점|

(1) The baby has four _____. (tooth)
(2) I saw two _____ on the wall. (fly)

20 우리말과 일치하도록 괄호 안의 단어를 이용하여 문장을 완성하시오. (단, one은 쓰지 말 것) |2점, 각 1점|

나는 오렌지 한 개와 감자 두 개가 필요하다.
(orange, potato)

→ I need _____ and
_____.

21 그림의 내용과 일치하도록 괄호 안의 단어를 이용하여 문장을 완성하시오. |4점, 각 2점|

My mom bought four (1) _____
_____ _____ and two (2) _____
_____ _____ for us. (glass, slice, pizza, Coke)

22 빈칸에 공통으로 들어갈 알맞은 관사를 쓰시오.　|3점|

- Please close _____ door. It's cold.
- I bought a hat for Mom. She liked _____ hat very much.

23 그림을 보고, 〈조건〉에 맞게 대화를 완성하시오.　|6점, 각 3점|

조건　1. cake와 coffee를 사용할 것
　　　2. 각각 4단어로 쓸 것

A What do you want for dessert?
B I want _____ and
_____ .

[24-25] 어법상 틀린 부분을 찾아 바르게 고쳐 쓰시오.
|6점, 각 3점|

24
I eat an apple for the breakfast every day.

_____ → _____

25
Steve plays cello on weekends.

_____ → _____

26 그림을 보고, 〈조건〉에 맞게 문장을 완성하시오.
|6점, 각 2점|

조건　1. 정확한 수량을 표현할 것
　　　2. (1)에는 slice, (2)에는 a나 an을 사용할 것

Let's make a sandwich! We need
(1) _____ ,
(2) _____ , and (3) _____ .

27 밑줄 친 ⓐ~ⓔ 중 어법상 틀린 것을 찾아 바르게 고쳐 쓰시오.　|5점|

It rained a lot today. I didn't have ⓐ an umbrella, so I got wet. My mom made ⓑ a bowl of soup for me. ⓒ The soup was really good. I went to ⓓ the bed early after ⓔ dinner.

(　) → _____

고난도

28 다음 표를 보고, 두 가지 표현 중 알맞은 것을 골라 Eric을 설명하는 문장들을 〈조건〉에 맞게 완성하시오.
|6점, 각 2점|

등교 방법	by subway / by the subway
방과 후 활동	play soccer / play the soccer
좋아하는 과목	math / the math

조건　1. 괄호 안의 말을 이용하되 필요하면 형태를 바꿀 것
　　　2. (3)에는 be동사를 사용할 것

(1) Eric _____ .
　　　　　(go to school)
(2) He _____ .
　　　　　(after school)
(3) His _____ .
　　　　　(favorite subject)

chapter

4

대명사

Q. "It's 12 o'clock."이 의미하는 것은?

☐ 그것은 12시야.   ☐ 지금 12시야.

인칭대명사, 비인칭 주어

1 인칭대명사

인칭대명사는 사람이나 사물을 가리키는 말로 단수와 복수가 있으며, 인칭과 격에 따라 형태가 달라진다.

수	인칭	주격(~은/는/이/가)	소유격(~의)	목적격(~을/를)	소유대명사(~의 것)
단수	1인칭	I	my	me	mine
	2인칭	you(너)	your	you	yours
	3인칭	he she it	his her its	him her it	his hers 없음
복수	1인칭	we	our	us	ours
	2인칭	you(너희들)	your	you	yours
	3인칭	they	their	them	theirs

주의 it의 소유격 its와 it is의 줄임말 it's를 혼동해서 쓰지 않도록 주의한다.

(1) 주격과 목적격: 주격은 주어 역할, 목적격은 목적어 역할을 한다.

Minji met her friends at the COEX Mall yesterday.
　　주어　　　목적어

→ **She** met **them** at the COEX Mall yesterday.
　　주격　　목적격

(2) 소유격과 소유대명사: 소유격은 '~의'라는 뜻으로 뒤에 명사가 오지만, 소유대명사는 '~의 것'이라는 뜻으로 뒤에 명사가 오지 않는다.

This is **my** umbrella. → This umbrella is **mine**.
　　　　소유격　　　　　　　　　　　　　　　소유대명사 (= my umbrella)

▶ 사람이나 동물을 나타내는 명사의 소유격과 소유대명사는 뒤에 -'s를 붙여 나타낸다.

This is **Paul's** cap. (Paul의 모자)　　　That bag is **Nancy's**. (Nancy의 것)

2 비인칭 주어 it

시간, 날짜, 요일, 날씨, 계절, 거리 등을 나타낼 때 주어 자리에 쓰며, 이때의 it은 '그것'이라고 해석하지 않는다.

시간	It's six o'clock.	날씨	It's very hot.
날짜	It's September 2.	계절	It's summer.
요일	It's Tuesday today.	거리	It's five kilometers from here.

비교 point

비인칭 주어 it vs. 대명사 it

비인칭 주어 it을 '그것'으로 해석하지 않도록 주의한다.

It is ten thirty now.	지금은 10시 30분이다. 〈비인칭 주어〉
It is my watch.	**그것은** 내 시계이다. 〈대명사〉

개념 우선 확인 | 옳은 표현 고르기

1 그의 신발
- ☐ his shoes
- ☐ he's shoes

2 그녀의 것
- ☐ her's
- ☐ hers

3 날씨가 맑다.
- ☐ It's sunny.
- ☐ Its sunny.

A   괄호 안에서 알맞은 것을 고르시오.

1 Mr. Park is (us / our) new math teacher.

2 These yellow boots are (my / mine).

3 She lost (her / hers) house keys on the bus.

4 Tim came to the party with (his / him) girlfriend.

B   빈칸에 알맞은 말을 〈보기〉에서 골라 대화를 완성하시오.

보기	it	he	her	their

1 A Who is that boy?   B _____ is Jim's brother.

2 A _____ is five o'clock.   B Hurry up! We're late.

3 A Do you know Sally?   B No, I don't know _____.

4 A Where do they live?   B _____ house is on the hill.

C   우리말과 일치하도록 빈칸에 알맞은 말을 넣어 문장을 완성하시오.

1 밖은 매우 덥다.

→ _____ is very hot outside.

2 모두가 너의 아름다운 목소리를 아주 좋아한다.

→ Everybody loves _____ beautiful voice.

3 Joe에게 그의 책이 없어서 내 것을 같이 봤다.

→ Joe didn't have _____ book, so I shared _____ with him.

4 그는 그녀를 먼저 도와줄 것이다. 그리고 그는 우리 또한 도와줄 것이다.

→ He will help _____ first. And he will help _____, too.

30초 완성 map

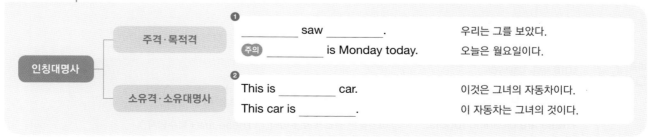

인칭대명사	주격·목적격	❶ _____ saw _____.
		주의 _____ is Monday today.
	소유격·소유대명사	❷ This is _____ car.
		This car is _____.

우리는 그를 보았다.
오늘은 월요일이다.
이것은 그녀의 자동차이다.
이 자동차는 그녀의 것이다.

지시대명사, 부정대명사, 재귀대명사

1 지시대명사

> this는 단수, these는 복수를 가리킨다.

this / these (가까이에 있는 사람이나 사물)	This is her computer. (이것) This is my little sister. (이 아이) These are famous pictures. (이것들)
that / those (멀리 떨어져 있는 사람이나 사물)	That is an old museum. (저것) That is my grandfather. (저분) Those are interesting books. (저것들)

> that은 단수, those는 복수를 가리킨다.

▶ this, these, that, those는 명사 앞에서 형용사로 쓰이기도 한다.

This *music* is great. (이 ~) / **That** *backpack* is mine. (저 ~)

2 부정대명사 one

one은 앞에서 말한 것과 같은 종류의 불특정한 것 하나를 가리킬 때 사용하며, 복수형은 ones이다.

one	My bike is very old. I'll buy a new **one**. ⟨one = a bike⟩
ones	I lost my glasses. I need new **ones**. ⟨ones = glasses⟩

▶ 앞에서 언급된 특정한 대상을 가리킬 때는 it이나 them을 쓴다.

This is my guitar. I like **it** very much. ⟨it = my guitar⟩

3 재귀대명사

인칭대명사의 소유격이나 목적격에 -self/-selves를 붙인 것으로 '~ 자신'이라는 뜻이다.

I → **myself**	you → **yourself**	he → **himself**	she → **herself**
it → **itself**	we → **ourselves**	you → **yourselves**	they → **themselves**

주의 단수 you와 복수 you는 재귀대명사가 yourself와 yourselves로 형태가 다르다.
Know **yourself**. (너 자신을 알라.)　　Know **yourselves**. (너희들 자신을 알라.)

자기 자신	We love **ourselves**. ⟨We = ourselves⟩ She talked to **herself**. ⟨She = herself⟩
직접, 스스로 (생략 가능)	He (**himself**) did it. (그가 **직접** 그것을 했다.) I made dinner (**myself**). (나는 저녁을 **직접** 만들었다.)

비교
point

this vs. these

This is a cleaning robot.	이것은 청소용 로봇이다.	⟨This is+단수명사.⟩
These are cleaning robots.	이것들은 청소용 로봇이다.	⟨These are+복수명사.⟩

개념 우선 확인 | 밑줄 친 부분의 옳은 해석 고르기

1 <u>This</u> is our teacher.
- ☐ 이분
- ☐ 이것

2 <u>These</u> are his pencils.
- ☐ 그것들
- ☐ 이것들

3 <u>Those</u> are my friends.
- ☐ 저것들
- ☐ 저 사람들

A 괄호 안에서 알맞은 것을 고르시오.

1 (This / These) watches are expensive.

2 I'll introduce (myself / me) to you.

3 They want a new house. They want a big (one / ones).

B 빈칸에 들어갈 말로 알맞은 것을 〈보기〉에서 골라 대화를 완성하시오.

보기	one	ones	myself	himself

1 **A** Which shoes do you like?   **B** I like the red _____.

2 **A** These cookies are really good.   **B** Tom made them _____.

3 **A** Michael lost his cell phone.   **B** Will he buy a new _____?

4 **A** Do you need help?   **B** It's okay. I can do it _____.

C 우리말과 일치하도록 괄호 안의 말을 배열하여 문장을 완성하시오.

1 이 흰색 양말들은 너무 더럽다. (socks, these, white)
→ _____ _____ _____ are too dirty.

2 그녀는 우리 집을 직접 방문하였다. (visited, she, herself)
→ _____ _____ _____ my house.

3 그들은 스스로 그 문제를 풀었다. (problem, solved, the, themselves)
→ They _____ _____ _____ _____.

4 내 책상은 너무 낡았다. 나는 새것이 하나 필요하다. (one, new, need, a)
→ My desk is too old. I _____ _____ _____ _____.

30초 완성 map

대명사	지시대명사	❶ **this** book 이 책 _____ books 이 책들 **That** is a book. 저것은 책이다. _____ are books. 저것들은 책이다.
	부정대명사	❷ I broke my cup. I'll buy a new _____. I like those pants. Do you have blue _____, too?
	재귀대명사	❸ He loves **himself**. 그는 _____ 사랑한다. He **himself** drew it. 그가 그것을 _____ 그렸다.

서술형 대비 문장 쓰기

□ 빈칸 완성 밑줄 친 부분을 대명사로 바꿔 빈칸 완성하기

01 Sujin and I took many pictures.

→ _____ many pictures.

02 I didn't meet Tim and Cathy last weekend.

→ _____ last weekend.

03 They came to Minho's house yesterday.

→ _____ yesterday.

04 I don't have a ruler. Can I use your ruler?

→ I don't have a ruler. _____

✔ 오류 수정 어법에 맞게 문장 고쳐 쓰기

05 Those building are very tall.

→ _____ very tall.

06 We looked at ourself in the mirror.

→ We _____ .

07 The phone is not mine phone.

→ The phone _____ .

08 My shoes are small. I need a new one.

→ My shoes are small. _____

☰ 배열 영작 괄호 안의 말을 바르게 배열하기

09 그 갈색 안경은 그의 것이다. (his, the, glasses, brown, are)

→ _____

10 우리는 이 노래들을 좋아한다. (like, songs, we, these)

→ _____

11 오늘은 10월 15일이다. (October 15, it, is, today)

→ _____

12 그녀가 직접 그 드레스를 만들었다. (made, she, herself, the dress)

→ _____

시험에 꼭 나오는 출제 포인트

Answers p. 8

출제 포인트 1   인칭대명사의 격에 따른 형태 변화를 익혀 두자!

괄호 안의 대명사를 알맞은 형태로 바꿔 쓰시오.

(1) I like _____ paintings. (he)

(2) We saw _____ at the bus stop. (they)

(3) That electric car is _____. (we)

고득점 POINT   소유격과 소유대명사의 형태

우리말과 일치하도록 빈칸에 알맞은 말을 쓰시오. (한 단어씩 쓸 것)

(1) Tim의 고양이는 예쁘다. 그것의 눈은 파란색이다.

  → _____ cat is pretty. _____ eyes are blue.

(2) 그 비옷은 그의 것이 아니다. 그것은 내 것이다.

  → The raincoat is not _____. It's _____.

출제 포인트 2   해석하지 않는 비인칭 주어 It의 쓰임을 기억하자!

밑줄 친 It의 쓰임이 나머지와 다른 것은?

① It's July 14.
② It's snowing.
③ It's eleven o'clock.
④ It's not my schoolbag.
⑤ It's Sunday today.

출제 포인트 3   지시대명사의 단수와 복수를 구분하자!

괄호 안에서 알맞은 것을 고르시오.

(1) (This / These) is my friend Lucy.

(2) Are (that / those) your puppies?

(3) I bought (this / these) sunglasses last weekend.

출제 포인트 4   부정대명사 one은 같은 종류의 불특정한 것 하나를 나타낸다!

빈칸에 들어갈 말로 알맞은 것은?

> I lost my umbrella. I need a new _____.

① it   ② this   ③ them
④ one   ⑤ ones

고득점 POINT   부정대명사 one vs. 지시대명사 it

빈칸에 it이나 one 중 알맞은 말을 쓰시오.

(1) I don't have a pen. Do you have _____?

(2) I like this cap. I'll buy _____.

01 빈칸에 들어갈 말로 알맞지 <u>않은</u> 것은? |2점|

> Those _____ are for my grandmother.

① socks   ② juice   ③ jeans
④ flowers   ⑤ vegetables

[02-03] 빈칸에 들어갈 말로 알맞은 것을 고르시오.
|6점, 각 3점|

02

> This is my favorite dress. _____ color is beautiful.

① It   ② Its   ③ It's
④ They   ⑤ Their

03

> Jane bought a black cap, and I bought a red _____.

① it   ② its   ③ them
④ one   ⑤ ones

[04-06] 빈칸에 들어갈 말이 순서대로 바르게 짝지어진 것을 고르시오. |9점, 각 3점|

04

> • I'll call Tom. Do you know _____ phone number?
> • I lost my pen. Can I use _____?

① him – mine   ② him – yours
③ his – mine   ④ his – yours
⑤ he's – your

05

> • This shirt is black. I need a white _____.
> • I got a present from Jinho. _____ was a cute doll.

① it – It   ② it – One
③ one – It   ④ one – One
⑤ ones – It

06

> • Is _____ April 4 today?
> • I bought _____ pants two years ago.

① it – this   ② it – these
③ this – that   ④ this – those
⑤ that – this

07 밑줄 친 부분의 쓰임이 나머지와 <u>다른</u> 것은? |3점|

① What's <u>that</u>?
② <u>She's</u> a famous artist.
③ <u>That's</u> not my cup.
④ <u>It's</u> his favorite movie.
⑤ <u>David's</u> father is always busy.

08 다음 중 밑줄 친 부분을 생략할 수 있는 것은? |3점|

① He talked to <u>himself</u>.
② We should love <u>ourselves</u>.
③ I'll introduce <u>myself</u> to you.
④ She fixed the computer <u>herself</u>.
⑤ The bird cleans <u>itself</u> every day.

09 우리말과 일치하도록 할 때 빈칸에 들어갈 말이 순서대로 바르게 짝지어진 것은? |3점|

> 내가 직접 이 장갑을 만들었어.
> → I made _____ gloves _____.

① this – itself
② this – myself
③ these – myself
④ these – themselves
⑤ that – themselves

10 밑줄 친 It의 쓰임이 〈보기〉와 같은 것은? |3점|

> 보기　It isn't my bike.

① It's Thursday today.
② It's not Jane's idea.
③ It is already 10 o'clock.
④ It will be warm tomorrow.
⑤ It is one kilometer from here.

[고난도]

11 다음 중 대화가 어법상 틀린 것은? |5점|

① A What time is it now?
　 B It's four forty.
② A How was the weather yesterday?
　 B It was cloudy.
③ A Are these Amy's books?
　 B Yes, they are.
④ A I bought this T-shirt for you.
　 B Thank you. I like one very much.
⑤ A I really like these sunglasses.
　 B I like them, too.

12 밑줄 친 her의 쓰임이 〈보기〉와 다른 것은? |3점|

> 보기　I like her hairstyle.

① It is her son's diary.
② This is her new laptop.
③ I visited her in Busan.
④ Jenny loves her sister.
⑤ She made this for her mom.

13 다음 중 밑줄 친 부분이 어법상 옳은 것은? |4점|

① That is Sam bike.
② This backpack is not he's.
③ I looked at me in the mirror.
④ The boy is running with its dog.
⑤ Our classroom isn't clean, but theirs is clean.

14 대화의 빈칸에 들어갈 말이 순서대로 바르게 짝지어진 것은? |4점|

> A Are these Sarah's colored pencils?
> B No, they are not _____. They're mine.
> A Can I use the green pencil?
> B Sorry, but I have to use _____ now.

① her – it　　　　② her – one
③ hers – it　　　　④ hers – one
⑤ her – ones

15 다음 중 어법상 틀린 문장은? |4점|

① Can I borrow your pen?
② It snowed a lot last winter.
③ This yellow bag is mine.
④ This is my favorite singers.
⑤ The students washed their hands.

16 다음 중 밑줄 친 부분을 잘못 고친 것은? |4점|

① That hat is <u>Ann</u>.
　　　　　　(→ Ann's)
② My <u>cat</u> name is Yeppi.
　　　(→ cat's)
③ We can do it <u>ourself</u>.
　　　　　　　　(→ ourselves)
④ <u>These</u> is Wednesday today.
　　(→ This)
⑤ <u>Their</u> are my grandparents.
　　(→ They)

17 (A)~(C)에 들어갈 말이 바르게 짝지어진 것은? |3점|

> **A** Tom, how's the weather outside?
> **B** (A) │It / That│ is cold and windy.
> **A** I see. I can't find my coat.
> **B** Is this (B) │your / yours│ coat?
> **A** No, (C) │my / mine│ is brown.

	(A)	(B)	(C)
①	It	your	my
②	It	yours	my
③	It	your	mine
④	That	your	my
⑤	That	yours	mine

18 다음 대화의 빈칸 ⓐ~ⓔ에 들어갈 말로 알맞지 <u>않은</u> 것은? |4점|

> **A** May I help you?
> **B** ＿＿ⓐ＿＿ shoes are too old. I need new ＿＿ⓑ＿＿.
> **A** How about ＿＿ⓒ＿＿ shoes? ＿＿ⓓ＿＿ are on sale.
> **B** Great! I'll take ＿＿ⓔ＿＿.

① ⓐ: My　　　　　② ⓑ: it
③ ⓒ: these　　　　④ ⓓ: They
⑤ ⓔ: them

서술형

19 밑줄 친 부분을 대신하는 알맞은 대명사를 빈칸에 쓰시오. |3점, 각 1점|

(1) <u>That woman</u> is our new music teacher.
　＿＿＿＿＿＿ is very tall.

(2) <u>Jiho and Jihun</u> are my brothers.
　I love ＿＿＿＿＿＿ so much.

(3) Look at <u>the rabbit</u>.
　＿＿＿＿＿＿ ears are long.

20 괄호 안의 말을 알맞은 형태로 바꿔 빈칸에 쓰시오. |2점|

> Did you see ＿＿＿＿＿ at the party? (we)

21 대화의 빈칸에 공통으로 들어갈 말을 쓰시오. |3점|

> **A** ＿＿＿＿＿ is raining outside. Where's my umbrella?
> **B** ＿＿＿＿＿ is behind the chair.

22 어법상 틀린 부분을 찾아 바르게 고쳐 쓰시오. |4점|

> Mom, I lost my cell phone. I need a new one. Can you buy it for me?

＿＿＿＿＿＿＿　→　＿＿＿＿＿＿＿

23 우리말과 일치하도록 대화의 빈칸에 알맞은 말을 쓰시오.

|3점, 각 1점|

> **A** Is this bag _____ ?
> (이 가방은 Tom의 것이니?)
> **B** No, that's not _____ . It's _____ .
> (아니, 그건 그의 것이 아니야. 그건 내 거야.)

24 그림의 내용과 일치하도록 대화의 빈칸에 알맞은 대답을 쓰시오.

|4점, 각 2점|

(1)

> **A** What time is it now?
> **B** _____

(2)

May						
Sun	Mon	Tue	Wed	Thu	Fri	Sat
9	10	11 (Today)	12	13	14	15

> **A** What day is it today?
> **B** _____

25 괄호 안의 말을 이용하여 우리말을 영작하시오.

|8점, 각 4점|

(1) 저 남자아이들은 너의 사촌들이니?
(boys, cousins)

→ _____

(2) 여러분은 여러분들 자신을 믿어야 한다.
(you, should, trust)

→ _____

26 우리말과 일치하도록 〈조건〉에 맞게 빈칸에 알맞은 말을 쓰시오.

|3점|

> **A** I really like this picture.
> **B** Thanks. _____
> (내가 직접 그것을 그렸어.)

조건 1. 재귀대명사를 사용할 것
2. drew를 포함하여 총 4단어로 쓸 것

27 Cindy가 자신을 소개한 글을 다음과 같이 바꿀 때, 빈칸에 알맞은 말을 쓰시오.

|4점, 각 2점|

Cindy
I live in France.
My favorite subject is science.
Look at these pictures. These are mine.

↓

My Friend Cindy
She lives in France.
(1) _____ science.
Look at these pictures.
(2) These _____ .

28 다음 글의 밑줄 친 ⓐ~ⓒ를 어법에 맞게 고쳐 쓰시오.

|6점, 각 2점|

> Today was ⓐJenny birthday. She invited ⓑI to her birthday party. I made a birthday cake for her. She really liked ⓒone.

ⓐ → _____

ⓑ → _____

ⓒ → _____

chapter

5

시제

우리는 지금 요리를 하고 있어.

Q. "우리는 지금 요리를 하고 있어."를 영어로 표현하면?

☐ We cook now.　　☐ We are cooking now.

현재시제, 과거시제

동사의 형태 변화로 동작이나 상태가 언제 일어나는지를 나타낼 수 있는데 이것을 시제라고 한다.
시제에는 현재시제, 과거시제, 미래시제와 진행형이 있다.

1 현재시제

현재시제는 현재의 상태나 사실, 현재의 반복되는 일이나 습관, 변함없는 진리 등을 나타낼 때 쓴다.

현재의 상태나 사실	My uncle **lives** in Sydney. He **likes** camping and fishing.
현재의 반복되는 일이나 습관	I usually **go** to bed at 10. She **eats** cereal for breakfast.
변함없는 진리	Two plus three **is** five. The sun **rises** in the east.

> 현재시제는 always(항상), usually(보통, 대개), every ~(매 ~) 등과 함께 자주 쓰인다.
> She *always* **goes** to school by bus.
> Daniel *usually* **plays** basketball after school.
> Tony **rides** his bike *every day*.

2 과거시제

과거시제는 과거의 특정 시점에 일어난 일이나 상태, 역사적 사실을 나타낼 때 쓴다.

과거에 일어난 일이나 상태	I **lost** my umbrella yesterday. We **went** to an Italian restaurant last night.
역사적 사실	The Korean War **broke** out in 1950. Edison **invented** the light bulb in 1879.

> 과거시제는 yesterday(어제), last ~(지난 ~), ~ ago(~ 전에), 「in+과거 연도」 등과 함께 자주 쓰인다.
> Susan **cooked** pasta for dinner *yesterday*.
> It **snowed** a lot *last winter*.
> We **had** lunch together *a week ago*.

시험
point

시제와 시간을 나타내는 표현

시제를 판단할 때는 시간을 나타내는 표현에 주의하자.

1 I (visit / visited) my grandparents every Sunday.

2 I (visit / visited) my grandparents yesterday.

개념 우선 확인 | 옳은 문장 고르기

1 나는 영어를 공부했다.
   □ I study English.
   □ I studied English.

2 너는 항상 늦는다.
   □ You are always late.
   □ You were always late.

3 그녀는 매일 아침 조깅한다.
   □ She jogs every morning.
   □ She jogged every morning.

A 괄호 안에서 알맞은 것을 고르시오.

1 The earth (is / was) round.

2 She (calls / called) me 30 minutes ago.

3 There (are / were) 12 months in a year.

4 Chris and I (go / went) to the movies last night.

B 밑줄 친 부분을 바르게 고쳐 쓰시오.

1 The moon went around the earth. _____

2 The Berlin Wall comes down in 1989. _____

3 They buy a new house last month. _____

4 Rabbits had long ears. _____

C 우리말과 일치하도록 괄호 안의 동사를 알맞은 형태로 바꿔 쓰시오.

1 나는 매일 7시간 잔다.
   → I _____ seven hours every day. (sleep)

2 그 가게는 어젯밤 9시에 문을 닫았다.
   → The store _____ at 9 last night. (close)

3 Tina는 매년 여름 해변에 간다.
   → Tina _____ to the beach every summer. (go)

4 그녀는 오늘 아침 8시에 아침을 먹었다.
   → She _____ breakfast at 8 this morning. (have)

5 나의 아버지는 보통 오후 7시에 집에 오신다.
   → My father usually _____ home at 7 p.m. (come)

30초 완성 map

현재시제	현재의 상태·사실 반복되는 일이나 습관 변함없는 진리	❶ He _____ many friends. (have) Jimin always _____ to school at 8. (go) The sun _____ in the west. (set)
과거시제	과거에 일어난 일·상태 역사적 사실	❷ I _____ Rachel yesterday. (meet) The Wright brothers _____ the airplaine in 1903. (invent)

1 미래시제

미래에 일어날 일이나 앞으로의 계획은 will과 be going to를 사용하여 나타낼 수 있다.
will과 be going to 다음에는 동사원형을 쓴다.

Tina	**will**	leave	soon.
	is going to		

Tina는 곧 떠날 **것이다**.

> 미래시제는 tomorrow(내일), next ~(다음 ~), this weekend(이번 주말), soon(곧) 등과 함께 자주 쓰인다.
> Mom **will** make spaghetti for us *tomorrow*.
> We **are going to** go on a picnic *this Friday*.

2 미래시제의 부정문

will의 부정문은 「will not+동사원형」, be going to의 부정문은 「be동사+not going to+동사원형」의 형태로
쓴다. will not은 won't로 줄여 쓸 수 있다.

I	**will**	not		download the app.
	am		**going to**	

나는 그 앱을 다운로드 **하지 않을 것이다**.

The store **won't**(**will not**) open this Sunday.
She **isn't**(**is not**) **going to** wear this dress tonight.

3 미래시제의 의문문

will의 의문문은 「Will+주어+동사원형 ~?」, be going to의 의문문은 「Be동사+주어+going to+동사원형 ~?」
의 형태로 쓴다.

Will	he		buy a new cap?
Is		**going to**	

그가 새 모자를 살**까**?

A **Will** you come to the party?
B Yes, I will. / No, I won't.

A **Are** you **going to** go shopping tomorrow?
B Yes, I am. / No, I'm not.

시험
point

be동사의 미래시제

be동사의 원형은 be이므로 will이나 be going to 뒤에 be를 써야 한다.

1 It is sunny today. It (will / **will be**) cold and windy tomorrow.

2 Mom and Dad (are going to / **are going to be**) busy this weekend.

개념 우선 확인 | 옳은 문장 고르기

1 그녀는 우리에게 전화할 것이다.
- ☐ She will call us.
- ☐ She will calls us.

2 그는 곧 떠날 것이다.
- ☐ He's going to leave soon.
- ☐ He's going to leaves soon.

3 그들은 올 것이다.
- ☐ They will going to come.
- ☐ They are going to come.

A 괄호 안에서 알맞은 것을 고르시오.

1 The teachers (will / is going to) come here with us.

2 Suji and I (am / are) going to meet at 6.

3 He (willn't / won't) go camping alone.

4 I (will / am going) to read detective stories this weekend.

B 두 문장의 의미가 같도록 빈칸에 알맞은 말을 쓰시오.

1 I am going to listen to pop songs.
→ I _____ _____ to pop songs.

2 Mia and Sam are not going to join the club.
→ Mia and Sam _____ _____ the club.

3 My sister won't buy a new bag.
→ My sister _____ _____ _____ _____ a new bag.

C 우리말과 일치하도록 괄호 안의 말을 이용하여 문장을 완성하시오.

1 그녀는 언젠가 전 세계를 여행할 것이다. (travel, will)
→ She _____ _____ around the world someday.

2 Jack은 내일 회의에 참석하지 않을 것이다. (attend, will)
→ Jack _____ _____ _____ the meeting tomorrow.

3 영화가 12시에 시작할 예정이니? (start, be going to)
→ _____ the movie _____ _____ _____ at 12?

30초 완성 map

미래시제

will
① 긍정문: He **will** come back next month.
부정문: He _____ come back next month.
의문문: _____ come back next month?

be going to
② 긍정문: Dad **is going to** go fishing tomorrow.
부정문: Dad _____ go fishing tomorrow.
의문문: _____ go fishing tomorrow?

1 현재진행형

현재진행형은 '~하고 있다'의 의미로 현재에 진행 중인 일을 나타내며 「be동사의 현재형(am / are / is) + 동사원형-ing」의 형태로 쓴다.

I	am			나는 지금 게임을 **하고 있다.**
Tony	is	playing	a game now.	Tony는 지금 게임을 **하고 있다.**
We	are			우리는 지금 게임을 **하고 있다.**

I **am waiting** for the bus now.
Mr. Kim **is taking** pictures in the park.
My sisters **are swimming** in the pool.

＊동사원형-ing형 만드는 법

대부분의 동사	동사원형＋-ing	work**ing** listen**ing** teach**ing** play**ing**
-e로 끝나는 동사	e를 빼고＋-ing	com**ing** rid**ing** danc**ing** writ**ing**
-ie로 끝나는 동사	ie를 y로 고치고＋-ing	lie → l**ying** tie → t**ying** die → d**ying**
「단모음＋단자음」으로 끝나는 동사	자음을 한 번 더 쓰고＋-ing	stop → stop**ping** run → run**ning** plan → plan**ning** shop → shop**ping** cut → cut**ting** jog → jog**ging**

2 현재진행형의 부정문

'~하고 있지 않다'라는 의미의 현재진행형 부정문은 「be동사의 현재형＋not＋동사원형-ing」의 형태로 쓴다.

| I | am | not | sleeping. | 나는 자고 있지 않다. |

Andy **isn't(is not) playing** the guitar.
They **aren't(are not) having** lunch.

3 현재진행형의 의문문

'~하고 있니?'라는 의미의 현재진행형 의문문은 「Be동사의 현재형＋주어＋동사원형-ing ~?」의 형태로 쓰며, 대답은 「Yes, 주어＋be동사.」 또는 「No, 주어＋be동사＋not.」으로 한다.

| Are | you | cleaning your room now? | 너는 지금 네 방을 청소하고 있니? |

A **Is** your father **fixing** the computer now?
B Yes, he is. / No, he isn't.

A **Are** they **looking** for their cat?
B Yes, they are. / No, they aren't.

개념 우선 확인 | 옳은 문장 고르기

1 나는 책을 읽는다.
☐ I read books.
☐ I am reading books.

2 그는 수영하고 있다.
☐ He swims.
☐ He is swimming.

3 그들은 달리고 있다.
☐ They running.
☐ They are running.

A 괄호 안에서 알맞은 것을 고르시오.

1 She (writing / is writing) a story.

2 They're (play / playing) basketball outside.

3 My sister is (not using / using not) my computer.

4 Are Jack and Mina (talks / talking) on the phone?

B 밑줄 친 동사를 현재진행형으로 바꿔 써서 문장을 완성하시오.

1 I take a shower every day.

→ I _____ _____ a shower now.

2 He jogs in the park every morning.

→ He _____ _____ in the park now.

3 Ron and Jane ride their bikes to school.

→ Ron and Jane _____ _____ their bikes to school now.

C 괄호 안의 지시대로 문장을 바꿔 쓰시오.

1 He is reading a newspaper. (의문문)

→ _____

2 I am chatting on my smartphone. (부정문)

→ _____

3 They are surfing the Internet. (의문문)

→ _____

4 Mom and Dad are cooking in the kitchen. (부정문)

→ _____

30초 완성 map

현재진행형	긍정문	❶ Mina _____ _____ on the stage. (dance)	미나는 무대에서 춤추고 있다.
	부정문	❷ I _____ _____ _____. (lie)	나는 거짓말하고 있지 않아.
	의문문	❸ _____ you _____ the paper now? (cut)	너는 지금 그 종이를 자르고 있니?

서술형 대비 문장 쓰기

Answers p. 10

↻ 문장 전환 밑줄 친 부분을 시제에 맞게 알맞은 형태로 바꿔 쓰기

01 Alex and Dave <u>play</u> computer games every night.

→ Alex and Dave _____ computer games right now.

02 Jina <u>goes</u> to school at 8 every day.

→ Jina _____ to school at 8 yesterday.

03 Toby and I <u>went</u> shopping last weekend.

→ Toby and I _____ shopping next weekend.

04 The children <u>fly</u> kites in the park every weekend.

→ The children _____ kites in the park right now.

✓ 오류 수정 어법에 맞게 문장 고쳐 쓰기

05 Olivia writing an email now.

→ _____ now.

06 Is Mr. Park waits for us right now?

→ _____ right now?

07 We won't going to watch a movie tonight.

→ _____ tonight.

08 My cousin and I am going to have some dessert.

→ My cousin and I _____ .

≡ 배열 영작 괄호 안의 말을 바르게 배열하기 (필요시 형태를 바꿀 것)

09 그녀는 어젯밤에 늦게 집에 왔다. (come, late, home, she)

→ _____ last night.

10 우리는 점심으로 프라이드 치킨을 먹을 것이다. (eat, we, be going to, fried chicken)

→ _____ for lunch.

11 나는 지금 진호에게 문자를 보내고 있다. (send, be, a text message, I)

→ _____ to Jinho now.

12 Ben과 Mike는 숙제를 하고 있니? (Mike, be, their homework, Ben, do, and)

→ _____

시험에 꼭 나오는 출제 포인트

출제 포인트 1 시간 표현을 통해 시제를 판단하자!

우리말과 일치하도록 괄호 안의 동사를 알맞은 형태로 바꿔 쓰시오.

(1) 그 기차는 매일 아침 9시에 온다.

→ The train _____ at 9 every morning. (come)

(2) 나는 한 시간 전에 빨래를 했다.

→ I _____ the laundry an hour ago. (do)

출제 포인트 2 현재시제나 과거시제만 쓰이는 경우를 구분하자!

괄호 안에서 알맞은 것을 고르시오.

(1) The moon (moves / moved) around the earth.

(2) Kim Yuna (wins / won) an Olympic gold medal in 2010.

출제 포인트 3 미래시제를 나타내는 두 가지 표현을 익혀 두자!

두 문장의 의미가 같도록 빈칸에 알맞은 말을 쓰시오.

Ryan will tell the truth.

→ Ryan _____ _____ _____
  tell the truth.

> **고득점 POINT** 미래시제의 부정문과 의문문 형태
>
> **다음 중 어법상 틀린 문장은?**
>
> ① I won't eat noodles for lunch.
> ② We will not attend the meeting.
> ③ Will you meet your friend tonight?
> ④ Are you going to watch the musical?
> ⑤ He is going to not visit the museum.

출제 포인트 4 현재진행형의 형태에 유의하자!

빈칸에 들어갈 말로 알맞은 것은?

My brother _____ a snack now.

① eat   ② is eat   ③ ate
④ is eating   ⑤ does eating

> **고득점 POINT** 헷갈리는 동사원형-ing의 형태
>
> **괄호 안의 말을 이용하여 문장을 완성하시오.**
>
> (1) We are _____ a trip to Paris. (plan)
> (2) Ben is _____ on the grass now. (lie)

실전 Test

[01-02] 빈칸에 들어갈 말로 알맞은 것을 고르시오.

|6점, 각 3점|

01

The earth _____ around the sun.

① go   ② goes
③ went   ④ will go
⑤ is going to go

02

King Sejong _____ Hangul in 1443.

① invents   ② invented
③ will invent   ④ is inventing
⑤ is going to invent

[03-04] 빈칸에 공통으로 들어갈 말로 알맞은 것을 고르시오.

|6점, 각 3점|

03

• My brother _____ watching TV now.
• Ann _____ going to stay here next year.

① be   ② is   ③ was
④ will   ⑤ does

04

A _____ John come to the party this weekend?
B Yes, he _____ .

① Is(is)   ② Was(was)   ③ Will(will)
④ Did(did)   ⑤ Does(does)

05 빈칸에 들어갈 말로 알맞지 <u>않은</u> 것을 <u>모두</u> 고르면? |3점|

We saw a rainbow _____ .

① now   ② last week
③ next year   ④ this morning
⑤ three days ago

06 다음 중 밑줄 친 부분이 틀린 것은? |3점|

① I am <u>lying</u> on the bed.
② Jane is <u>riding</u> her bike.
③ It is <u>rainning</u> a lot now.
④ Mike is <u>running</u> over there.
⑤ The students are <u>working</u> hard.

07 빈칸에 들어갈 말이 순서대로 바르게 짝지어진 것은?

|3점|

• Tom _____ busy next Friday.
• I _____ a new computer yesterday.

① was – buy   ② was – bought
③ will is – buy   ④ will be – bought
⑤ will be – will buy

08 대화의 빈칸에 들어갈 말로 알맞은 것은? |3점|

A _____ a comic book?
B No, I'm not. I'm studying English.

① Do I read   ② Do you read
③ Am I reading   ④ Are you reading
⑤ Did you read

09 다음 중 밑줄 친 부분이 어법상 옳은 것은? |3점|

① Eva <u>learns</u> French last year.
② My parents <u>are eating</u> dinner now.
③ They <u>watch</u> a baseball game tomorrow.
④ Alice <u>made</u> a cheesecake next weekend.
⑤ We <u>will play</u> soccer together a week ago.

10 주어진 질문에 대한 대답으로 알맞은 것은? |3점|

> What are you doing now?

① I study art history.
② I went on a picnic.
③ I'm making a robot.
④ I will do my homework.
⑤ I'm going to clean my room.

11 우리말을 영어로 바르게 옮긴 것은? |3점|

① 그는 내일 그녀를 만날 것이다.
  → He will meets her tomorrow.
② 그 꽃들은 하얀색이었다.
  → The flowers are white.
③ 나는 지금 음악을 듣고 있지 않다.
  → I'm not listening to music now.
④ 나는 오늘 밤 TV를 보지 않을 것이다.
  → I am going not to watch TV tonight.
⑤ 소라는 숙제를 끝내지 않았다.
  → Sora didn't finished her homework.

12 다음 중 대화가 어법상 틀린 것은? |4점|

① A Will Ron come back next week?
  B No, he won't.
② A Are you going to read this magazine?
  B Yes, I am.
③ A Is Michael going to be busy next week?
  B Yes, he is.
④ A Are your friends going to join the club?
  B No, they aren't.
⑤ A Are Grandpa and Grandma going to the mall now?
  B Yes, they will.

13 다음 중 어법상 틀린 문장은? |4점|

① He always gets up early.
② It rained a lot last night.
③ Will you eat out tonight?
④ I'm not playing the piano.
⑤ He is bring some food to the table.

14 다음 중 밑줄 친 부분을 잘못 고친 것은? |3점|

① The movie is going <u>to not start</u> soon.
  (→ is not going to start)
② My parents <u>won't</u> home next weekend.
  (→ won't are)
③ <u>Is</u> Sam and Eric going to sing together?
  (→ Are)
④ <u>Will you going</u> to the library tomorrow?
  (→ Are you going to go)
⑤ We <u>will have</u> a lot of snow last winter.
  (→ had)

15 (A)~(C)에 들어갈 말이 바르게 짝지어진 것은? |3점|

> • He won't (A) go / going to the concert.
> • I (B) eat / am eating breakfast at 8 every morning.
> • It is going to (C) is / be windy tomorrow.

	(A)	(B)	(C)
①	go	eat	is
②	go	eat	be
③	go	am eating	be
④	going	eat	is
⑤	going	am eating	be

16 어법상 옳은 문장의 개수는? |4점|

ⓐ They are tired yesterday.
ⓑ I'm wearing blue jeans now.
ⓒ She will be at school last Friday.
ⓓ They lived in Busan three years ago.
ⓔ We are going to having hamburgers after school.

① 1개 ② 2개 ③ 3개
④ 4개 ⑤ 5개

최신기출

17 Kate의 일정표와 일치하지 <u>않는</u> 것은? |4점|

MON.	read a book
TUE.	visit my aunt
WED.	TODAY
THU.	have a math test
FRI.	watch a movie with Susan
SAT.	go camping with my family

① Kate read a book on Monday.
② Kate visited her aunt on Tuesday.
③ Kate will have a math test on Thursday.
④ Kate is going to watch a movie on Friday.
⑤ Kate won't go camping this weekend.

고난도

18 밑줄 친 ⓐ~ⓔ 중 대화의 흐름상 <u>어색한</u> 것은? |5점|

A Jim, did you have a good weekend?
B Yes. ⓐ<u>I went hiking with my father.</u> What about you?
A ⓑ<u>I'm staying home.</u> ⓒ<u>I read a lot of books.</u>
B I see. ⓓ<u>Are you going to stay home this weekend, too?</u>
A No. ⓔ<u>I'm going to play basketball with John.</u> Will you join us?
B Sure!

① ⓐ ② ⓑ ③ ⓒ ④ ⓓ ⑤ ⓔ

서술형

19 어법상 <u>틀린</u> 부분을 찾아 바르게 고쳐 쓰시오. |3점|

A Is Dan going to takes Spanish lessons?
B Yes, he is.

_____ → _____

20 내용상 자연스러운 문장이 되도록 괄호 안의 동사를 알맞은 형태로 바꿔 쓰시오. |3점|

I _____ hard last month, so I passed the test. (study)

21 자연스러운 대화가 되도록 빈칸에 알맞은 대답을 세 단어로 쓰시오. |3점|

A Is Yumi studying for the exam?
B _____ She's playing a computer game.

22 밑줄 친 ⓐ~ⓒ의 동사를 어법에 맞게 고쳐 쓰시오.
|3점, 각 1점|

• I ⓐ<u>be</u> sick a week ago, but I ⓑ<u>be</u> not sick now.
• Minho ⓒ<u>travel</u> to Europe next year.

ⓐ → _____
ⓑ → _____
ⓒ → _____

23 그림을 보고, 괄호 안의 단어를 이용하여 대화를 완성하시오. |4점, 각 2점|

(1)

(2)

(1) **A** What _____ Alex doing?

B _____ _____ _____ in the river. (swim)

(2) **A** What _____ Peter and Sue doing?

B _____ _____ _____ on the stage. (dance)

24 괄호 안의 지시대로 문장을 바꿔 쓰시오. |6점, 각 3점|

(1) I am late. (will을 사용한 부정문으로)

→ _____

(2) They left the party. (현재진행형 의문문으로)

→ _____

25 자연스러운 대화가 되도록 〈조건〉에 맞게 빈칸에 알맞은 말을 쓰시오. |5점|

A _____

these sneakers?

B Yes, I am. I like them.

조건 1. 미래시제로 쓸 것

2. be동사와 buy를 사용할 것

26 어법상 틀린 부분을 찾아 바르게 고쳐 문장을 다시 쓰시오. (가능한 답 두 개를 모두 쓸 것) |4점, 각 2점|

Will he going to visit Paris next year?

→ _____

→ _____

27 Joe의 계획표를 보고, 〈조건〉에 맞게 빈칸에 알맞은 말을 쓰시오. |4점, 각 2점|

Yesterday	Today	Tomorrow
내 방 청소하기	쇼핑하기	축구하기

조건 1. clean, play를 사용하여 각각 세 단어로 쓸 것

2. be동사는 사용하지 말 것

Joe _____ yesterday.
He went shopping today.
He _____ tomorrow.

28 밑줄 친 ⓐ~ⓔ 중 대화의 흐름상 어색한 것을 찾아 기호를 쓰고, 바르게 고쳐 쓰시오. |5점|

A ⓐI am going to go to Canada next month.

B That's great! ⓑAre you going to stay at a hotel?

A No. I'm going to stay at my grandmother's house.

B Oh, ⓒdoes your grandmother live in Canada?

A Yes. ⓓShe will move to Toronto in 2010.

ⓔI will travel around Canada with her.

( ) → _____

chapter

6

조동사

Jason **can** speak English.
Mia **may** speak English.

Q. 위 두 문장으로 보아 남자는 누구에게 길을 물어보면 좋을까?

☐ Jason   ☐ Mia

1 조동사의 특징

조동사는 be동사나 일반동사를 도와서 능력, 추측, 의무, 허가 등의 의미를 더해 준다.
조동사는 주어의 인칭이나 수에 관계없이 형태가 같고, 뒤에 항상 동사원형이 온다.

I	**can**		나는 하와이에 **갈 수 있다.**
He	**may**	go to Hawaii.	그는 하와이에 **갈지도 모른다.**
You	**must**		너는 하와이에 **가야만 한다.**
They	**should**		그들은 하와이에 **가야 한다.**

2 조동사의 부정문

조동사의 부정문은 조동사 바로 뒤에 not을 붙여 만든다.

You	**must**		run here.	너는 여기서 뛰어서는 **안 된다.**
He	**should**	not	go there.	그는 그곳에 가면 **안 된다.**
It	**may**		be true.	그것은 사실이 **아닐지도 모른다.**
I	**cannot**		swim.	나는 수영을 하지 **못한다.**

주의 can의 부정을 can not으로 쓰지 않고 may not을 mayn't로 줄여 쓰지 않도록 주의한다.

You **shouldn't** be late again.
Jane and I **can't** go to the party.

3 조동사의 의문문

조동사의 의문문은 조동사를 주어 앞으로 보내 「조동사＋주어＋동사원형 ~?」의 형태로 쓰며,
긍정의 대답은 「Yes, 주어＋조동사.」로, 부정의 대답은 「No, 주어＋조동사＋not.」으로 한다.

Can	she	drive a car?	그녀는 자동차를 운전할 **수 있니?**
May	I	use your pen?	네 펜을 사용**해도 되니?**

A **Can** you play the violin?
B Yes, I can. / No, I can't.

개념 우선 확인 | 옳은 형태 고르기

1 He can _____ .
☐ swim
☐ swims

2 They may _____ busy.
☐ are
☐ be

3 Can she _____ French?
☐ speak
☐ speaks

A 괄호 안에서 알맞은 것을 고르시오.

1 Daniel (must / musts) finish the work today.

2 Can you (help / helping) me now?

3 You (don't should / should not) park your car here.

4 She (mayn't / may not) be home now.

B 밑줄 친 부분을 부정형으로 바꿔 쓰시오.

1 You <u>should shout</u> in the library.
→ You _____ in the library.

2 I <u>can find</u> this word in the dictionary.
→ I _____ this word in the dictionary.

3 He <u>may go</u> to the meeting tomorrow.
→ He _____ to the meeting tomorrow.

C 괄호 안의 지시대로 문장을 바꿔 쓰시오.

1 We can go home now. (의문문)
→ _____

2 Mike may join our tennis club. (부정문)
→ _____

3 We must play the piano at night. (부정문)
→ _____

4 You should drink a lot of coffee. (부정문)
→ _____

30초 완성 map

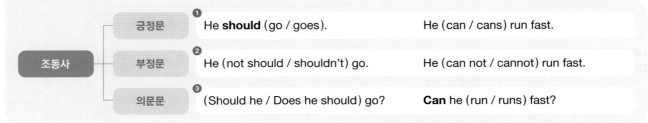

긍정문 ❶	He **should** (go / goes).	He (can / cans) run fast.
조동사 부정문 ❷	He (not should / shouldn't) go.	He (can not / cannot) run fast.
의문문 ❸	(Should he / Does he should) go?	**Can** he (run / runs) fast?

1 can

~할 수 있다 〈능력〉	I **can** speak Spanish. She **can't**(**cannot**) ride a bike. (~할 수 없다) A **Can** you play the guitar? B Yes, I **can**. / No, I **can't**.
~해도 좋다 〈허가〉	You **can** use my cell phone. You **can't**(**cannot**) eat food here. (~하면 안 된다) A **Can** I take pictures here? B Yes, you **can**. / No, you **can't**.
~해 줄래? 〈요청〉	A **Can** you do the dishes? B OK(Sure). / Sorry, but I'm busy.

▶ can이 '~할 수 있다'의 의미로 쓰일 때는 be able to로 바꿔 쓸 수 있다. 이때 be동사는 주어의 인칭과 수에 따라 형태가 바뀐다.

Mike **is able to** come to the party.
We **are not able to** use the Internet now.
She **will be able to** pass the exam.

2 may

~일지도 모른다 〈약한 추측〉	Susie **may** be sick. He **may not** come to school today. (~이 아닐지도 모른다)
~해도 좋다 〈허가〉	You **may** close the window. You **may not** wear your shoes here. (~하면 안 된다) A **May** I go home now? B Yes, you **may**. / No, you **may not**.

▶ can과 may는 모두 허가를 나타내지만 may가 더 공손한 표현이다.

Can I borrow your book? (네 책을 빌려 줄래?)
May I borrow your book? (당신 책을 빌려도 될까요?)

시험
point

두 개를 나란히 쓸 수 없는 조동사

능력을 나타내는 can을 다른 조동사와 같이 쓸 때는 「조동사+be able to」 형태로 쓴다.

1 Mike will (can / be able to) solve the problem.

2 We may (can / be able to) go to the moon soon.

개념 우선 확인 | 밑줄 친 부분의 옳은 해석 고르기

1 I <u>can</u> play tennis.
  ☐ ~할 수 있다
  ☐ ~해도 좋다

2 He <u>may</u> be hungry.
  ☐ ~해도 좋다
  ☐ ~일지도 모른다

3 <u>May</u> I sit here?
  ☐ ~해도 좋다
  ☐ ~일지도 모른다

A 괄호 안에서 알맞은 것을 고르시오.

1 (Can / May) you do magic tricks?

2 Tyler (will can / will be able to) win the match.

3 We (can / are able) visit many cities in Canada.

4 John is very busy. He (may / may not) play soccer with us.

B 우리말과 일치하도록 밑줄 친 부분을 바르게 고쳐 쓰시오.

1 내일 아침에 나에게 전화해 주겠니?
  → <u>May</u> you call me tomorrow morning? _____

2 아빠가 우리에게 스파게티를 만들어 주실 수 있을 것이다.
  → Dad will <u>can</u> make spaghetti for us. _____

3 그녀는 집에 일찍 오지 않을지도 모른다.
  → She <u>cannot</u> come home early. _____

C 〈보기〉에서 알맞은 동사를 고른 후 **may** 또는 **can**을 사용하여 대화를 완성하시오.

보기	pass	be	walk	borrow

1 A The traffic is very heavy.
  B Julia _____ _____ late for the contest.

2 A I broke my leg. I _____ _____ very well.
  B That's too bad.

3 A _____ you _____ me the spoon?
  B Sure. Here you are.

4 A It's raining a lot. _____ I _____ your umbrella?
  B Yes, of course.

30초 완성 map

조동사
  can
  ❶ He **can** sing well. (능력 / 허가) **Can** we sing here? (능력 / 허가)
  Can you sing for us? (능력 / 요청) 주의 He will (can / be able to) go there.

  may
  ❷ She **may** be busy. (추측 / 허가) **May** I go with you? (추측 / 허가)

unit 3 must, have to, should

1 must

~해야 한다 〈강한 의무〉	You **must** return the book today. You **must not** cross the street on a red light.
~임에 틀림없다 〈강한 추측〉	I saw Nancy's car outside. She **must** be at home.

▶ '~일 리가 없다'의 의미로 강한 부정의 추측을 나타낼 때는 must not이 아니라 can't를 쓴다.

   That **must** be true. (~임에 틀림없다)
   That **can't** be true. (~일 리가 없다)

2 have to

have to는 의무를 나타내는 must와 바꿔 쓸 수 있으며, 시제와 주어의 인칭이나 수에 따라 have의 형태가 바뀐다.

~해야 한다 〈의무〉	You **have to** wear a seat belt. She **has to** come home before 9. We **had to** leave early this morning.

주의 조동사는 두 개를 나란히 쓸 수 없으므로 의무를 나타내는 must가 다른 조동사와 쓰일 때는 have to를 쓴다.
   I **will have to** lose weight. (~해야 할 것이다)
   ‾‾‾‾‾‾‾‾‾‾‾
   will must (x)

▶ must와 have to는 의무를 나타내는 같은 의미로 쓰일 수 있지만 부정형일 때는 의미가 달라진다.

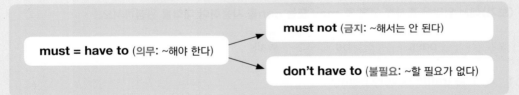

You **must** (**have to**) finish the report today.
You **must not** be late for the train. It leaves on time.
You **don't have to** hurry. The store isn't open yet.

3 should

~해야 한다 〈(도덕적) 의무〉	You **should** be honest with your parents.
~하는 게 좋다 〈충고〉	You **should** exercise for your health. You **shouldn't** be late for school.

비교
point **must not vs. don't have to**

You **must not** run here.	너는 여기서 뛰어**서는 안 된다.** 〈금지〉
You **don't have to** run here.	너는 여기서 뛸 **필요가 없다.** 〈불필요〉

개념 우선 확인 | 옳은 문장 고르기

1 그는 졸린 것이 틀림없다.
- ☐ He must be sleepy.
- ☐ He can't be sleepy.

2 너는 그것을 할 필요가 없다.
- ☐ You must not do it.
- ☐ You don't have to do it.

3 우리는 가야만 했다.
- ☐ We had to go.
- ☐ We did must go.

A 괄호 안에서 알맞은 것을 고르시오.

1 It's snowing. You (should / must not) wear your gloves.

2 They were late for class. They (have to / had to) run.

3 It's too late. We (will must / will have to) do it tomorrow.

4 We have enough milk. We (have to / don't have to) buy more.

B have to와 괄호 안의 동사를 이용하여 문장을 완성하시오. (시제에 유의할 것)

1 He _____ _____ _____ his homework now. (do)

2 I _____ _____ _____ for two hours yesterday. (wait)

3 You _____ _____ _____ _____ here tomorrow. (leave)

4 They _____ _____ _____ for the test last night. (study)

C 우리말과 일치하도록 괄호 안의 말을 이용하여 문장을 완성하시오.

1 그는 지금 자고 있다. 피곤한 게 틀림없다. (must, be)

→ He is sleeping now. He _____ _____ tired.

2 이 근처에서는 뛰면 안 된다. (should, run)

→ You _____ _____ _____ around here.

3 너는 미래를 위해 저축을 해야 해. (must, save)

→ You _____ _____ money for the future.

4 일요일이야. 나는 일찍 일어날 필요가 없어. (have to, get up)

→ It's Sunday. I _____ _____ _____ _____ _____ early.

30초 완성 map

조동사

- must
  - ❶ You **must** run. 너는 _____.
  - You **must** be hungry. 너는 _____.
- have to
  - ❷ She _____ _____ leave now. 그녀는 지금 떠나야 한다.
  - 주의 You **don't have to** hurry. 너는 (서두르지 말아야 한다 / 서두를 필요가 없다).
- should
  - ❸ We **should** be quiet in the library. 우리는 도서관에서 _____.
  - It's late. You **should** take a taxi. 늦었다. 너는 _____.

서술형 대비 문장 쓰기

Answers p. 12

□ 빈칸 완성 괄호 안의 말을 이용하여 빈칸 완성하기

01 수업 시간에 휴대전화를 사용해서는 안 된다. (use, must)

→ You ＿＿＿＿＿＿＿＿＿＿＿＿＿＿＿＿＿＿ your cell phones in class.

02 수진이는 롤러코스터를 타지 못한다. (ride, can)

→ Sujin ＿＿＿＿＿＿＿＿＿＿＿＿＿＿＿＿ roller coasters.

03 너는 지금 그것에 대해 걱정할 필요가 없다. (worry, have to)

→ You ＿＿＿＿＿＿＿＿＿＿＿＿＿＿＿＿＿ about it now.

04 우리는 오후 2시까지 그곳에 도착할 수 있었다. (get, be able to)

→ We ＿＿＿＿＿＿＿＿＿＿＿＿＿＿＿＿＿ there by 2 p.m.

↻ 문장 전환 괄호 안의 지시대로 문장 바꿔 쓰기

05 You must make noise in the museum. (부정문)

→ ＿＿＿＿＿＿＿＿＿＿＿＿＿＿＿＿＿＿ in the museum.

06 You can carry the box for me. (의문문)

→ ＿＿＿＿＿＿＿＿＿＿＿＿＿＿＿＿＿＿ for me?

07 Tim can speak Korean well. (미래시제)

→ ＿＿＿＿＿＿＿＿＿＿＿＿＿＿＿＿＿＿ Korean well.

08 She must wear her seat belt. (have to 이용)

→ ＿＿＿＿＿＿＿＿＿＿＿＿＿＿＿＿＿＿ her seat belt.

≡ 배열 영작 괄호 안의 말을 바르게 배열하기

09 이곳에서는 뛰면 안 된다. (run, you, not, may)

→ ＿＿＿＿＿＿＿＿＿＿＿＿＿＿＿＿＿＿ here.

10 저를 위해 이것을 해주실 수 있나요? (do, you, can, this)

→ ＿＿＿＿＿＿＿＿＿＿＿＿＿＿＿＿＿＿ for me?

11 우리는 웅변대회에 늦어서는 안 된다. (not, should, be, late, we)

→ ＿＿＿＿＿＿＿＿＿＿＿＿＿＿＿＿＿＿ for the speech contest.

12 너는 내일 일찍 오지 않아도 된다. (have, don't, to, you, come)

→ ＿＿＿＿＿＿＿＿＿＿＿＿＿＿＿＿＿＿ early tomorrow.

시험에 나오는 **출제 포인트**

Answers p. 12

출제 포인트 ❶ 조동사의 특징을 기억하자!

괄호 안에서 알맞은 것을 고르시오.

(1) She (may / mays) understand you.

(2) My uncle can (fix / fixes) my bike.

> **고득점 POINT** 조동사는 두 개를 나란히 쓸 수 없다.
>
> **우리말과 일치하도록 밑줄 친 부분을 어법에 맞게 고쳐 쓰시오.**
>
> He <u>may can</u> skate well.
> (그는 스케이트를 잘 탈 수 있을지도 모른다.)
> → _____

출제 포인트 ❷ 조동사의 여러 의미를 각각 구분하자!

밑줄 친 May(may)의 의미가 나머지와 다른 것은?

① <u>May</u> I open the window?
② The news <u>may</u> not be true.
③ <u>May</u> I have some water?
④ You <u>may</u> go to the bathroom now.
⑤ You <u>may</u> not play music loudly at night.

출제 포인트 ❸ 조동사 can, must와 바꿔 쓸 수 있는 표현을 익혀 두자!

두 문장의 의미가 같도록 빈칸에 알맞은 말을 쓰시오.

(1) I can make Mexican food.

→ I _____ _____ _____ make
   Mexican food.

(2) He must listen to his father.

→ He _____ _____ listen to his father.

> **고득점 POINT** be able to와 have to의 형태 변화
>
> **우리말과 일치하도록 빈칸에 알맞은 말을 쓰시오.**
>
> (1) 나는 그곳에 제시간에 도착할 수 있을 것이다.
>   → I _____ _____ _____
>   arrive there on time.
>
> (2) 우리는 규칙을 따라야 했다.
>   → We _____ _____ follow the rules.

출제 포인트 ❹ must not과 don't have to의 의미 차이를 구분하자!

우리말과 일치하도록 괄호 안에서 알맞은 것을 고르시오.

(1) 너는 시간을 낭비해서는 안 된다.

→ You (must not / don't have to) waste your time.

(2) 그녀는 그 버스를 기다릴 필요가 없다.

→ She (must not / doesn't have to) wait for the bus.

유형	문항수	배점	점수
객관식	18	60	
서술형	10	40	

01 빈칸에 들어갈 말로 알맞지 <u>않은</u> 것은? |2점|

Sam _____ come here on time.

① is　　② may　　③ can
④ must　　⑤ should

02 빈칸에 들어갈 말로 알맞은 것은? |3점|

I'm very busy. I _____ play with you now.

① can　　② can't　　③ may
④ must　　⑤ should

[03-04] 빈칸에 공통으로 들어갈 말로 알맞은 것을 고르시오.
|6점, 각 3점|

03
• You _____ not run in the museum.
• You look sick. You _____ see a doctor.

① will　　② can　　③ should
④ have to　　⑤ are able to

04
• I _____ finish my homework before dinner.
• You may go first. You don't _____ wait for me.

① could　　② may　　③ be able to
④ should　　⑤ have to

05 빈칸에 may(May)가 들어갈 수 <u>없는</u> 것은? |3점|

① You _____ wear my hat.
② _____ I use your eraser?
③ Sally _____ be bored now.
④ Mark _____ be at his office.
⑤ _____ you close the window?

06 밑줄 친 can(Can)의 의미가 〈보기〉와 같은 것은? |3점|

> 보기　I <u>can</u> play the flute.

① You <u>can</u> use my camera.
② <u>Can</u> I borrow your bike?
③ <u>Can</u> you turn on the TV, please?
④ I <u>can</u> sing many K-pop songs.
⑤ You <u>can</u> have the cookies.

[07-08] 밑줄 친 부분의 쓰임이 나머지와 <u>다른</u> 것을 고르시오.
|6점, 각 3점|

07 ① You <u>must</u> do your best.
② He <u>must</u> pass the exam.
③ We <u>must</u> follow the traffic rules.
④ They <u>must</u> clean the classroom.
⑤ My English teacher <u>must</u> be angry today.

08 ① The news <u>may</u> be true.
② You <u>may</u> go out and play.
③ He <u>may</u> have lots of money.
④ It <u>may</u> rain a lot tomorrow.
⑤ She <u>may</u> come back next week.

09 (A)~(C)에 들어갈 말이 바르게 짝지어진 것은? |3점|

> • The man (A) may / mays be diligent.
> • Can Emily (B) do / does the work?
> • He (C) have to / has to buy a new bag.

      (A)   (B)   (C)

① may ····· do ····· have to
② may ····· does ····· has to
③ may ····· do ····· has to
④ mays ····· does ····· have to
⑤ mays ····· do ····· has to

10 밑줄 친 부분을 의미가 같도록 바꿔 쓸 때, 알맞지 <u>않은</u> 것은? |4점|

① Can I use the bathroom?
   (→ May)
② We can make Korean food.
    (→ are able to)
③ You must study for the English test.
     (→ have to)
④ My grandma can't send text messages.
      (→ isn't able to)
⑤ You must not turn on your computer.
     (→ don't have to)

11 다음 중 대화가 자연스럽지 <u>않은</u> 것은? |4점|

① A Can you help me?
   B Of course.
② A May I see your student ID?
   B Sure. Here it is.
③ A Can I try this skirt on?
   B Sorry, you can't.
④ A Can you answer the question?
   B Yes, I can.
⑤ A Should I bring my sunglasses?
   B Yes. You won't need them.

12 표지판을 보고, 대화의 빈칸에 들어갈 말로 알맞은 것을 고르면? |3점|

> A Can I park my car here?
> B _____ Look at this sign.

① Yes, I can.   ② Yes, you can.
③ No, I don't.   ④ No, you can't.
⑤ Sorry, but I can't.

13 다음 중 어법상 옳은 문장은? |4점|

① You mayn't sit here.
② It may is difficult for him.
③ Tom must not goes there.
④ You shouldn't use plastic bags.
⑤ They may can solve the puzzle.

14 어법상 <u>틀린</u> 부분을 찾아 바르게 고친 것은? |4점|

> It's not cold today. You have not to wear a coat.

① It's → That's
② It's not → It's
③ have → must
④ have not to → don't have to
⑤ to wear → wear

15 어법상 옳은 문장의 개수는? |5점|

> ⓐ He musts be nervous.
> ⓑ They may not come to the festival.
> ⓒ Peter will can eat lunch with us.
> ⓓ Do I may drink some milk now?
> ⓔ Mr. White can speak three languages.

① 1개   ② 2개   ③ 3개
④ 4개   ⑤ 5개

16 다음은 세 사람이 할 수 있는 것과 할 수 없는 것을 나타낸 표이다. 표의 내용과 일치하지 <u>않는</u> 것은? |3점|

	ride a bike	play tennis	speak Chinese
Sumi	○	×	○
Jiho	×	○	○
Mina	○	○	×

① Sumi can ride a bike.
② Jiho cannot ride a bike.
③ Sumi isn't able to play tennis.
④ Jiho and Sumi are able to speak Chinese.
⑤ Mina can play tennis and speak Chinese.

[17-18] 다음 글을 읽고, 물음에 답하시오.

> Kelly goes to school by bus. Every morning, the traffic is very heavy. So she is often late for school. Today, she was late again.
>
> ↓
>
> **Teacher** You ___ⓐ___ not be late again. You ___ⓑ___ arrive before 8:30. It's our rule. (A) 내일은 제시간에 올 수 있겠니?

17 빈칸 ⓐ와 ⓑ에 공통으로 들어갈 말로 알맞은 것은? |3점|

① will   ② can   ③ must
④ may   ⑤ have to

18 밑줄 친 (A)의 우리말을 영어로 바르게 옮긴 것은? |4점|

① Can you will come on time tomorrow?
② Will you can come on time tomorrow?
③ Can you be able to come on time tomorrow?
④ Will you be able to come on time tomorrow?
⑤ Are you be able to come on time tomorrow?

19 다음 그림을 보고, 괄호 안의 단어와 can을 이용하여 문장을 완성하시오. |4점, 각 2점|

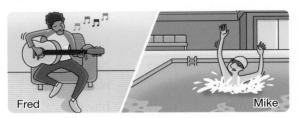

(1) Fred _____ the guitar. (play)
(2) Mike _____ well. (swim)

20 우리말과 일치하도록 괄호 안의 말을 바르게 배열하시오. (단, 조동사를 추가할 것) |3점|

> 그녀는 소풍을 가지 않을지도 모른다.
> (not, she, go on a picnic)

→ _____

21 우리말과 일치하도록 빈칸에 알맞은 말을 쓰시오. |3점|

> 일요일이야. 너는 학교에 갈 필요가 없어.

→ It's Sunday. You _____
to school.

최신기출

22 다음 문장을 의문문으로 바꿔 쓰고, 답을 완성하시오. |3점|

> Peter can fix the computer.

A _____ _____ _____ _____
_____?
B No, _____.

23 괄호 안의 말과 조동사를 사용하여 대화를 완성하시오.

|3점|

> **A** I don't have a pen. _____
>
> _____ (use, I, yours)
>
> **B** Okay. Here it is.

24 그림을 보고, 각 장소에서 지켜야 할 규칙을 〈조건〉에 맞게 쓰시오.

|4점, 각 2점|

(1)   (2)

> 조건 1. 괄호 안의 말을 반드시 사용할 것
>   2. 긍정문과 부정문을 한 번씩 쓸 것

(1) You _____

in the museum. (must, pictures)

(2) You _____

in the library. (should, quiet)

25 주어진 문장을 〈보기〉와 같이 충고하는 문장으로 바꿔 쓰시오.

|4점, 각 2점|

> 보기 Don't eat a lot of fast food.
>   → You shouldn't eat a lot of fast food.

(1) Clean your room every day.

→ _____

(2) Don't buy the jacket.

→ _____

26 괄호 안의 지시대로 문장을 바꿔 쓰시오.

|6점, 각 3점|

(1) He can't come home soon. (미래시제)

→ _____

(2) We must get up early. (과거시제)

→ _____

27 괄호 안의 말을 이용하여 밑줄 친 우리말을 〈조건〉에 맞게 영작하시오.

|4점, 각 2점|

> **A** (1) <u>너는 그 화병을 만지면 안 돼.</u>
>   (touch the vase)
>
> **B** Why not?
>
> **A** (2) <u>그것이 깨질지도 몰라.</u> (break)

> 조건 1. will, may, must 중 하나를 선택하여 한 번씩만 쓸 것
>   2. 부정어는 줄임말로 쓰지 말 것

(1) _____

(2) _____

28 어법상 <u>틀린</u> 부분을 <u>두 군데</u> 찾아 바르게 고쳐 쓰시오.

|6점, 각 3점|

> **A** Look at that skateboard. It looks cool.
>
> **B** Wow, it must is expensive.
>
> **A** I'm going to start saving money for it.
>
> **B** That's great! You will can buy it someday.

(1) _____ → _____

(2) _____ → _____

chapter

7

to부정사와 동명사

우리는 기타 치는 것을 좋아해.

Q. "우리는 기타 치는 것을 좋아해."를 영어로 표현하면?

☐ We like play the guitar.　　☐ We like to play the guitar.

to부정사의 명사적 용법

1 to부정사

to부정사는 「to+동사원형」의 형태로 문장 안에서 명사, 형용사, 부사의 역할을 한다.

		동사원형	
to	**+**	**eat** (먹다)	┌ **먹는 것, 먹기** 〈명사 역할〉 ├ **먹을** 〈형용사 역할〉 └ **먹기 위해** 〈부사 역할〉

2 to부정사의 명사적 용법

to부정사가 명사처럼 문장 안에서 주어, 목적어, 보어로 쓰일 때는 '~하는 것', '~하기'로 해석한다.

(1) 주어 역할: ~하는 것은, ~하기는

To learn English	is fun.	영어 **배우기는** 재미있다.
To follow school rules	is important.	학교 규칙을 **따르는 것은** 중요하다.

> **주의** to부정사구가 문장에서 주어 역할을 할 경우, 단수 취급한다.

> ▶ to부정사구가 주어로 쓰일 때, 보통 주어 자리에 가주어 It을 쓰고, to부정사구를 문장의 맨 뒤로 보낸다.
>
> **To swim** in this river isn't safe.
> → **It** isn't safe **to swim** in this river.
> ⌐➤ 가주어 It은 '그것'이라고 해석하지 않는다.

(2) 목적어 역할: ~하는 것을

to부정사가 동사 want, hope, plan, need, decide, promise, expect, agree, like 등의 목적어로 쓰인다.

They	want	**to see** the movie.	그들은 그 영화를 **보는 것을** 원한다.
I	hope	**to pass** the exam.	나는 시험에 **합격하기를** 바란다.
We	decided	**not to go** to Laos.	우리는 라오스에 **가지 않기로** 결정했다.

> **주의** to부정사를 부정할 때는 to부정사 앞에 not이나 never를 쓴다.

(3) 보어 역할: ~하는 것(이다)

to부정사가 주격보어로 쓰여 주어를 보충 설명한다.

My dream is	**to become** a pilot.	내 꿈은 비행기 조종사가 **되는 것**이다.
His goal is	**to save** a lot of money.	그의 목표는 많은 돈을 **모으는 것**이다.
Her plan is	**to finish** it today.	그녀의 계획은 오늘 그것을 **끝내는 것**이다.

개념 우선 확인 | 밑줄 친 to부정사의 옳은 해석 고르기

1 It is fun <u>to swim</u>.
- ☐ 수영하기를
- ☐ 수영하기는

2 My goal is <u>to swim</u> fast.
- ☐ 수영하는 것
- ☐ 수영하기를

3 I want <u>to swim</u> fast.
- ☐ 수영하기를
- ☐ 수영하기는

A 괄호 안에서 알맞은 것을 고르시오.

1 My plan is (buy / to buy) a new tablet PC.

2 He likes (to ride / rides) his bike in the park.

3 It is important (learn / to learn) history.

4 They need (exercise / to exercise) regularly.

5 (It / This) is difficult to make new friends.

B 빈칸에 들어갈 말을 〈보기〉에서 골라 알맞은 형태로 쓰시오. (단, 한 번씩만 사용할 것)

보기	learn	invite	become	join

1 I decided _____ the guitar club.

2 He promised _____ me to his party.

3 My dream is _____ a famous artist.

4 It is interesting _____ a foreign language.

C 우리말과 일치하도록 괄호 안의 말을 이용하여 문장을 완성하시오.

1 그녀의 목표는 3개 국어를 말하는 것이다. (be, speak)

→ Her goal _____ _____ _____ three languages.

2 그는 농구 선수가 되기를 희망한다. (hope, become)

→ He _____ _____ _____ a basketball player.

3 그 일을 오늘 끝내는 것은 쉽지 않을 것이다. (finish)

→ _____ won't be easy _____ _____ the work today.

4 그는 다시는 나에게 거짓말을 하지 않기로 약속했다. (promise, lie)

→ He _____ _____ _____ _____ to me again.

30초 완성 map

to부정사 — 명사적 용법

주어
❶ **To ski** is exciting. _____ 신난다.
= _____ is exciting **to ski**.

목적어
❷ I like **to ski**. 나는 _____ 좋아한다.

보어
❸ My plan is **to ski**. 내 계획은 _____ 이다.

to부정사의 형용사적 용법과 부사적 용법

1 to부정사의 형용사적 용법

to부정사가 명사나 대명사를 뒤에서 꾸며주는 형용사 역할을 할 때는 '~할', '~해야 할'로 해석한다.

| We have | a problem. | | 우리는 문제가 있다. |
| We have | a problem | **to solve.** | 우리는 **해결해야 할** 문제가 있다. 〈명사 수식〉 |

| I want | something. | | 나는 어떤 것을 원한다. |
| I want | something | **to eat.** | 나는 **먹을** 무언가를 원한다. 〈대명사 수식〉 |

2 to부정사의 부사적 용법

to부정사가 부사처럼 동사나 형용사, 문장 전체를 꾸며주며 목적, 원인, 결과 등의 의미를 나타낸다.

(1) 목적: ~하기 위해

행동	행동의 목적(~하기 위해)	
She exercised	**to lose** weight.	그녀는 체중을 **줄이기 위해** 운동했다.
I saved money	**to buy** new sneakers.	나는 새 운동화를 **사기 위해** 돈을 모았다.

(2) 감정의 원인: ~해서, ~하여

감정	감정의 원인(~해서)	
I'm glad	**to see** you again.	나는 너를 다시 **만나서** 기쁘다.
We were sad	**to leave** the city.	우리는 그 도시를 **떠나게 되어서** 슬펐다.

> 원인을 나타내는 부사적 용법의 to부정사는 주로 happy, glad, sad, sorry, surprised 등 감정을 나타내는 형용사 뒤에 쓰인다.

(3) 결과: (…해서) (결국) ~하다

자연적으로 일어난 일(…해서)	일의 결과(~하다)	
She grew up	**to be** a painter.	그녀는 자라서 화가가 **되었다.**
He lived	**to be** 99 years old.	그는 살아서 99살이 **되었다.**

비교 point

형용사적 용법 vs. 부사적 용법

| I have enough money **to buy** a T-shirt. | 티셔츠를 **살** | 〈명사를 수식하는 형용사적 용법〉 |
| I went to the mall **to buy** a T-shirt. | 티셔츠를 **사기 위해** | 〈목적을 나타내는 부사적 용법〉 |

개념 우선 확인 | 밑줄 친 부분의 옳은 해석 고르기

1 He wants <u>something to drink</u>.
☐ 마실 무언가
☐ 무언가를 마시기 위해

2 I was happy <u>to win the game</u>.
☐ 경기를 이기기 위해
☐ 경기를 이겨서

3 We have <u>lots of work to do</u>.
☐ 해야 할 많은 일
☐ 많은 일을 하기 위해

A 자연스러운 의미의 문장이 되도록 알맞게 연결하시오.

1 I turned on the computer •　　　• ⓐ to be 90 years old.

2 The children were happy •　　　• ⓑ to play with snow.

3 My grandfather lived •　　　• ⓒ to read on the train.

4 She needs a magazine •　　　• ⓓ to check my email.

B 빈칸에 들어갈 말을 〈보기〉에서 골라 알맞은 형태로 쓰시오. (단, 한 번씩만 사용할 것)

보기	buy	become	hear	see

1 I have enough money _____ the shoes.

2 We went outside _____ the stars in the sky.

3 They were sad _____ the news.

4 She grew up _____ a famous writer.

C 우리말과 일치하도록 괄호 안의 말을 이용하여 문장을 완성하시오.

1 그들은 시험에 합격하기 위해 열심히 공부했다. (pass, the test)

→ They studied hard _____ _____ _____ _____.

2 냉장고에는 먹을 것이 하나도 없었다. (eat, nothing)

→ There was _____ _____ _____ in the refrigerator.

3 나는 그 실수를 해서 유감이었다. (make, that mistake)

→ I was sorry _____ _____ _____ _____.

4 그는 자라서 위대한 과학자가 되었다. (become, grow up)

→ He _____ _____ _____ _____ a great scientist.

30초 완성 map

to부정사

형용사적 용법
❶
I have many books **to read**.　　나는 _____ 책을 많이 가지고 있다.
I want something **to eat**.　　나는 _____ 무언가를 원한다.

부사적 용법
❷
She tried hard **to become** a singer.　　그녀는 가수가 _____ 열심히 노력했다.
She was happy **to become** a singer.　　그녀는 가수가 _____ 행복했다.
She grew up **to become** a singer.　　그녀는 _____ 가수가 _____.

1 동명사

동명사는 「동사원형＋-ing」의 형태로 동사의 의미와 성질을 가지면서 명사의 역할을 한다.

동사원형			동명사	
study (공부하다) **eat** (먹다)	**+**	**-ing** →	**study**ing **eat**ing	공부하기 먹기

2 동명사의 역할

동명사는 명사처럼 문장 안에서 주어, 목적어, 보어 역할을 한다.

(1) 주어 역할: ~하는 것은, ~하기는

Learning	is very important.	배우는 것은 매우 중요하다.
Learning history		역사를 **배우는 것은** 매우 중요하다.

> 동명사(구)가 주어 역할을 할 경우, 단수 취급한다.
> **Watching** sports **is** exciting.

(2) 목적어 역할: ~하는 것을

동명사가 동사 enjoy, finish, mind, avoid, practice, stop, quit, give up 등의 목적어로 쓰인다.

I	enjoy	**listening** to classical music.	나는 클래식 음악 **듣는 것을** 즐긴다.
She	stopped	**playing** mobile games.	그녀는 모바일 게임 **하는 것을** 멈췄다.

(3) 보어 역할: ~하는 것(이다)

Her hobby is	**collecting** coins.	그녀의 취미는 동전을 **모으는 것**이다.
His job is	**taking care of** sick animals.	그의 직업은 아픈 동물들을 **돌보는 것**이다.

3 동명사의 관용 표현

go -ing	~하러 가다	We **went fishing** last weekend.
be busy -ing	~하느라 바쁘다	She **is busy doing** her homework.
feel like -ing	~하고 싶다	I **feel like dancing** with you.
How(What) about -ing ~?	~하는 게 어때?	**How about going** hiking this weekend?

비교 point

동명사 vs. 진행형

His job is **making** cookies.	그의 직업은 쿠키를 **만드는 것**이다.	〈그의 직업 = 쿠키 만들기 → 동명사〉
He is **making** cookies.	그는 쿠키를 **만드는 중**이다.	〈그 ≠ 쿠키 만들기 → 진행형〉

1 eating pizza
   ☐ 피자 먹기
   ☐ 먹을 피자

2 running every day
   ☐ 매일 달리기 위해
   ☐ 매일 달리는 것

3 calling her
   ☐ 전화하는 그녀를
   ☐ 그녀에게 전화하기

A 괄호 안에서 알맞은 것을 고르시오.

1 My hobby is (do / doing) yoga.

2 Meeting new people (is / are) always exciting.

3 Amy is busy (to write / writing) a speech.

4 I enjoy (to watch / watching) singing contests on TV.

B 빈칸에 들어갈 말을 〈보기〉에서 골라 동명사 형태로 바꿔 문장을 완성하시오. (단, 한 번씩만 사용할 것)

보기	draw	camp	clean	eat	play

1 _____ fresh vegetables is good for you.

2 My favorite activity is _____ cartoons.

3 My brother stopped _____ computer games.

4 He likes to go _____ with his family.

5 I don't feel like _____ my room.

C 우리말과 일치하도록 괄호 안의 말을 배열하여 문장을 완성하시오.

1 그는 친구들과 채팅하느라 바쁘다. (busy, is, chatting)

   → He _____ _____ _____ with his friends.

2 그녀에게 미안하다고 말하는 게 어때? (about, sorry, how, saying)

   → _____ _____ _____ _____ to her?

3 나는 아무것도 하고 싶지 않았다. (feel, anything, like, doing)

   → I didn't _____ _____ _____ _____.

4 나는 주말마다 수영하러 갈 것이다. (swimming, will, weekend, every, go)

   → I _____ _____ _____ _____ _____.

30초 완성 map

동명사	주어	❶ **Drawing** pictures _____ his job.	_____ 그의 직업이다.
	목적어	❷ He stopped **drawing** pictures.	그는 _____ 멈췄다.
	보어	❸ His hobby is **drawing** pictures.	그의 취미는 _____ 이다.
		주의 He is drawing a picture.	그는 _____.

서술형 대비 문장 쓰기

Answers p. 14

☐ **빈칸 완성** 괄호 안의 말을 이용하여 빈칸 완성하기

01 우리는 너를 곧 다시 보기를 바란다. (hope, see)

→ We _____ you again soon.

02 그들은 나와 이야기하는 것을 즐거워했다. (enjoy, talk)

→ They _____ with me.

03 이탈리아에는 방문할 곳들이 많이 있다. (place, visit)

→ There are many _____ in Italy.

04 이 호수에서 수영하는 것은 위험하다. (dangerous, swim)

→ It is _____ in this lake.

✔ **오류 수정** 어법에 맞게 문장 고쳐 쓰기

05 He promised to not be late again.

→ He promised _____.

06 Do you mind to open the window?

→ Do you mind _____?

07 She doesn't have a dress wear to the party.

→ She doesn't have _____.

08 How about to eat out tonight?

→ How about _____?

≡ **배열 영작** 괄호 안의 말을 바르게 배열하기

09 나는 그 소식을 듣고 놀랐다. (surprised, was, I, hear, to)

→ _____ the news.

10 나는 케이크를 사기 위해 빵집에 갔다. (to, went, buy, the bakery, I, to)

→ _____ a cake.

11 하루에 8시간 자는 것이 필요하다. (is, necessary, it, sleep, to)

→ _____ eight hours a day.

12 우리는 오늘 해야 할 숙제가 많이 있다. (have, homework, do, we, to, a lot of)

→ _____ today.

시험에 꼭 나오는 출제 포인트

출제 포인트 **1** to부정사의 문장 속 의미를 파악하자!

밑줄 친 부분을 바르게 해석하시오.

(1) They wanted to travel abroad.

→ 그들은 해외로 _____ 원했다.

(2) It is easy to find the answer.

→ 답을 _____ 쉽다.

> **고득점 POINT** 가주어 it
>
> **두 문장의 의미가 같도록 빈칸에 알맞은 말을 쓰시오.**
>
> To win a gold medal is hard.
>
> → _____ a gold medal.

출제 포인트 **2** to부정사가 있는 문장의 어순을 익히자!

우리말과 일치하도록 괄호 안의 말을 배열하시오.

(1) 마실 무언가를 원하니? (drink, to, something)

→ Do you want _____?

(2) 나는 나를 도와줄 누군가가 필요해.
(help, to, me, someone)

→ I need _____.

> **고득점 POINT** to부정사의 부정
>
> **우리말과 일치하도록 괄호 안의 말을 배열하시오.**
>
> 나는 그 가방을 사지 않기로 결정했다.
> (to, the bag, buy, not)
>
> → I decided _____.

출제 포인트 **3** to부정사의 쓰임은 해석으로 구분하자!

밑줄 친 부분의 쓰임이 〈보기〉와 같은 것은?

| 보기 | He has nothing to say. |

① We were sad to leave Hawaii.
② My dad likes to play the guitar.
③ It is very easy to send an email.
④ She went to Paris to study French.
⑤ I have many friends to invite to the party.

출제 포인트 **4** to부정사와 동명사를 각각 목적어로 취하는 동사들을 익히자!

밑줄 친 부분을 바르게 고쳐 쓰시오.

(1) We hope win the game. → _____

(2) Did you finish paint the wall? → _____

유형	문항수	배점	점수
객관식	17	60	
서술형	10	40	

[01-03] 빈칸에 들어갈 말로 알맞은 것을 고르시오.

|9점, 각 3점|

01

My dream is _____ in a big house.

① live   ② lives   ③ lived
④ to live   ⑤ to living

02

I enjoy _____ the Internet.

① surf   ② surfs   ③ surfing
④ to surf   ⑤ to surfing

03

He went to the airport _____ his friend.

① pick up   ② picks up
③ picked up   ④ to pick up
⑤ to picking up

04 다음 우리말을 영작할 때, 빈칸에 알맞은 것을 모두 고르면?

|3점|

TV를 너무 많이 보는 것은 눈에 좋지 않다.
→ _____ too much TV is not good for your eyes.

① Watch   ② To watch
③ To watching   ④ Watching
⑤ Don't watch

05 두 문장의 의미가 같도록 할 때, 빈칸에 들어갈 말이 순서대로 바르게 짝지어진 것은?

|3점|

To follow the class rules is important.
= _____ is important _____ the class rules.

① It – follow   ② It – to follow
③ That – following   ④ That – to follow
⑤ This – follow

06 빈칸에 들어갈 말이 순서대로 바르게 짝지어진 것은?

|3점|

• _____ the drums is my hobby.
• I need _____ my friends tonight.

① Play – to meet   ② To play – meet
③ Playing – meet   ④ To play – meeting
⑤ Playing – to meet

07 빈칸에 들어갈 말로 알맞지 않은 것은?

|3점|

My family _____ eating dessert after dinner.

① loved   ② enjoyed   ③ stopped
④ planned   ⑤ liked

08 다음 중 밑줄 친 It의 쓰임이 나머지와 다른 것은? |4점|

① It is dangerous to swim here.
② It is fun to read comic books.
③ It is two kilometers to the airport.
④ It must be exciting to see an aurora.
⑤ It is difficult to learn a new language.

09 주어진 우리말을 영어로 바르게 옮긴 것은? |3점|

그는 다시는 늦지 않겠다고 약속했다.

① He didn't promise to be late again.
② He promised to don't be late again.
③ He promised not being late again.
④ He promised to not be late again.
⑤ He promised not to be late again.

10 밑줄 친 부분의 쓰임이 〈보기〉와 <u>다른</u> 것은? |4점|

보기 <u>Walking</u> is good exercise.

① My job is <u>baking</u> cookies.
② <u>Biting</u> your nails is a bad habit.
③ I will go <u>swimming</u> with my dad.
④ Why are you <u>looking</u> at that girl?
⑤ His sister is busy <u>painting</u> the wall.

11 밑줄 친 부분의 쓰임이 〈보기〉와 <u>같은</u> 것은? |4점|

보기 I have a problem <u>to solve</u>.

① I'm sorry <u>to hear</u> that.
② We're happy <u>to see</u> you again.
③ I want a cap <u>to wear</u> to the picnic.
④ She went to the mall <u>to buy</u> new pants.
⑤ His son grew up <u>to be</u> a famous dancer.

12 다음 중 어법상 <u>틀린</u> 문장은? |4점|

① I feel like crying now.
② He is busy cleaning his room.
③ She decided moving to New York.
④ Becky doesn't like listening to music.
⑤ He didn't want to stop exercising.

13 우리말과 일치하도록 괄호 안의 말을 바르게 배열할 때, 세 번째로 오는 말은? |3점|

그녀는 먹을 무언가를 가져왔다.
(brought, to, she, eat, something)

① to　　　　② eat　　　　③ she
④ something　　⑤ brought

14 대화의 밑줄 친 ⓐ~ⓔ 중 어법상 틀린 부분을 잘못 고친 것은? |5점|

A John, did you finish ⓐ<u>practice</u> the violin?
B Yes. I'm ⓑ<u>look</u> for something ⓒ<u>read</u> now.
A How about ⓓ<u>ask</u> Jane? She has many interesting books ⓔ<u>reading</u>.

① ⓐ → practicing
② ⓑ → looking
③ ⓒ → to read
④ ⓓ → to ask
⑤ ⓔ → to read

15 다음 중 어법상 옳은 문장의 개수는? |5점|

> ⓐ This is hard to use chopsticks.
> ⓑ I have an old computer to fix.
> ⓒ My goal is save a lot of money.
> ⓓ Teaching children are not easy.

① 0개   ② 1개   ③ 2개
④ 3개   ⑤ 4개

[16-17] 다음 대화를 읽고, 물음에 답하시오.

> A I'm planning (A) [to go / going] on a picnic this
> Sunday. Do you want (B) [to join / joining] me?
> B I really want to, but I can't. I have to finish
> (C) [to do / doing] my science project.
> A Don't worry. We still have time ⓐto do it.
> B You're right. See you on Sunday, then.

16 (A)~(C)에 들어갈 말이 바르게 짝지어진 것은? |3점|

	(A)	(B)	(C)
①	to go	to join	to do
②	to go	joining	doing
③	to go	to join	doing
④	going	to join	to do
⑤	going	joining	to do

17 밑줄 친 ⓐ와 쓰임이 다른 것은? |4점|

① I want some water to drink.
② He has many friends to help him.
③ She was surprised to hear the news.
④ The Louvre is a great museum to visit.
⑤ I had a chance to meet my favorite singer.

---

18 빈칸에 공통으로 들어갈 말을 쓰시오. |3점|

> • She was glad _____ see her old friends.
> • I came home early _____ help my mom.

19 우리말과 일치하도록 괄호 안의 말을 이용하여 문장을 완성하시오. |6점, 각 3점|

(1) 나는 너에게 할 말이 있어.
(you, something, tell)

→ I have _____ _____ _____

_____ .

(2) 그녀는 커피를 마시지 않기로 결심했다.
(drink coffee)

→ She decided _____ _____

_____ _____ .

[20-21] 빈칸에 알맞은 말을 〈보기〉에서 골라 to부정사나 동명사를 이용하여 문장을 완성하시오. |6점, 각 3점|

보기	• run in the park
	• borrow some books

20 Tony went to the library _____

_____

21 I didn't feel like _____

this morning. The weather was too bad.

22 두 문장의 의미가 같도록 빈칸에 알맞은 말을 쓰시오.

|3점|

> To meet new friends is always exciting.

→ _____ is always exciting _____

_____ _____ _____.

23 대화의 내용과 일치하도록 괄호 안의 말을 어법에 맞게 사용하여 문장을 완성하시오. |4점|

> **Eric** Can you help me with my homework, Kate?
>
> **Kate** Of course.

→ Kate doesn't mind _____

with his homework. (help Eric)

24 그림을 보고, 여자아이가 남자아이들에게 할 수 있는 말을 〈조건〉에 맞게 쓰시오. |4점|

조건 1. 괄호 안에 주어진 말 중 2개만 사용할 것
　　　2. 필요하면 형태를 바꿀 것

→ We're in the library now. You should be quiet
here. Please _____.
　　　　　　　　　　　(enjoy, stop, eat, talk)

25 대화에서 어법상 틀린 부분을 찾아 바르게 고쳐 쓰시오.

|4점|

> **A** How was your trip?
>
> **B** It was great. I enjoyed to visit new places.

_____ → _____

26 다음 두 문장을 〈조건〉에 맞게 한 문장으로 완성하시오.

|4점|

> The girl grew up.
> She became the first woman pilot.

조건 1. to부정사를 이용할 것
　　　2. 8단어로 쓸 것

→ The girl _____

_____.

27 대화의 밑줄 친 ⓐ~ⓔ 중 어법상 틀린 것을 두 개 찾아 바르게 고쳐 쓰시오. |6점, 각 3점|

> **A** What do you want ⓐto do this summer vacation?
>
> **B** I want to go ⓑfish with my dad. How about you?
>
> **A** I want to go to Gangwon-do or Jeju-do. It's hard ⓒdecide.
>
> **B** How about ⓓgoing to Gangwon-do? There are many interesting places ⓔto visit there.

(1) (　　) → _____

(2) (　　) → _____

chapter

08

의문사

Q. 남자아이의 말에 대한 대답으로 알맞은 것은?

☐ I'm Genie.   ☐ Yes, I am.

who, whom, whose, what, which

1 의문사

의문사는 '누가, 언제, 어디서, 무엇을, 어떻게, 왜' 등의 정보를 물을 때 사용하는 말이다.
의문사는 문장의 맨 앞에 위치하며 의문사가 있는 의문문에는 Yes나 No로 대답하지 않는다.

	의문문	대답
의문사가 없는 경우	Is she your mom?	Yes, she is. 〈긍정〉 No, she isn't. 〈부정〉
의문사가 있는 경우	**Who** is she?	She is my mom.

2 who, whom, whose

who	누구, 누가	**Who** is that girl? **Who** made this salad? 〈의문사가 주어로 쓰인 경우〉
whom	누구를	**Who(m)** do you want to meet?
whose	누구의	**Whose** backpack is this? 〈whose+명사〉

주의 의문사가 주어로 쓰일 때는 3인칭 단수 취급한다.
Who **teaches** English?

3 what, which

what	무엇	**What** is your favorite color? **What** did you do last weekend?
	무슨 ~	**What** subjects do you like? 〈what+명사〉
which	어느 것	**Which** is better, this one or that one? **Which** do you prefer, yogurt or ice cream?
	어떤 ~	**Which** sport do you like better, soccer or baseball? 〈which+명사〉

비교
point
what vs. which

정해진 범위 없이 물을 때는 what을 쓰고, 정해진 범위 안에서 물을 때는 which를 쓴다.

1 (What / Which) is your favorite fruit?

2 (What / Which) do you like better, apples or oranges?

개념 우선 확인 | 옳은 의문사 고르기

1 누가 이것을 했니?

_____ did this?

☐ Who ☐ Whom

2 너는 무엇을 보았니?

_____ did you see?

☐ What ☐ Which

3 이것은 누구의 자전거니?

_____ bike is this?

☐ Whom ☐ Whose

A 괄호 안에서 알맞은 것을 고르시오.

1 (Who / Whose) computer is that?

2 (Who / Whom) painted this picture?

3 (Whose / Whom) did you call last night?

4 (Who / Which) do you want, chicken or beef?

B 〈보기〉에서 알맞은 의문사를 골라 대화를 완성하시오. (단, 한 번씩만 쓸 것)

보기	whose	who	what	which

1 A _____ idea was this? B It was Jim's.

2 A _____ made this doll? B I made it.

3 A _____ do you need, a pen or a pencil? B A pen, please.

4 A _____ did you do for the class project? B We made a video clip.

C 우리말과 일치하도록 괄호 안의 말을 배열하여 문장을 완성하시오.

1 너는 누구를 만나고 싶니? (do, whom, want, you)

→ _____ to meet?

2 이것과 저것 중 어느 것을 더 좋아하니? (prefer, which, do, you)

→ _____, this one or that one?

3 누가 수학을 가르치시니? (teaches, math, who)

→ _____

4 너는 무슨 색깔을 좋아하니? (do, what, you, colors, like)

→ _____

30초 완성 map

의문사

who, whom, whose

- ❶ _____ called me? — **누가** 나에게 전화했니?
- _____ did you meet yesterday? — 너는 어제 **누구를** 만났니?
- _____ bag is this? — 이것은 **누구의** 가방이니?

what, which

- ❷ _____ do you want to buy? — 너는 **무엇을** 사고 싶니?
- _____ do you want to buy, this one or that one? — 이것과 저것 중 **어느 것을** 사고 싶니?

where, when, why, how

1 where, when, why, how

where	어디에(서)	**Where** is the library? **Where** did you go yesterday?
when	언제	**When** is your birthday? **When** does the bus leave?
why	왜	**Why** were you late for class? **Why** do you want to be a singer?
how	어떻게	**How** is the weather? 〈상태〉 **How** did she go to Daegu? 〈방법〉

2 how + 형용사/부사

「how+형용사/부사」는 '얼마나 ~한/하게'의 의미로 정도나 수치를 물을 때 사용한다.

how old	몇 살의	**How old** are you?
how tall	얼마나 키가 큰	**How tall** is Max?
how long	얼마나 긴, 얼마 동안	**How long** is this pencil? 〈길이〉 **How long** did you wait? 〈기간〉
how far	얼마나 먼	**How far** is the bus stop from here?
how often	얼마나 자주	**How often** do you call your grandma?
how much	얼마의	**How much** is this skirt?
how many +셀 수 있는 명사 (복수형)	얼마나 많은 (수의) ~	**How many** pets do you have?
how much +셀 수 없는 명사	얼마나 많은 (양의) ~	**How much** sugar do you want?

비교
point **how long의 두 가지 의미**

How long is this river?	이 강은 **얼마나 기니?**	〈길이〉
How long will you stay here?	너는 여기에 **얼마 동안** 머무를 거니?	〈기간〉

개념 우선 확인 | 옳은 표현 고르기

1 얼마나 긴

☐ how long
☐ how tall

2 얼마나 자주

☐ how far
☐ how often

3 얼마나 많은 소금

☐ how many salt
☐ how much salt

A 질문에 대한 답을 보고 괄호 안에서 알맞은 의문사를 고르시오.

1 **A** (When / Where) is today's newspaper?　**B** It's over there.

2 **A** (When / How) are the final exams?　**B** They start next week.

3 **A** (Why / How) does she go to school?　**B** By bus.

4 **A** (Why / How) are you so upset?　**B** Because I lost the game.

5 **A** (How / Where) is Eric today?　**B** He is very sick.

B 자연스러운 대화가 되도록 질문과 답을 알맞게 연결하시오.

1 How long is your winter vacation?　•　　•　ⓐ One month.

2 How old is your sister?　•　　•　ⓑ Two glasses.

3 How much milk do you want?　•　　•　ⓒ About 200 meters.

4 How far is your house from our school?　•　　•　ⓓ She is 12 years old.

C 우리말과 일치하도록 괄호 안의 말을 배열하여 문장을 완성하시오.

1 너는 열쇠를 어디에서 찾았니? (find, where, you, did)

→ _____ the key?

2 너는 왜 액션 영화를 좋아하니? (like, why, you, do)

→ _____ action movies?

3 너의 남동생은 키가 얼마나 크니? (tall, is, your brother, how)

→ _____

4 너는 얼마나 자주 외식을 하니? (you, often, how, eat out, do)

→ _____

30초 완성 map

의문사

where, when, why, how

_____ did you meet him?　너는 그를 **언제** 만났니?
_____ did you meet him?　너는 그를 **어떻게** 만났니?
_____ did you meet him?　너는 그를 **왜** 만났니?

how + 형용사/부사

How (many / much) is the sweater?　그 스웨터는 **얼마**니?
How (far / long) did you live there?　너는 그곳에서 **얼마 동안** 살았니?
How (often / many) do you exercise?　너는 운동을 **얼마나 자주** 하니?

서술형 대비 문장 쓰기

Answers p. 16

□ 빈칸 완성 괄호 안의 말과 의문사를 이용하여 빈칸 완성하기

01 이것은 누구의 노래니? (song)

→ _____ is this?

02 어제 얼마나 많은 학생들이 시험을 봤니? (students)

→ _____ took the test yesterday?

03 우리는 얼마 동안 기다려야 하니? (long)

→ _____ do we have to wait?

04 너는 얼마나 자주 이 앱을 사용하니? (often)

→ _____ do you use this app?

✓ 오류 수정 대답을 참고하여 어법에 맞게 문장 고쳐 쓰기

05 A What is your favorite singer?　　　　B Justin Bieber.

→ _____ your favorite singer?

06 A Where did you go to Busan?　　　　B Three days ago.

→ _____ to Busan?

07 A How long is the subway station?　　　B About 200 meters from here.

→ _____ the subway station?

08 A What flavor do you want, strawberry or vanilla?　　B Vanilla.

→ _____, strawberry or vanilla?

≡ 배열 영작 괄호 안의 말을 바르게 배열하기

09 너는 왜 그들과 함께 그곳에 갔었니? (did, you, there, go, why)

→ _____ with them?

10 너는 그 표에 얼마를 지불했니? (much, did, pay, you, how)

→ _____ for that ticket?

11 너희는 어디에서 축구를 할 거니? (you, soccer, will, where, play)

→ _____

12 누가 이 그림을 좋아하니? (this, who, painting, likes)

→ _____

시험에 나오는 출제 포인트

Answers p. 16

출제 포인트 1 의문사의 의미를 익히자!

괄호 안에서 알맞은 의문사를 고르시오.

(1) (Who / What) are you going to do tomorrow?

(2) (What / Which) do you like better, pizza or spaghetti?

고득점 POINT who, whom, whose의 쓰임

우리말과 일치하도록 빈칸에 알맞은 의문사를 쓰시오.

(1) 너는 누구에게 전화하고 있니?

→ _____ are you calling?

(2) 소파 위에 있는 저것은 누구의 코트니?

→ _____ coat is that on the sofa?

출제 포인트 2 의문사가 있는 의문문의 어순을 익히자!

괄호 안의 말을 바르게 배열하여 의문문 문장을 완성하시오.

(1) (are, so, you, why, excited)

→ _____ ?

(2) (did, buy, you, the bag, where)

→ _____ ?

고득점 POINT 의문사가 주어로 사용된 경우

우리말과 일치하도록 괄호 안의 말을 어법에 맞게 이용하여 문장을 쓰시오.

누가 정답을 아니? (know, the answer)

→ _____

출제 포인트 3 의문사가 있는 의문문에 어울리는 대답을 익히자!

다음 중 대화가 자연스럽지 <u>않은</u> 것은?

① A Who are those children?   B They are my sons.

② A Why did he cry?   B Because he lost his cat.

③ A When do you get up every morning?   B At seven.

④ A Where did she go in Busan?   B By train.

⑤ A How tall is this building?   B It's 15 meters tall.

출제 포인트 4 「how+형용사/부사」의 쓰임을 익혀 두자!

자연스러운 대화가 되도록 빈칸에 알맞은 의문사를 쓰시오.

(1) A _____ is your dog?

B She is 10 years old.

(2) A _____ is the bookstore from here?

B About 50 meters.

고득점 POINT how many vs. how much

many와 much 중 알맞은 것을 빈칸에 쓰시오.

(1) How _____ time do you need?

(2) How _____ cookies did you eat?

[01-03] 빈칸에 들어갈 말로 알맞은 것을 고르시오.
|9점, 각 3점|

01

A _____ did you run this morning?
B Because I was late for school.

① Who   ② Why   ③ What
④ When   ⑤ Where

02

A _____ do you want for your birthday,
a bag or a cap?
B I want a cap.

① How   ② Whose   ③ Why
④ Whom   ⑤ Which

03

A How _____ do they go swimming?
B Twice a week.

① much   ② many   ③ far
④ often   ⑤ long

04 빈칸에 들어갈 말로 알맞지 않은 것은? |3점|

_____ does Daniel play basketball?

① What   ② Where   ③ Why
④ When   ⑤ How often

[05-06] 질문에 대한 대답으로 알맞은 것을 고르시오.
|6점, 각 3점|

05

A How many comic books do you have?
B _____

① They are 20 dollars.
② At four twenty.
③ Four times a month.
④ About fifty.
⑤ I bought them online.

06

A Which season do you like better, spring or
fall?
B _____

① Spring.   ② Yes, I do.
③ No, I don't.   ④ Yes, it's spring.
⑤ I don't like winter.

07 밑줄 친 부분의 쓰임이 어색한 것은? |3점|

① When is your concert?
② Where is my cell phone?
③ How much did his uncle stay here?
④ Why does he look so angry?
⑤ How old is your English teacher?

08 주어진 대답에 대한 질문으로 알맞은 것은? |3점|

A _____
B It's Andrew's.

① What is his name?
② Where is your brother?
③ Who is your best friend?
④ Whom did you see there?
⑤ Whose smartphone is this?

09 다음 정보를 보고, 대답할 수 없는 질문은? |3점|

Name	Age
Tony	13
Date of Birth	
November 14	
Address	123 Insa-dong, Jongro-gu, Seoul
Cell phone	010-1234-5678

① How old is Tony?
② Where does Tony live?
③ When is Tony's birthday?
④ How does Tony go to school?
⑤ What is Tony's phone number?

10 다음 빈칸에 공통으로 들어갈 말로 알맞은 것은? |4점|

A _____ did you spend your weekend?
B I went to Busan with my cousins.
A _____ did you get there?
B By train.

① Who   ② How   ③ What
④ Why   ⑤ Where

11 다음 중 대화가 자연스럽지 <u>않은</u> 것은? |4점|

① A How is the weather?
   B It's sunny.
② A Where do you practice basketball?
   B At the school gym.
③ A When are you going to visit the museum?
   B This Saturday.
④ A What is your favorite color?
   B Blue.
⑤ A How long was your vacation?
   B Last weekend.

12 다음 중 어법상 <u>틀린</u> 문장은? |4점|

① Who's that pretty girl?
② How long is this bridge?
③ Whose gloves are they?
④ How much pens do you have?
⑤ Who did you call last night?

13 주어진 우리말을 영어로 바르게 옮긴 것은? |4점|

누가 수업 시간에 네 옆에 앉니?

① Who sit next to you in class?
② Whom sits next to you in class?
③ Who sits next to you in class?
④ Who do you sit next to in class?
⑤ Who does sit next to you in class?

14 다음 수미의 영수증을 보고 답을 할 수 <u>없는</u> 질문은? |4점|

HAPPY STORE		
Postcard	1	$2.50
Pencil	3	$3.25
T-shirt	1	$6.00
Total		$11.75
Thank you for shopping!		

① What did Sumi buy?
② How much was the postcard?
③ When did Sumi buy the items?
④ Where did Sumi buy the items?
⑤ How many pencils did Sumi buy?

15 빈칸에 How가 들어갈 수 있는 것을 <u>모두</u> 고르면? |4점|

① _____ made this tomato juice?

② _____ tall is the boy next to her?

③ _____ movie did you see last Friday?

④ _____ can I get to the subway station?

⑤ _____ city do you like better, Rome or Venice?

고난도

16 어법상 옳은 문장을 <u>모두</u> 골라 바르게 짝지은 것은? |5점|

ⓐ Whom is your favorite actor?

ⓑ Why were you so upset yesterday?

ⓒ How far the park is from here?

ⓓ How many hours do you sleep?

ⓔ Who know the title of the song?

① ⓐ, ⓑ   ② ⓐ, ⓒ, ⓔ   ③ ⓑ, ⓓ

④ ⓑ, ⓓ, ⓔ   ⑤ ⓒ, ⓔ

17 (A)~(C)에 들어갈 말이 바르게 짝지어진 것은? |4점|

A Jenny, (A) | how / where | was your vacation?

B It was great. I went to Jeju-do with my family.

A (B) | When / How long | did you stay in Jeju-do?

B For three days.

A (C) | What / Which | did you do there?

B I climbed Hallasan and swam in the sea.

	(A)	(B)	(C)
①	how	When	Which
②	how	How long	What
③	how	How long	Which
④	where	When	What
⑤	where	How long	What

서 술 형

18 빈칸에 들어갈 알맞은 의문사를 쓰시오. |4점, 각 2점|

(1)
A _____ does she do on weekends?

B She usually goes to the movies.

(2)
A _____ book is this on the table?

B It's Mike's.

19 대화의 흐름에 맞게 빈칸에 들어갈 알맞은 말을 쓰시오. |3점|

A _____ book did you read first, the blue one _____ the red one?

B I read the red book first.

[20-21] 우리말과 일치하도록 괄호 안의 말을 바르게 배열하시오. |6점, 각 3점|

20 그녀는 무슨 과목을 좋아하니?

(like, what, she, subjects, does)

→ _____

21 우리에게 설탕이 얼마나 있나요?

(we, sugar, how, have, do, much)

→ _____

22 주어진 대답의 밑줄 친 부분을 묻는 질문이 되도록 〈조건〉에 맞게 쓰시오. |4점|

> 조건 1. 의문사를 반드시 사용할 것
> 2. 6단어의 완전한 문장으로 쓸 것

A _____

B I heard the news <u>yesterday</u>.

23 대화의 빈칸에 들어갈 알맞은 말을 각각 쓰시오. |4점, 각 2점|

A How _____ do you call your grandma?
B Once a week.
A How _____ is your hometown from here?
B It takes three hours to get there by car.

최신기출
24 세 사람이 지난주 금요일에 한 일을 보고, 빈칸에 알맞은 말을 〈조건〉에 맞게 쓰시오. |6점, 각 3점|

Sam	read a comic book
Mike	go to the movies with Jessy
Jessy	go to the movies with Mike

> 조건 1. 알맞은 의문사와 괄호 안의 말을 사용할 것
> 2. 필요하면 형태를 바꿀 것

A (1) _____ last Friday? (do)
B He read a comic book.
A (2) _____ last Friday? (go)
B Mike and Jessy.

고난도
25 Daniel의 어제 일정표를 보고, 주어진 대답에 알맞은 질문이 되도록 〈조건〉에 맞게 쓰시오. |5점|

| **12:00** | have lunch | **13:00** | meet Sora |

> 조건 1. 의문사와 Daniel을 반드시 사용할 것
> 2. 과거시제로 5단어로 쓸 것

Q _____
A At noon.

[26-27] 다음 대화를 읽고, 물음에 답하시오.

A How can I help you?
B ___(A)___ are the children's books? I'm looking for a book for my son.
A Children's books are here in Section 12. Let me see… How about this book?
B ___(B)___ wrote this book?
A J.K. Rowling.
B It looks fun. _____(C)_____
A It's 10 dollars.
B Okay. I'll take it.

26 빈칸 (A)와 (B)에 들어갈 알맞은 의문사를 쓰시오. |4점, 각 2점|

(A) _____ (B) _____

27 빈칸 (C)에 알맞은 질문을 네 단어로 쓰시오. |4점|

_____

chapter

9

다양한 문장

What a tall building!

Q. "What a tall building!"이 의미하는 것은?

☐ 높은 건물은 무엇일까? ☐ 정말 높은 건물이구나!

명령문, Let's ~, There is/are ~

1 명령문

명령문은 상대방에게 '~해라'와 같이 명령이나 요청할 때 사용하는 문장으로, 주어 없이 동사원형으로 시작한다.
'~하지 마라'의 의미인 부정 명령문은 동사원형 앞에 Don't를 붙인다.

	Use	my computer.	내 컴퓨터를 **사용해라**.
Don't(Do not)	use	my computer.	내 컴퓨터를 **사용하지 마라**. 〈부정 명령문〉

Wash your hands.   **Don't waste** water.
Be careful.   **Don't be** late.

▶ 명령문의 앞이나 뒤에 please를 붙이면 좀 더 공손한 표현이 된다.
    Please be quiet. / Take off your shoes, **please**.

2 Let's ~

Let's ~.는 '~하자'의 의미로 제안하거나 권유할 때 사용하며 「Let's+동사원형 ~.」으로 나타낸다.
'~하지 말자'는 「Let's not+동사원형 ~.」으로 나타낸다.

Let's		**drink**	coffee.	커피를 **마시자**.
Let's	not	**drink**	coffee.	커피를 **마시지 말자**.

Let's dance together.
Let's not eat fast food.

3 There is/are ~

There is/are ~.는 '~가 있다'라는 뜻으로 There is 뒤에는 단수명사 또는 셀 수 없는 명사가 오고, There are 뒤에는 복수명사가 온다. 이 문장의 주어는 There is/are 뒤에 오는 명사(구)이며, There는 '그곳에'라고 해석하지 않는다.

There	**is**	a book	on the desk.	책상 위에 책이 한 권 **있다**.
	are	three books		책상 위에 책이 세 권 **있다**.

There is *some water* in the bottle.
There are *five oranges* in the refrigerator.
There isn't *a problem*. 〈부정문〉
Are there *three apples* in the basket? 〈의문문〉

시험
point

be동사가 있는 명령문

be동사가 있는 명령문에서는 be를 빠트리지 않도록 주의하자.

1 (Nice / Be nice) to your brother and sister.

2 Please (don't / don't be) angry with me.

개념 우선 확인 | 옳은 문장 고르기

1 조용히 해라!
☐ Do quiet!
☐ Be quiet!

2 여기서 뛰지 마라.
☐ Run not here.
☐ Don't run here.

3 그곳에 가지 말자.
☐ Let's not go there.
☐ Don't let's go there.

A 괄호 안에서 알맞은 것을 고르시오.

1 (Be / Do) careful! A car is coming!

2 I'm hungry. (Let / Let's) have lunch together.

3 (Don't / Not) call him. He's busy now.

4 (There is / There are) many tall buildings in this town.

B 우리말과 일치하도록 괄호 안의 말을 이용하여 문장을 완성하시오.

1 이 호수에서 수영하지 말자. (swim)

→ _____ _____ _____ in this lake.

2 다른 사람들에게 공손해라. (polite)

→ _____ _____ to other people.

3 밤 늦게 문자 메시지를 보내지 마! (send)

→ _____ _____ text messages late at night!

4 거실에 피아노가 한 대 있다. (there)

→ _____ _____ a piano in the living room.

C 상황에 가장 어울리는 표현을 〈보기〉에서 골라 빈칸에 쓰시오.

보기	• Do your best!	• Let's buy a present.
	• Don't make noise.	• Let's not eat here.

1 Tomorrow is Jane's birthday. _____

2 _____ You will pass the test.

3 _____ You are in the library.

4 This restaurant is not clean. _____

30초 완성 map

명령문/ Let's ~
❶
_____ the door. (문 닫아.) ↔ _____ _____ the door. (문 닫지 마.)
주의 _____ nice to your friends! (친구들에게 친절하게 대해라!)
_____ go outside. (밖으로 나가자.) ↔ _____ _____ go outside. (밖으로 나가지 말자.)

There is/are ~
❷
There (is / are) two birds in the tree.   나무에 새 두 마리가 있다.
(Is / Are) there a grocery store near here?   이 근처에 식료품 가게가 있나요?

감탄문, 부가의문문

1 감탄문

감탄문은 기쁨, 놀라움, 슬픔 등의 감정을 표현하는 문장으로, '정말 ~하구나!'라는 의미로 해석한다.

What	a/an	형용사	명사	(주어+동사)!
How		형용사/부사		(주어+동사)!

What a smart girl she **is!**
What an interesting story it **is!**
How expensive the watch **is!**
How fast he **runs!**

> **주의** what으로 시작하는 감탄문에서 명사가 복수형일 때는 a/an을 쓰지 않는다.
> **What** cute *puppies* he has!

2 부가의문문

부가의문문은 앞에서 말한 내용을 확인하거나 상대방에게 동의를 구하기 위해 평서문 뒤에 「동사+주어?」의 형태로 덧붙이는 의문문으로, '그렇지?' 또는 '그렇지 않니?'라고 해석한다.

(1) 부가의문문 만드는 방법

형태	동사	주어
• 긍정문 → 부정의 부가의문문 • 부정문 → 긍정의 부가의문문	• be동사/조동사 → 그대로 • 일반동사 → do/does/did **주의** 평서문과 같은 시제로	대명사로 바꾸기

This movie *is* interesting,	**isn't it?**
You *can't* come to the party,	**can you?**
Tina *studies* hard,	**doesn't she?**
Andy *didn't break* the window,	**did he?**

(2) 부가의문문에 대한 대답

질문의 형태와 상관없이 대답의 내용이 긍정이면 Yes, 부정이면 No로 답한다.

A Justin enjoys sports, **doesn't he?**
B **Yes**, he **does.** (= He enjoys sports.)
  No, he **doesn't.** (= He doesn't enjoy sports.)

비교 point

감탄문과 의문문의 어순 비교

1 How tall (he is / is he)!   그는 정말 키가 크구나! 〈감탄문〉
2 How tall (he is / is he)?   그는 키가 얼마나 크니? 〈의문문〉

개념 우선 확인 | **옳은 해석 고르기**

1 How cute!

☐ 얼마나 귀여운지!
☐ 어떻게 귀여운지!

2 What a beautiful song it is!

☐ 어떤 노래가 아름다운지!
☐ 정말 아름다운 노래구나!

3 She will come, won't she?

☐ 그녀는 올 거야, 안 올 거야?
☐ 그녀는 올 거야, 그렇지 않니?

A 괄호 안에서 알맞은 것을 고르시오.

1 (How / What) deep the river is!

2 (How / What) a nice person she is!

3 (How / What) high the mountain is!

4 (How / What) beautiful eyes she has!

B 빈칸에 알맞은 말을 넣어 부가의문문을 완성하시오.

1 The weather is very hot, _____ _____?

2 Luna can drive a car, _____ _____?

3 The mall wasn't crowded, _____ _____?

4 You didn't tell a lie, _____ _____?

5 Henry likes to play baseball, _____ _____?

C 우리말과 일치하도록 괄호 안의 말을 배열하여 감탄문을 쓰시오.

1 저 다리는 정말 길구나! (that, how, bridge, is, long)

→ _____

2 그는 정말 힘이 센 소년이구나! (what, is, a, boy, strong, he)

→ _____

3 너의 여동생은 정말 친절하구나! (your, kind, is, how, sister)

→ _____

4 그것은 정말로 흥미진진한 시합이구나! (what, match, exciting, an, is, it)

→ _____

30초 완성 map

① 감탄문

(How / What) fast he runs!
= (How / What) a fast runner he is!

② 부가의문문

Jason swims well, _____ _____?
You can't go to the festival, _____ _____?
Mom and Dad are great singers, _____ _____?

서술형 대비 문장 쓰기

Answers p. 18

□ 빈칸 완성 괄호 안의 말을 이용하여 빈칸 완성하기

01 그녀는 정말 빨리 말하는구나! (quickly)

→ _____ she speaks!

02 도서관에서 3시에 만나자. (meet)

→ _____ in the library at 3.

03 Tim은 내일 안 올 거지, 그렇지? (will)

→ Tim won't come tomorrow, _____ ?

04 이 도시에는 공항이 두 개 있다. (there, airport)

→ _____ in this city.

✓ 오류 수정 어법에 맞게 문장 고쳐 쓰기

05 Be not too nervous about it.

→ _____ about it.

06 How a beautiful painting it is!

→ _____ it is!

07 Ethan knows the answer, isn't he?

→ Ethan knows _____ ?

08 Is there many parks in your town?

→ _____ many _____ in your town?

☰ 배열 영작 괄호 안의 말을 바르게 배열하기

09 이곳에서 야영하지 말자. 안전하지 않아. (not, let's, here, camp)

→ _____ It's not safe.

10 이 거리에는 재미있는 가게들이 많이 있다. (interesting, there, stores, many, are)

→ _____ on this street.

11 저것은 정말 높은 산이구나! (high, a, mountain, what, is, that)

→ _____

12 너는 그의 이름을 모르지, 그렇지? (don't, you, do, know, name, his, you)

→ _____

시험에 꼭 나오는 출제 포인트

Answers p. 18

출제 포인트 1 명령문과 Let's ~. 문장의 형태에 유의하자!

괄호 안에서 알맞은 것을 고르시오.

(1) (Sit / Sits) on that chair.

(2) (Not / Don't) enter the room.

(3) (Let's not / Don't let's) talk loudly.

> **고득점 POINT** be동사가 있는 명령문을 만들 때 be를 빠트리지 않도록 유의해야 한다.
>
> **우리말과 일치하도록 괄호 안의 말을 이용하여 문장을 완성하시오.**
>
> 다른 사람들에게 무례하게 굴지 마라. (rude)
>
> → _____ to others.

출제 포인트 2 There is/are ~. 문장의 be동사는 뒤에 오는 명사의 수에 맞게 쓰자!

우리말과 일치하도록 빈칸에 알맞은 말을 쓰시오.

(1) 컵에 물이 조금 있다.

   → _____ _____ some water in the cup.

(2) 그 동물원에는 많은 동물들이 있지 않다.

   → _____ _____ many animals in the zoo.

출제 포인트 3 What과 How로 시작하는 감탄문의 어순을 기억하자!

다음 중 어법상 <u>틀린</u> 문장은?

① What an amazing story!

② What a pretty girl she is!

③ How dirty your shoes are!

④ How slowly he walks!

⑤ How an expensive phone you have!

출제 포인트 4 부가의문문 만드는 방법을 익히자!

빈칸에 알맞은 부가의문문을 쓰시오.

(1) Harry is very handsome, _____?

(2) Amy plays the flute well, _____?

(3) You won't do it again, _____?

> **고득점 POINT** 부가의문문에 대한 대답은 대답의 내용이 긍정이면 Yes, 부정이면 No로 한다.
>
> **자연스러운 대화가 되도록 빈칸에 알맞은 말을 쓰시오.**
>
> A Justin didn't tell a lie, _____?
>
> B _____ He always tells the truth.

01 빈칸에 들어갈 말로 알맞은 것은? |3점|

_____ kind to your classmates.

① Be ② Do ③ Don't
④ Are ⑤ Have

02 다음 질문에 대한 대답으로 알맞은 것은? |3점|

A Are there many Koreans in California?
B _____

① Yes, they are. ② No, they aren't.
③ Yes, there is. ④ Yes, there are.
⑤ No, there isn't.

[03-04] 빈칸에 공통으로 들어갈 말로 알맞은 것을 고르시오. |6점, 각 3점|

03
• It's very cold. _____ go swimming today.
• The light is red. _____ cross the street.

① Do ② Be ③ Let's
④ Not ⑤ Don't

04
A _____ play computer games.
B Sorry, but I have to finish my homework.
   _____ play tomorrow.

① Do ② Let's ③ Does
④ Be ⑤ Please

[05-06] 빈칸에 들어갈 말이 바르게 짝지어진 것을 고르시오. |6점, 각 3점|

05
• _____ tall the tower is!
• _____ a wonderful day it is!

① It's – What ② How – How
③ What – It's ④ How – What
⑤ What – How

06
• You are tired, _____?
• Kevin can't play the guitar, _____?

① are you – can he
② are you – can't he
③ aren't you – can he
④ aren't you – can't he
⑤ don't you – can Kevin

07 빈칸에 들어갈 말이 나머지와 다른 것은? (단, 시제는 현재시제) |3점|

① There _____ two balls in the box.
② There _____ many clouds in the sky.
③ There _____ some flowers in the vase.
④ There _____ lots of apples in the basket.
⑤ There _____ some snow on the mountain.

08 두 문장의 의미가 같도록 할 때, 빈칸에 들어갈 말로 알맞은 것은? |3점|

You must not park your car here.
= _____ park your car here.

① No ② Let's ③ Do
④ Don't ⑤ Let's not

09 빈칸에 들어갈 말로 알맞지 <u>않은</u> 것을 <u>모두</u> 고르면? |3점|

> You _____, don't you?

① like traveling
② work at a bank
③ can speak English
④ run every morning
⑤ went shopping with Sam

10 주어진 문장을 감탄문으로 <u>잘못</u> 바꾼 것은? |4점|

① You are very diligent.
  → How diligent you are!
② They are really kind.
  → How kind they are!
③ These are very nice pants.
  → What nice pants these are!
④ It is a great idea.
  → What a great idea it is!
⑤ The robot is very smart.
  → How a smart robot it is!

11 밑줄 친 부분이 어법상 옳은 것은? |4점|

① Let's <u>quiet</u> in the library.
② <u>What carefully</u> she drives!
③ <u>Is there</u> birds under the tree?
④ <u>What</u> expensive shoes they are!
⑤ Mom and Dad won't come home early, <u>will she</u>?

12 대화의 빈칸에 들어갈 말로 알맞은 것은? |4점|

> A Tom doesn't live in Busan, does he?
> B _____ He lives in Daegu.

① Yes, he is.
② Yes, he does.
③ No, he isn't.
④ No, he didn't.
⑤ No, he doesn't.

13 다음 중 어법상 <u>틀린</u> 문장은? |4점|

① Don't afraid of spiders.
② How lovely the baby is!
③ Let's not waste our time.
⑤ What a great movie it was!
④ She isn't reading a book, is she?

14 (A)~(C)에 들어갈 말이 바르게 짝지어진 것은? |3점|

> • There (A) [was / were] no bread in the bakery.
> • (B) [How / What] interesting the story is!
> • Susan studied hard, (C) [did / didn't] she?

	(A)	(B)	(C)
①	was	How	didn't
②	was	How	did
③	was	What	did
④	were	How	didn't
⑤	were	What	did

최신기출

15 빈칸에 들어갈 말을 괄호 안의 단어들을 배열하여 쓸 때, 세 번째로 오는 단어로 알맞은 것은? |4점|

> A I'm looking for a scarf.
> B How about this one?
> A _____! I'll take it.
> (a, is, what, scarf, beautiful, it)

① a
② is
③ scarf
④ it
⑤ beautiful

16 다음 중 우리말을 영어로 바르게 옮긴 것은? |3점|

① 부끄러워 하지 마.
→ Don't shy.
② 배드민턴을 치자.
→ Let's to play badminton.
③ 그것들은 정말 비싼 차들이구나!
→ What an expensive cars they are!
④ 너는 나를 도와줄 거지, 그렇지 않니?
→ You will help me, won't you?
⑤ 공원에는 아이들이 많이 있었다.
→ There was a lot of children in the park.

[19-20] 어법상 틀린 부분을 찾아 바르게 고쳐 쓰시오.
|6점, 각 3점|

19

I'm thirsty. Let's drinks something.

_____ → _____

20

Don't late for school.

_____ → _____

최신기출 고난도

17 대화의 밑줄 친 ⓐ~ⓔ 중 어법상 틀린 것은? |5점|

A Andy got an A on the test, didn't he?
            ⓐ   ⓑ   ⓒ

B Yes, he did. How smart boy he is!
                      ⓓ   ⓔ

① ⓐ   ② ⓑ   ③ ⓒ   ④ ⓓ   ⑤ ⓔ

21 그림을 보고, 조건에 맞게 문장을 완성하시오. |4점|

조건 1. 괄호 안의 단어를 사용할 것 (there, book, cat)
     2. 명사의 개수를 반드시 포함할 것

_____ _____ _____ _____ on
the table, and _____ _____ _____
_____ under the table.

18 밑줄 친 ⓐ~ⓔ 중 어법상 틀린 것은? |4점|

ⓐ Let's look at the trees in the garden.
There ⓑis some flowers in the garden, too.
The flowers are beautiful, ⓒaren't they?
Please don't ⓓpick them. Just ⓔenjoy the
view.

① ⓐ   ② ⓑ   ③ ⓒ   ④ ⓓ   ⑤ ⓔ

22 빈칸에 알맞은 말을 넣어 대화를 완성하시오. |4점|

A Mr. Park didn't play basketball with you,
_____ _____ ?

B _____ , _____ _____ . He was
too busy yesterday.

23 괄호 안의 말을 사용하여 주어진 문장을 감탄문으로 바꿔 쓰시오. |4점, 각 2점|

(1) You have very good friends. (What)

→ _____ you have!

(2) The vase is very pretty. (How)

→ _____

24 우리말과 일치하도록 괄호 안의 말을 바르게 배열하시오. |3점|

그 미술관 안에는 그림들이 많이 있었다.
(many, paintings, gallery, there, the, in, were)

→ _____
_____

25 그림의 내용과 일치하도록 〈조건〉에 맞게 대화를 완성하시오. |4점|

조건 1. 명령문으로 쓸 것
2. pictures를 사용하여 3단어로 쓸 것

A Look at this sign. _____
here.

B Sorry, I didn't see it.

26 질문에 대한 대답을 〈조건〉에 맞게 쓰시오. |5점|

You don't want to go shopping with your sister today. What should you say to her?

조건 1. let's를 반드시 사용할 것
2. shopping과 today를 사용하여 5단어로 쓸 것

→ _____

27 밑줄 친 부분이 어법상 틀린 것을 찾아 기호를 쓰고, 바르게 고쳐 쓰시오. |4점|

ⓐ Don't turn right.
ⓑ Open your textbook.
ⓒ Pass me the salt, please.
ⓓ The books are interesting, isn't it?
ⓔ Michael dances very well, doesn't he?

( ) → _____

28 다음 대화를 읽고, 괄호 안의 말을 바르게 배열하시오. |4점|

A It was an awful day yesterday. I missed the school bus in the morning. Then it started raining, and I got wet.

B _____!
(it, what, day, unlucky, was, an)

chapter

10

문장의 구조

She looks happy.

Q. "She looks happy."가 의미하는 것은?

☐ 그녀는 행복해 보인다.　　☐ 그녀는 행복하게 보고 있다.

목적어가 두 개 있는 문장

1 목적어가 있는 문장

목적어가 하나인 문장	He	bought		**a pen**.	그는 **펜을** 샀다.
목적어가 두 개인 문장	He	bought	*me*	**a pen**.	그는 *나에게* **펜을** 사 줬다.

2 수여동사가 있는 문장

수여동사는 '~에게 …을 해 주다'라는 의미로 두 개의 목적어를 필요로 하는 동사이다. '~에게'에 해당하는 것을 간접목적어, '…을'에 해당하는 것을 직접목적어라고 한다.

주어	수여동사	간접목적어(~에게)	직접목적어(…을)	
Dad	**gave**	*me*	a present.	아빠가 *내게* 선물을 **주셨다**.
Kate	**showed**	*him*	her blog.	Kate는 *그에게* 자신의 블로그를 **보여 주었다**.

I **sent** *Tom* an email.
Ms. Baker **teaches** *us* English.
They **asked** *Mr. Brown* difficult questions.

> **수여동사의 종류**
> give, show, send, teach, bring, tell, lend, write, buy, make, cook, get, ask 등

3 수여동사가 있는 문장의 전환

「수여동사＋간접목적어＋직접목적어」는 「수여동사＋직접목적어＋전치사(to/for)＋간접목적어」의 형태로 바꿔 쓸 수 있다. 이때 간접목적어 앞에 쓰이는 전치사는 동사에 따라 다르다.

	수여동사	간접목적어	직접목적어
Joan	**showed**	*me*	a picture.

	수여동사			
Joan	**showed**	a picture	to	*me.*

We **sent** *Grandma* postcards.
→ We **sent** postcards **to** *Grandma*.

Tom **bought** *her* a silver ring.
→ Tom **bought** a silver ring **for** *her*.

> 간접목적어 앞에 전치사 to를 쓰는 동사
> give, send, show, teach, tell, lend, write 등
> 간접목적어 앞에 전치사 for를 쓰는 동사
> buy, make, cook, get 등

시험 point

간접목적어와 직접목적어의 순서

직접목적어가 간접목적어 앞에 오는 경우에는 간접목적어 앞에 전치사를 쓴다.

1 Mr. Wilson teaches (us math / to us math).

2 Mr. Wilson teaches (math us / math to us).

개념 우선 확인 | 목적어 모두 고르기

1 He loves music.
☐ loves
☐ music

2 They gave me a gift.
☐ gave
☐ a gift

3 She bought me a hot dog.
☐ me
☐ a hot dog

A 괄호 안에서 알맞은 것을 고르시오.

1 Mr. Jung teaches science (of / to) us.

2 Alex made dinner (for / of) his friends.

3 My aunt bought a nice jacket (to / for) me.

4 We will give a birthday present (to / for) him.

B 〈보기〉에서 알맞은 동사를 골라 과거형으로 바꿔 문장을 완성하시오. (단, 한 번씩만 사용할 것)

보기	tell	cook	show	ask

1 She _____ us her new house.

2 My uncle _____ me a difficult question.

3 He _____ them an interesting story.

4 Sarah _____ ramen for her friends.

C 우리말과 일치하도록 괄호 안의 말을 배열하여 문장을 완성하시오.

1 할머니께서 나에게 손목시계를 사 주셨다. (me, watch, a, bought)
→ Grandma _____ _____ _____ _____.

2 내 친구가 그에게 이메일을 보냈다. (an, him, email, sent)
→ My friend _____ _____ _____ _____.

3 우리는 우리 선생님께 꽃을 드렸다. (our, gave, teacher, flowers)
→ We _____ _____ _____ _____.

4 Luis는 나에게 그의 사진을 보여 주었다. (his, showed, to, photos, me)
→ Luis _____ _____ _____ _____ _____.

30초 완성 map

수여동사
(~에게 …을 해 주다)

❶ He **teaches** _____ _____.   그는 우리에게 영어를 가르친다.
= He **teaches** English _____ us.

❷ Mom **made** _____ _____.   엄마가 나에게 쿠키를 만들어 주었다.
= Mom **made** cookies _____ me.

Chapter 10 문장의 구조 **131**

보어가 있는 문장

1 감각동사 + 형용사

look, sound, smell, taste, feel과 같이 감각을 나타내는 동사를 감각동사라고 한다.
감각동사 뒤에는 보어로 형용사가 쓰여 주어의 상태나 성질을 설명해 준다.

주어	**look** **sound** **smell** **taste** **feel**	형용사	~하게 보이다 ~하게 들리다 ~한 냄새가 나다 ~한 맛이 나다 ~한 느낌이 나다

That **sounds** *great*.   It **smells** *sweet*.
The soup **tastes** *good*.   The blanket **feels** *soft*.

> 감각동사 뒤에 명사가 올 때는 「감각동사+like+명사」의 형태로 쓴다.
> He **looks like** *an actor*.

2 목적격보어가 필요한 동사

목적어 뒤에서 그 목적어에 대해 보충 설명해 주는 말을 목적격보어라고 하며, 목적격보어 자리에는 주로 명사나
형용사가 쓰인다.

(1) 목적격보어로 명사를 쓰는 경우

주어	동사	목적어	목적격보어(명사)	
The song	**made**	him	**a star**.	그를 스타로 만들었다 〈him = a star〉
Jake	**called**	me	**an angel**.	나를 천사라고 불렀다 〈me = an angel〉
We	**named**	the cat	**Cookie**.	그 고양이를 쿠키라고 이름 지었다 〈the cat = Cookie〉

(2) 목적격보어로 형용사를 쓰는 경우

주어	동사	목적어	목적격보어(형용사)	
This coat	**kept**	me	**warm**.	나를 따뜻하게 유지했다 〈me = warm〉
We	**made**	him	**angry**.	그를 화나게 만들었다 〈him = angry〉

비교 point

주격보어 vs. 목적격보어

주격보어는 주어를 보충 설명해 주는 말이고, 목적격보어는 목적어를 보충 설명해 주는 말이다.

The song sounds **sad**. (그 노래는 슬프게 들린다.)	sad: 주어 The song을 설명해 주는 주격보어
The song made me **sad**. (그 노래는 나를 슬프게 만들었다.)	sad: 목적어 me를 설명해 주는 목적격보어

개념 우선 확인 | 옳은 해석 고르기

1 She looks angry.
- ☐ 그녀는 화가 나 보인다.
- ☐ 그녀는 화가 나서 본다.

2 The music sounds great.
- ☐ 그 음악과 소리는 멋지다.
- ☐ 그 음악은 멋지게 들린다.

3 He called me a fool.
- ☐ 그는 나를 바보라고 불렀다.
- ☐ 그는 나에게 바보라고 전화했다.

A 괄호 안에서 알맞은 것을 고르시오.

1 The story sounds (nice / nicely).

2 The news made me (sad / sadly).

3 The apple juice tastes (sweet / sweetly).

4 These gloves will keep your hands (warm / warmly).

B 〈보기〉에서 알맞은 말을 골라 문장을 완성하시오. (단, 한 번씩만 사용할 것)

보기	tastes	smells	sounds	looks

1 This candle _____ sweet.

2 She _____ great in her new dress.

3 His voice _____ strange these days.

4 This lemon _____ too sour.

C 우리말과 일치하도록 괄호 안의 말을 배열하여 문장을 완성하시오.

1 우리 엄마는 나를 공주라고 부르신다. (me, a, calls, princess)

→ My mom _____ _____ _____ _____ .

2 저 구름은 곰처럼 보인다. (like, a, looks, bear)

→ That cloud _____ _____ _____ _____ .

3 이 소설은 그를 부유하게 만들 것이다. (make, will, rich, him)

→ This novel _____ _____ _____ _____ .

4 그 영화는 그녀를 유명한 여배우로 만들었다. (her, a, actress, famous, made)

→ The movie _____ _____ _____ _____ _____ .

30초 완성 map

보어
- 주격보어
  - 감각동사+형용사
    - ❶ The robot looks (old / oldly). 그 로봇은 오래돼 보인다.
    - 주의 The robot looks (a cat / like a cat). 그 로봇은 고양이처럼 보인다.
- 목적격보어
  - 명사
    - ❷ We **called** the dog **Max**. 우리는 _____ 불렀다.
  - 형용사
    - ❸ The ice **keeps** the water **cold**. 얼음은 _____ 유지한다.

서술형 대비 문장 쓰기

Answers p. 20

☐ **빈칸 완성** 괄호 안의 말을 이용하여 빈칸 완성하기

01 아빠는 나에게 새 헬멧을 사 주실 것이다. (me)

→ Dad will _____ a new helmet.

02 이 병은 물을 따뜻하게 유지한다. (the water)

→ This bottle _____ warm.

03 그 이야기는 이상하게 들린다. (strange)

→ The story _____ .

04 그녀는 나에게 비밀을 말해 주었다. (a secret)

→ She _____ .

✓ **오류 수정** 어법에 맞게 문장 고쳐 쓰기

05 The wind feels coldly today.

→ The wind _____ .

06 His smile made everyone happily.

→ His smile _____ .

07 They call Coco their dog.

→ They call _____ .

08 The students made a big card to their teacher.

→ The students made _____ .

☰ **배열 영작** 괄호 안의 말을 바르게 배열하기

09 윤호는 그의 부모님께 티켓 두 장을 사 드렸다. (his, for, parents, bought, tickets, two)

→ Yunho _____ .

10 너는 어제 수업 시간에 정말 졸려 보였다. (sleepy, looked, you, really)

→ _____ in class yesterday.

11 선생님은 우리에게 몇 가지 질문을 하셨다. (us, asked, questions, some)

→ The teacher _____ .

12 그는 어젯밤에 우리에게 무서운 이야기를 해 주었다. (told, us, to, a, story, scary, he)

→ _____ last night.

시험에 꼭 나오는 출제 포인트

Answers p. 20

출제 포인트 1 간접목적어와 직접목적어의 순서에 주의하자!

우리말과 일치하도록 괄호 안의 말을 배열하시오.

(1) 그는 나에게 카메라를 빌려주었다. (lent, his camera, me)

→ He _____ .

(2) 그녀는 아들에게 장갑을 만들어 주었다. (gloves, for, made, her son)

→ She _____ .

출제 포인트 2 수여동사에 따라 간접목적어 앞에 쓰이는 전치사를 구별하자!

빈칸에 알맞은 말이 순서대로 바르게 짝지어진 것은?

> • He sent a postcard _____ me.
> • She bought chocolate cookies _____ her children.

① to – to   ② for – for   ③ for – to
④ to – of   ⑤ to – for

출제 포인트 3 감각동사 뒤에는 형용사를 쓴다!

빈칸에 들어갈 말로 알맞지 <u>않은</u> 것은?

> That sounds _____ .

① good   ② greatly   ③ nice
④ exciting   ⑤ perfect

고득점 POINT 「감각동사+형용사」 vs. 「감각동사+like+명사」

우리말과 일치하도록 괄호 안의 말을 이용하여 문장을 완성하시오.

(1) 그 치즈케이크는 맛있어 보인다. (tasty)

→ The cheesecake _____ _____ .

(2) 그 구름은 새처럼 보인다. (like)

→ The cloud _____ _____ a bird.

출제 포인트 4 목적격보어로 명사나 형용사가 오는 문장을 익혀 두자!

우리말과 일치하도록 빈칸에 알맞은 말을 쓰시오.

(1) We named _____ _____ .

(우리는 그를 Paul이라고 이름 지었다.)

(2) This scarf kept _____ _____ .

(이 스카프가 나를 따뜻하게 유지해 주었다.)

고득점 POINT '~하게'라고 해석된다고 해서 목적격보어 자리에 부사를 쓰지 않도록 주의해야 한다.

어법상 틀린 부분을 찾아 바르게 고쳐 쓰시오.

The news made us sadly. _____ → _____

유형	문항수	배점	점수
객관식	18	60	
서술형	10	40	

[01-03] 빈칸에 들어갈 말로 알맞은 것을 고르시오.

|6점, 각 2점|

01

Lemons _____ sour.

① do ② have ③ taste
④ make ⑤ watch

02

I will _____ an apple pie to you.

① get ② buy ③ make
④ cook ⑤ give

03

The tree _____ a big mushroom.

① felt ② tasted ③ looked
④ looked like ⑤ sounded like

04 우리말과 일치하도록 할 때 빈칸에 들어갈 말로 알맞은 것은? |3점|

우리 엄마는 나에게 스웨터를 만들어 주셨다.
→ My mom made _____.

① I a sweater ② a sweater me
③ me a sweater ④ a sweater to me
⑤ for me a sweater

05 빈칸에 들어갈 말로 알맞지 <u>않은</u> 것은? |3점|

Their music makes me _____.

① happy ② calm ③ sleepy
④ sadly ⑤ lonely

06 밑줄 친 동사의 성격이 나머지와 <u>다른</u> 것은? |3점|

① This salad <u>tastes</u> fresh.
② The fish <u>smelled</u> terrible.
③ My cat <u>looks</u> healthy now.
④ He <u>told</u> his friends the news.
⑤ Your idea <u>sounds</u> interesting.

07 빈칸에 들어갈 말이 순서대로 바르게 짝지어진 것은? |3점|

• The singer sent an email _____ her fan.
• He made a kite _____ his son.

① to – to ② to – for
③ for – of ④ for – to
⑤ of – for

08 밑줄 친 **look**의 쓰임이 〈보기〉와 <u>다른</u> 것은? |3점|

보기 You <u>look</u> excited today.

① Ms. Kang <u>looked</u> tired.
② This building <u>looks</u> clean.
③ He <u>looks</u> great in that jacket.
④ I <u>looked</u> at the shining stars.
⑤ My dad <u>looked</u> angry this morning.

09 그림 속 남자가 할 말을 완성할 때, 빈칸에 들어갈 말로 알맞은 것은? |3점|

We call _____.

① an elephant that animal
② that animal an elephant
③ an elephant to that animal
④ that animal for an elephant
⑤ to that animal an elephant

10 다음 중 밑줄 친 부분이 어법상 틀린 것은? |4점|

① You look like an angel.
② Please keep the food cold.
③ Ted bought for Kate a ring.
④ Can you make us some cookies?
⑤ The song made the singer popular.

11 주어진 문장을 의미가 같도록 바꿔 쓸 때 잘못된 것은? |4점|

① He told me the secret.
   → He told the secret to me.
② He lent me his bike.
   → He lent his bike for me.
③ I will give you the letter later.
   → I will give the letter to you later.
④ She will cook us some food tonight.
   → She will cook some food for us tonight.
⑤ Dan showed his friends his new cell phone.
   → Dan showed his new cell phone to his friends.

12 주어진 우리말을 영어로 바르게 옮긴 것은? |3점|

그녀는 우리에게 영어를 가르쳐 주었다.

① She taught English of us.
② She taught for us English.
③ She taught English us.
④ She taught to us English.
⑤ She taught English to us.

13 다음 중 어법상 틀린 문장은? |4점|

① The soup smells bad.
② They named their son Brad.
③ My father gave me a present.
④ This candy tastes like strawberries.
⑤ They should keep their children quietly.

최신기출

14 빈칸에 들어갈 수 있는 말끼리 바르게 짝지어진 것은? |4점|

Jennifer made us _____.

| ⓐ cookies | ⓑ busily | ⓒ angry |
| ⓓ often | ⓔ easily | |

① ⓐ, ⓑ   ② ⓐ, ⓒ   ③ ⓑ, ⓓ
④ ⓒ, ⓓ   ⑤ ⓒ, ⓔ

고난도

15 다음 중 어법상 옳은 문장의 개수는? |5점|

ⓐ The fan kept me cool.
ⓑ He lent his money Susan.
ⓒ The baby looks so lovely.
ⓓ It sounded my dad's voice.
ⓔ The TV show made him a famous singer.

*fan 선풍기

① 1개   ② 2개   ③ 3개   ④ 4개   ⑤ 5개

16 밑줄 친 ⓐ~ⓔ 중 어법상 틀린 것은? |5점|

> A Your hands ⓐ<u>feel like ice</u>. Do you ⓑ<u>feel cold</u>?
> B Yes. Could you ⓒ<u>give me some hot tea</u>?
> A Sure. Here you are.
> B Thank you. Oh, it ⓓ<u>smells sweetly</u>. It ⓔ<u>tastes good</u>, too.

① ⓐ   ② ⓑ   ③ ⓒ   ④ ⓓ   ⑤ ⓔ

[17-18] 다음 대화를 읽고, 물음에 답하시오.

> A Jane, what will you do for Parents' Day?
> B I'll get some flowers ___ⓐ___ my parents. What about you?
> A Well, I (A) <u>wrote a letter my parents</u>.
> B That's great! Let's make cakes ___ⓑ___ them, too.
> A Good idea.

17 빈칸 ⓐ와 ⓑ에 공통으로 들어갈 말로 알맞은 것은? |3점|

① to   ② of   ③ with
④ for   ⑤ about

18 밑줄 친 (A)를 어법에 맞게 고쳐 쓴 것을 두 개 고르면? |4점|

① wrote a letter of my parents
② wrote a letter to my parents
③ wrote my parents to a letter
④ wrote my parents for a letter
⑤ wrote my parents a letter

서술형

19 〈보기〉에서 알맞은 말을 골라 문장을 완성하시오. |4점, 각 2점|

> 보기   buys   looks   gives   tastes like

(1) This apple pie _____ delicious.

(2) Grandma _____ birthday gifts for us every year.

20 우리말과 일치하도록 괄호 안의 말을 이용하여 **두 개의 문장**을 완성하시오. |4점, 각 2점|

> 소라는 Stella에게 빨간 장갑을 보냈다.
> (red gloves)

(1) Sora sent _____.
(2) Sora sent _____.

[21-22] 우리말과 일치하도록 괄호 안의 말을 바르게 배열하시오. |8점, 각 4점|

21
> 규칙적인 운동은 너를 건강하게 만든다.
> (you, makes, regular exercise, healthy)

→ _____

22
> 이 영화는 그를 슈퍼스타로 만들었다.
> (made, this movie, a superstar, him)

→ _____

23 우리말과 일치하도록 〈조건〉에 맞게 대화를 완성하시오.

|4점|

> A This bag is really cheap. It's 10 dollars.
> B Really? I can't believe it.
> _____
> (그것은 비싸 보여.)

> 조건 1. look을 사용할 것
>   2. 3단어로 쓸 것

[24-25] 그림을 보고, 빈칸에 알맞은 말을 〈조건〉에 맞게 쓰시오.

|8점, 각 4점|

24

> 조건 1. math를 사용할 것
>   2. 대명사를 사용하여 3단어로 쓸 것

> A What did Ms. Smith teach the students?
> B She _____.

25

> 조건 1. keep, clean을 사용할 것
>   2. 대명사를 사용하여 3단어로 쓸 것

> A John, your room is so messy. You must
>   _____.
> B OK, Mom.

[26-27] 다음 글을 읽고, 물음에 답하시오.

> Yesterday was Jihun's birthday. He had a big birthday party. (A) I bought him a nice bag. Cindy didn't come, but she sent him a cap. (B) 그 파티는 우리를 행복하게 했다. (made, the party, happy, us)

26 밑줄 친 (A)와 같은 의미가 되도록 빈칸에 알맞은 말을 쓰시오.

|3점|

→ I bought a nice bag _____.

27 밑줄 친 (B)의 우리말과 일치하도록 괄호 안의 말을 바르게 배열하시오.

|4점|

→ _____

28 밑줄 친 ⓐ~ⓓ 중 어법상 틀린 것의 기호를 쓰고, 바르게 고쳐 쓰시오.

|5점|

> Mr. Baker ⓐtold us about a new kind of car. It doesn't use gasoline. It needs only water. We call it ⓑto a hydrogen car. We asked ⓒMr. Baker many questions. He gave lots of interesting information about hydrogen cars ⓓto us.
>
> *gasline 휘발유   hydrogen car 수소차

(   ) → _____

chapter

11

형용사, 부사, 비교

Harry is faster than Ron.

Q. 위 문장으로 보아 먼저 학교에 도착하는 것은 누구일까?

☐ Harry　　☐ Ron

형용사

1 형용사의 쓰임

형용사는 명사와 대명사를 수식하거나 명사와 대명사의 상태를 설명한다.

She is	a **famous** artist.	그녀는 **유명한** 예술가이다. 〈명사 수식〉
The artist is	**famous**.	그 예술가는 **유명하다**. 〈명사 설명〉

▶ -thing, -body, -one으로 끝나는 대명사는 형용사가 뒤에서 수식한다.

I want *something* **cold**.

Is there *anybody* **new** here today?

2 수와 양을 나타내는 형용사

(1) many, much, a lot of, lots of

many	많은	셀 수 있는 명사의 복수형
much		셀 수 없는 명사
a lot of, lots of		셀 수 있는 명사의 복수형 / 셀 수 없는 명사

→ much는 주로 부정문에 쓴다.

He has **many** *friends*.

I don't have **much** *time* now.

The princess has **a lot of** *shoes*.

She has **lots of** *homework* to do.

(2) a few, a little, few, little

a few	약간의, 조금 있는	셀 수 있는 명사의 복수형
a little		셀 수 없는 명사
few	거의 없는	셀 수 있는 명사의 복수형
little		셀 수 없는 명사

→ few와 little에는 부정적인 의미가 있기 때문에 부정어와 함께 쓰지 않는다.

I have **a few** *questions* about the book.

She put **a little** *sugar* in her tea.

There were **few** *cars* on the road.

There is **little** *juice* in the bottle.

(3) some, any

some	약간의	긍정문, 권유문
any		부정문, 의문문

I bought **some** books. 〈긍정문〉

Would you like **some** water? 〈권유문〉

She doesn't have **any** homework today. 〈부정문〉

Do you have **any** problems? 〈의문문〉

개념 우선 확인 | 형용사 고르기

1 a tall building	2 an interesting game	3 something exciting	4 He is honest.
☐ ☐	☐ ☐	☐ ☐	☐ ☐

A 괄호 안에서 알맞은 것을 고르시오.

1 I need (something special / special something).

2 We had (few / little) rain last summer.

3 She doesn't have (many / much) time.

4 There were (a few / a little) people at the park.

B 빈칸에 알맞은 말을 〈보기〉에서 골라 문장을 완성하시오. (단, 한 번씩만 사용할 것)

보기	many	few	little	some	any

1 She can't buy it now. She has _____ money.

2 I'm going to buy _____ bread and milk.

3 He is not popular at all. He has _____ fans.

4 We don't have _____ classes today. Let's go hiking.

5 The store is crowded. _____ people are shopping.

C 우리말과 일치하도록 괄호 안의 말을 이용하여 문장을 완성하시오.

1 이 호수에는 물이 조금 있다. (water)

→ There is _____ _____ _____ in this lake.

2 그들은 여행에 대한 몇 가지 계획을 가지고 있다. (plan)

→ They have _____ _____ _____ for their trip.

3 나는 어제 학교에서 어리석은 어떤 짓을 했다. (foolish)

→ I did _____ _____ at school yesterday.

4 너는 동물원에서 많은 동물들을 볼 수 있다. (animal)

→ You can see _____ _____ _____ _____ at the zoo.

30초 완성 map

형용사
- 쓰임
  - ❶ I saw a (pretty girl / girl pretty). She was kind to everyone.
  - 주의 He met (famous somebody / somebody famous).
- 수량 형용사
  - ❷ (many / much) flowers   (a lot of / many) milk
  - (a few / a little) children   (few / little) salt
  - Do you have (some / any) questions?

unit 2 부사

1 부사의 쓰임

부사는 동사, 형용사, 다른 부사, 또는 문장 전체를 수식한다.

We	walked	quickly.		우리는 **빠르게** 걸었다. 〈동사 수식〉
It	is	really	long.	그것은 **정말로** 길다. 〈형용사 수식〉
He	studied	very	hard.	그는 **아주** 열심히 공부했다. 〈부사 수식〉

2 부사의 형태

(1) 기본 형태

| 대부분의 부사는 **형용사+-ly** | slow(느린) – slow**ly**(느리게)
careful(주의 깊은) – careful**ly**(주의 깊게) |
| -y로 끝나는 형용사의 부사는
y를 **i**로 고치고**+-ly** | easy(쉬운) – eas**ily**(쉽게)
happy(행복한) – happ**ily**(행복하게) |

Can you speak **slowly**?
My father fixed my computer **easily**.

(2) 주의해야 할 형태

| 형용사와 형태가 같은 부사 | fast(빠른) – **fast**(빠르게)   early(이른) – **early**(일찍)
late(늦은) – **late**(늦게)   hard(어려운) – **hard**(열심히)
high(높은) – **high**(높이) |
| -ly가 붙었을 때 다른 뜻을 갖는 부사 | **hard**(열심히) – **hardly**(거의 ~ 않다)
late(늦게) – **lately**(최근에)   **high**(높이) – **highly**(매우) |

The bus left an hour **late**. (늦게)
Daniel looks tired **lately**. (최근에)

> **주의** **-ly로 끝나는 형용사**: lovely(사랑스러운), friendly(친절한), ugly(못생긴), silly(어리석은) 등
> She has a **lovely** voice.   He is a **friendly** man.

3 빈도부사

빈도부사는 어떤 일이 얼마나 자주 일어나는지를 나타내는 말로, 주로 be동사나 조동사의 뒤, 일반동사의 앞에 쓴다.

always (항상)	He *is* **always** busy on weekends.
usually (보통, 대개)	I **usually** *sleep* nine hours a day.
often (자주)	She **often** *plays* online games.
sometimes (가끔, 때때로)	They **sometimes** *drink* coffee.
never (결코 ~ 않는)	I *will* **never** tell a lie.

개념 우선 확인 | 옳은 표현 고르기

1 천천히 먹다
- ☐ eat slow
- ☐ eat slowly

2 매우 열심히
- ☐ very hard
- ☐ very hardly

3 빠르게 뛰다
- ☐ run fast
- ☐ run fastly

A 괄호 안에서 알맞은 것을 고르시오.

1 He solved the problem (quick / quickly).

2 They talked (quiet / quietly) on the subway.

3 The train came (late / lately) because of the storm.

4 Our neighbors are not friendly. They (hard / hardly) smile.

B 괄호 안의 빈도부사를 알맞은 위치에 넣어 문장을 다시 쓰시오.

1 We go to school at 8. (usually)

→ _____

2 He will help you. (always)

→ _____

3 I lie to my parents. (never)

→ _____

C 우리말과 일치하도록 괄호 안의 말을 이용하여 문장을 완성하시오.

1 그는 공원에서 빠르게 걸었다. (walk, fast)

→ He _____ _____ in the park.

2 나는 가끔 아버지와 쇼핑하러 간다. (go, sometimes)

→ I _____ _____ shopping with my father.

3 그들은 그 퍼즐을 쉽게 풀었다. (solve, easy)

→ They _____ the puzzle _____.

4 나의 아버지는 눈 때문에 천천히 운전하셨다. (drive, slow)

→ My father _____ _____ because of the snow.

30초 완성 map

부사	쓰임·형태	They sang (happy / happily).	그들은 행복하게 노래했다.
		The man talks (fast / fastly).	그 남자는 빠르게 말한다.
		(주의) I woke up (late / lately) this morning.	나는 오늘 아침에 늦게 일어났다.
	빈도부사	He is (often / never) kind.	그는 결코 친절하지 않다.
		She (usually / sometimes) visits my house.	그녀는 가끔 나의 집을 방문한다.
		You should (always / often) be polite to others.	항상 다른 사람들에게 공손해야 한다.

1 비교 표현

Kevin is **tall**.	Kevin은 키가 크다.
Kevin is **taller than** Mark.	Kevin은 Mark보다 키가 더 크다. 〈비교급〉
Kevin is **the tallest**.	Kevin은 가장 키가 크다. 〈최상급〉

2 비교급: 형용사/부사의 비교급+than (…보다 더 ~한/하게)

My bag	is	**bigger than**	yours.
This movie	is	**more interesting than**	that one.

3 최상급: the+형용사/부사의 최상급 (가장 ~한/하게)

Joe	is	**the fastest** student	*in his class.*	〈in+장소/범위〉
Soccer	is	**the most popular** sport	*of the three.*	〈of+복수명사/기간〉

＊비교급과 최상급 만드는 방법   ∞ 부록 p. 171

			원급	비교급	최상급
규칙 변화	대부분의 경우	**+-er/-est**	fast	fast**er**	fast**est**
	-e로 끝나는 경우	**+-r/-st**	large	large**r**	large**st**
	-y로 끝나는 경우	**y를 i로 고치고** **+-er/-est**	easy	eas**ier**	eas**iest**
	「단모음+단자음」 으로 끝나는 경우	자음을 한 번 더 쓰고 **+-er/-est**	hot	hot**ter**	hot**test**
	3음절 이상인 경우	**more/most+원급**	important	**more** important	**most** important
불규칙 변화			good(좋은) – better(더 좋은) – best(가장 좋은) well(잘) – better(더 잘) – best(가장 잘) bad(나쁜) – worse(더 나쁜) – worst(가장 나쁜) many(수가 많은) – more(수가 더 많은) – most(수가 가장 많은) much(양이 많은) – more(양이 더 많은) – most(양이 가장 많은)			

Your camera is **better** than mine.
Autumn is **the best** season for reading.

주의 2음절 단어 중 –ful, -ous, -ing 등으로 끝나는 단어는 more/most를 사용하여 비교급과 최상급을 만든다.
   useful – more useful – most useful / famous – more famous – most famous
   boring – more boring – most boring

개념 우선 확인 | 옳은 표현 고르기

1 가장 추운
- ☐ the coldest
- ☐ the most cold

2 ~보다 더 가벼운
- ☐ more light than
- ☐ lighter than

3 ~보다 더 인기 있는
- ☐ popular than
- ☐ more popular than

A   주어진 단어의 비교급과 최상급을 순서대로 쓰시오.

1 hot   – _____ – _____

2 good – _____ – _____

3 strong – _____ – _____

4 useful – _____ – _____

5 large – _____ – _____

6 pretty – _____ – _____

7 bad   – _____ – _____

8 beautiful – _____ – _____

B   괄호 안의 말을 알맞은 형태로 바꿔 빈칸에 쓰시오.

1 This box is _____ than that box. (heavy)

2 Jina is the _____ girl of the five. (short)

3 Today is _____ than yesterday. (warm)

4 This is the _____ _____ building in the city. (famous)

C   우리말과 일치하도록 괄호 안의 말을 이용하여 문장을 완성하시오.

1 이 문제는 저 문제보다 더 쉽다. (easy)
- → This question is _____ _____ that one.

2 서울은 한국에서 가장 큰 도시이다. (big)
- → Seoul is _____ _____ _____ in Korea.

3 너의 아이디어가 내 아이디어보다 더 좋다. (good)
- → Your idea is _____ _____ my idea.

4 이 노트북 컴퓨터는 내 것보다 더 비싸다. (expensive)
- → This laptop is _____ _____ _____ mine.

5 그녀는 이곳에서 가장 중요한 사람이다. (important)
- → She is _____ _____ _____ person here.

30초 완성 map

비교급과 최상급

❶ 형태

young – _____ (더 어린) – youngest   busy – busier – _____ (가장 바쁜)

good – _____ (더 좋은) – best   much – more – _____ (가장 많은)

❷ 쓰임

China is _____ _____ India. (large)   중국은 인도보다 더 크다.

It is _____ _____ _____ thing here. (expensive)

그것은 이곳에서 가장 비싼 것이다.

서술형 대비 문장 쓰기

Answers p. 22

□ 빈칸 완성 괄호 안의 말을 이용하여 빈칸 완성하기

01 나는 달콤한 무언가를 먹고 싶다. (something)

→ I want to eat _____ _____ .

02 그들에게는 희망이 거의 없다. (hope)

→ They have _____ _____ .

03 그 소녀는 트램폴린 위에서 높이 뛰었다. (jump)

→ The girl _____ _____ on a trampoline.

04 그의 휴대전화가 내 것보다 더 좋다. (good)

→ His cell phone _____ _____ _____ mine.

✔ 오류 수정 어법에 맞게 문장 고쳐 쓰기

05 We have a few milk in the refrigerator.

→ We have _____ .

06 Dana met nice somebody at the concert.

→ Dana met _____ .

07 This is the most longest river in the world.

→ This is _____ .

08 The students worked hardly on the class project.

→ The students worked _____ .

≡ 배열 영작 괄호 안의 말을 바르게 배열하기

09 그는 다른 사람들 앞에서 절대 울지 않는다. (cries, he, never)

→ _____ in front of other people.

10 그 야구 경기는 비 때문에 늦게 시작했다. (the baseball game, late, started)

→ _____ because of the rain.

11 한국에서 가장 인기 있는 가수는 누구니? (most, singer, popular, is, the, who)

→ _____ in Korea?

12 너는 그 잡지에서 뭔가 재미있는 것을 찾았니? (find, anything, did, interesting, you)

→ _____ in the magazine?

시험에 꼭 나오는 출제 포인트

출제 포인트 ① 수와 양을 나타내는 형용사의 쓰임을 구분하자!

우리말과 일치하도록 밑줄 친 부분을 바르게 고쳐 쓰시오.

(1) 내 지갑에는 약간의 돈이 있다.

→ There is <u>a few</u> money in my wallet.　→ _____

(2) 그 부자는 친구가 거의 없다.

→ The rich man has <u>little</u> friends.　→ _____

출제 포인트 ② 형용사와 부사의 쓰임을 구분하고, 부사의 형태를 익히자!

괄호 안에서 알맞은 것을 고르시오.

(1) The actress wasn't very (happy / happily).

(2) I can't speak French very (good / well).

(3) She arrived at the airport (safe / safely).

> **고득점 POINT 혼동하기 쉬운 부사**
>
> **어법상 틀린 부분을 찾아 바르게 고쳐 쓰시오.**
>
> (1) Eric can run very fastly. _____ → _____
>
> (2) I usually get up lately. _____ → _____

출제 포인트 ③ 비교급의 변화형과 쓰임을 익히자!

괄호 안의 말을 알맞은 형태로 바꿔 쓰시오.

(1) Today is _____ than yesterday. (hot)

(2) This book is _____ than that one. (difficult)

출제 포인트 ④ 최상급의 변화형과 쓰임을 익히자!

우리말과 일치하도록 괄호 안의 말을 이용하여 문장을 완성하시오.

(1) Ryan은 우리 반에서 가장 키가 큰 학생이다. (tall)

→ Ryan is _____ student in my class.

(2) Tom은 우리 반에서 가장 인기 있는 소년이다. (popular)

→ Tom is _____ boy in my class.

> **고득점 POINT 비교급과 최상급의 불규칙 변화**
>
> **괄호 안의 말을 어법에 맞게 사용하여 문장을 완성하시오.**
>
> (1) 오늘은 내 인생 최악의 날이었다. (bad)
>
> → Today was _____ _____ day of my life.
>
> (2) 그녀는 Tom보다 축구를 더 잘한다. (well)
>
> → She plays soccer _____ _____ Tom does.

실전 Test

[01-03] 빈칸에 들어갈 말로 알맞지 <u>않은</u> 것을 고르시오.
|6점, 각 2점|

01

John always talks _____.

① fast ② slowly
③ quietly ④ silly
⑤ carefully

02

I want something _____.

① new ② cold
③ lovely ④ delicious
⑤ expensively

03

Snowboarding is more _____ than skiing.

① exciting ② better
③ difficult ④ interesting
⑤ dangerous

04 빈칸에 공통으로 들어갈 말로 알맞은 것은? |3점|

• He wants to make _____ money.
• We learn _____ things at school.

① many ② much
③ a few ④ a little
⑤ a lot of

05 빈칸에 some이 들어갈 수 <u>없는</u> 것은? |3점|

① Would you like _____ juice?
② I need _____ paper and pencils.
③ He wanted to buy _____ flowers.
④ They didn't take _____ pictures here.
⑤ There were _____ students in the classroom.

06 밑줄 친 부분의 위치가 어법상 어색한 것은? |3점|

① I will <u>never</u> tell the truth.
② Kathy <u>always</u> goes shopping with me.
③ He is <u>sometimes</u> late for work.
④ Minsu <u>usually</u> sleeps seven hours a day.
⑤ She reads <u>often</u> the newspaper in the morning.

07 어법상 <u>틀린</u> 부분을 찾아 바르게 고친 것은? |4점|

She hit the ball highly and started to run fast.

① hit → hitted
② highly → high
③ highly → more highly
④ fast → the fast
⑤ fast → fastly

08 밑줄 친 hard의 의미가 나머지와 <u>다른</u> 것은? |3점|

① Making a movie is <u>hard</u> work.
② To control your feelings is <u>hard</u>.
③ It is <u>hard</u> to read English books.
④ Did you practice the piano <u>hard</u>?
⑤ The teacher solved <u>hard</u> problems.

[09-10] 밑줄 친 부분이 어법상 옳은 것을 고르시오.

|8점, 각 4점|

09 ① You are my <u>goodest</u> friend.
② Science is <u>easyer</u> than history.
③ The <u>nearest</u> station is the City Hall station.
④ Yesterday was <u>hoter</u> than today.
⑤ Chopsticks are <u>usefuler</u> than forks.

10 ① Mr. Lee looks tired <u>late</u>.
② My dog can run <u>fastly</u>.
③ The train arrived too <u>lately</u>.
④ They will live <u>happily</u> forever.
⑤ We studied <u>hardly</u> for the exam.

[11-12] 빈칸에 들어갈 말이 순서대로 바르게 짝지어진 것을 고르시오.

|6점, 각 3점|

11

• Becky has _____ good friends.
• Please put _____ salt in the soup.

① little – many
② a little – a lot of
③ a little – a little
④ a few – a little
⑤ a few – many

12

I _____ get up early in the morning, so I'm _____ late for school.

① always – never
② usually – always
③ never – never
④ always – always
⑤ often – always

[13-14] 우리말을 영어로 바르게 옮긴 것을 고르시오.

|8점, 각 4점|

13

내 점수가 네 점수보다 더 안 좋다.

① My score is badder than you.
② My score is worse than you.
③ My score is worst than yours.
④ My score is worse than yours.
⑤ My score is more bad than yours.

14

이 주스에는 설탕이 거의 없다.

① This juice has few sugar.
② This juice has a few sugar.
③ This juice has little sugar.
④ This juice has a little sugar.
⑤ This juice doesn't have little sugar.

15 다음 표의 내용과 일치하는 문장은? |4점|

	A	B	C
MODEL			
PRICE	$1,500	$800	$1,000
POPULARITY	★★	★	★★★

① Model A is cheaper than Model C.
② Model A is the most popular of the three.
③ Model B is the cheapest phone of the three.
④ Model B is more popular than Model A.
⑤ Model C is the most expensive of the three.

16 (A)~(C)에 들어갈 말이 바르게 짝지어진 것은? |4점|

- Don't put too (A) much / many salt in my soup.
- I can solve the problem (B) easy / easily .
- His score was the (C) higher / highest in his class.

	(A)	(B)	(C)
①	much	easy	higher
②	much	easily	higher
③	much	easily	highest
④	many	easy	higher
⑤	many	easily	highest

고난도

17 다음 중 어법상 옳은 문장의 개수는? |5점|

ⓐ There is few money in my wallet.
ⓑ Rachel drinks a lot of water every day.
ⓒ This machine doesn't use much energy.
ⓓ They don't have some homework today.
ⓔ We bought a few book at the bookstore.

① 1개 ② 2개 ③ 3개
④ 4개 ⑤ 5개

최신기출 고난도

18 다음 글의 내용을 잘못 이해한 사람은? |5점|

My name is Suji. I am 14. I have three sisters. They are Sarah, Susan, and Sally. Susan is 17. Sarah is younger than Susan and older than Sally. I am younger than Sally.

① 태영: Susan is the oldest.
② 하나: Suji is older than Sarah.
③ 유준: Sarah is older than Suji.
④ 상운: Suji is the youngest of the four.
⑤ 지윤: Sally is younger than Susan.

19 happy를 이용하여 문장을 완성하시오. (필요시 형태를 바꿀 것) |3점|

- Mom looks _____.
- She looked at me _____.

20 우리말과 일치하도록 빈칸에 공통으로 알맞은 말을 쓰시오. |3점|

- I have a _____ pencils.
  (나에게 연필이 몇 자루 있다.)
- There were _____ cars in the parking lot. (주차장에는 차가 거의 없었다.)

21 그림을 보고, 조건에 맞게 글을 완성하시오. |4점, 각 2점|

조건 1. 비교급 또는 최상급을 사용할 것
2. fast를 사용할 것

Mike runs (1) _____ _____ Kevin. Sam is (2) _____ _____ runner of the four.

22

Her idea is more good than mine.
(그녀의 아이디어는 내 것보다 더 좋다.)

_____ → _____

23

There was a few milk in the bottle.
(그 병 안에는 우유가 거의 없었다.)

_____ → _____

24 괄호 안의 말을 이용하여 비교하는 문장을 완성하시오.
|4점|

My watch was 80 dollars.
Kelly's watch was 90 dollars.

→ Kelly's watch was _____

_____. (expensive)

25 그림을 보고, 〈조건〉에 맞게 문장을 완성하시오.
|6점, 각 2점|

보기	late	loud	slow

조건　1. 〈보기〉에 있는 단어를 사용할 것
　　　2. 필요하면 형태를 바꿀 것

(1) (2) (3)

(1) The elderly woman walked _____.

(2) He went to bed _____ last night.

(3) Don't speak _____ here.

26 다음 표를 보고, 세 명의 몸무게를 비교하는 문장을 〈조건〉에 맞게 완성하시오.　|4점, 각 2점|

Name	Mina	Jiho	Junsu
Weight	50 kg	65 kg	60 kg

조건　1. heavy 또는 light를 이용할 것
　　　2. 비교급 또는 최상급을 이용하여 문장을 완성할 것

(1) Junsu is _____ _____ Mina.

(2) Mina is _____ _____ of the three.

27 우리말과 일치하도록 괄호 안의 말을 바르게 배열하시오.
|4점|

Julie는 새로운 것을 배우고 싶어한다.
(Julie, new, learn, something, wants, to)

→ _____

_____

28 학생들이 좋아하는 과목을 조사한 그래프를 보고, 〈조건〉에 맞게 문장을 완성하시오.　|4점|

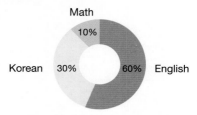

Math
10%
Korean 30%
60% English

조건　1. 비교급이나 최상급으로 쓸 것
　　　2. popular, subject를 사용할 것

→ English is _____

_____ of the three.

chapter

12

접속사와 전치사

It is between the rocks.

Q. 위 문장으로 보아 보물이 있는 곳은?

☐ ①　☐ ②　☐ ③　☐ ④

1 and, but, or

and, but, or는 문법적으로 대등한 단어와 단어, 구와 구, 절과 절을 연결한다.

and	그리고 〈내용이 비슷한 것 연결〉	I like *soccer* **and** *baseball*.
but	그러나 〈내용이 상반되는 것 연결〉	*He ran fast*, **but** *he missed the bus*.
or	또는 〈둘 이상 중에서 선택〉	Will you *stay home* **or** *play outside*?

주의 and, but, or는 문법적으로 대등한 것을 연결한다.
Sally likes *singing* **and** *dancing*. 〈동명사〉
Do you want *to play tennis* **or** (*to*) *watch TV*? 〈to부정사〉

2 when, because, if

when	~할 때 〈시간〉	I was glad **when** she visited me.
because	~이기 때문에 〈원인, 이유〉	I'll go swimming **because** it's very hot. (= It's very hot, **so** I'll go swimming.)
if	(만약) ~하면 〈조건〉	I will help you **if** you need my help.

When the rain stopped, they went out.
Because I broke my leg, I went to the hospital.
If you have any questions, you can call me.

▶ 접속사가 이끄는 부사절이 문장 앞에 오면 부사절 뒤에 콤마(,)를 쓴다.

3 that

접속사 that이 이끄는 절은 문장에서 목적어 역할을 할 수 있다. 이때 that은 생략할 수 있다.

I	think know believe hope	that	he will succeed.	나는 그가 성공할 거라고 **생각한다**. 나는 그가 성공할 거**라는 것을 안다**. 나는 그가 성공할 거**라고 믿는다**. 나는 그가 성공하기**를 바란다**.

I think (**that**) she dances very well.
I believe (**that**) he is honest.

시험 point

if가 이끄는 조건절에서 주의할 점

조건을 나타내는 접속사 if가 이끄는 부사절에서는 현재시제로 미래를 나타낸다.

If it (**rains** / will rain) tomorrow, we'll watch a movie on TV.

개념 우선 확인 | 옳은 표현 고르기

1 작지만 힘이 센
  ☐ small and strong
  ☐ small but strong

2 더웠기 때문에
  ☐ so it was hot
  ☐ because it was hot

3 나는 그가 옳다는 것을 안다.
  ☐ I know that he's right.
  ☐ I know when he's right.

A 괄호 안에서 알맞은 것을 고르시오.

1 They were sad, (or / but) they didn't cry.

2 He is a doctor, (and / or) his wife is a nurse.

3 Which do you want, a hot dog (and / or) a hamburger?

4 She studied hard (or / but) failed the test.

B 자연스러운 의미의 문장이 되도록 알맞게 연결하시오.

1 I couldn't call you   •   • ⓐ if you have time.

2 You should wear a helmet •   • ⓑ because I was busy.

3 I believe   •   • ⓒ that the rumor is true.

4 Please help me   •   • ⓓ when you ride a bike.

C 〈보기〉에서 알맞은 접속사를 골라 문장을 완성하시오. (단, 한 번씩만 사용할 것)

보기	that	but	because	if

1 I think _____ he is diligent.

2 I was late _____ the traffic was heavy.

3 You can have this book _____ you like it.

4 He was sick, _____ he went to school.

30초 완성 map

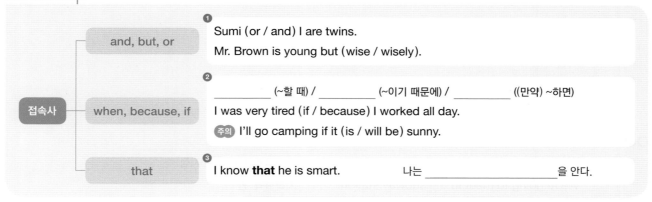

접속사
- and, but, or
  - ❶ Sumi (or / and) I are twins.
    Mr. Brown is young but (wise / wisely).
- when, because, if
  - ❷ _____ (~할 때) / _____ (~이기 때문에) / _____ ((만약) ~하면)
    I was very tired (if / because) I worked all day.
    주의 I'll go camping if it (is / will be) sunny.
- that
  - ❸ I know **that** he is smart.   나는 _____ 을 안다.

위치·장소를 나타내는 전치사

1 위치를 나타내는 전치사

(1) in, on, under

in	~ 안에	The baseballs are **in** the box.
on	~ 위에	There is a cheesecake **on** the table.
under	~ 아래에	I put my bag **under** the seat.

(2) in front of, behind

in front of	~ 앞에	There is a bench **in front of** the museum.
behind	~ 뒤에	I sit **behind** Angela in the classroom.

(3) next to, between A and B

next to	~ 옆에	A boy was standing **next to** my bicycle.
between A and B	A와 B 사이에	The bank is **between** the hospital **and** the bookstore.

2 장소를 나타내는 전치사

at	~에 〈장소의 한 지점〉	**at** home	**at** school	**at** the bus stop
		at the airport	**at** the subway station	**at** the corner
in	~ 안에, ~에 〈공간의 내부, 도시, 국가〉	**in** my room	**in** the building	**in** the library
		in Paris	**in** Korea	**in** the world

We have a festival **at** school this Thursday.
She lived **in** Canada three years ago.

비교 point

장소를 나타내는 전치사 at vs. in

We're going to meet **at** the subway station.	지하철역의 '어느 한 지점'
We're going to meet **in** the subway station.	지하철역 '안'

개념 우선 확인 | 옳은 표현 고르기

1 프랑스에
- ☐ at France
- ☐ in France

2 집 앞에
- ☐ behind the house
- ☐ in front of the house

3 은행 옆에
- ☐ next to the bank
- ☐ between the bank

A 괄호 안에서 알맞은 것을 고르시오.

1 My family lived (at / in) Germany ten years ago.

2 They are waiting for me (on / at) the bus stop.

3 Many people were standing (behind / between) me.

4 The supermarket is between the bank (and / or) the school.

B 그림을 보고, 〈보기〉에서 알맞은 전치사를 골라 문장을 완성하시오. (단, 한 번씩만 사용할 것)

보기	in	on	under	next to

1 The cat is _____ the box.

2 The desk is _____ the bed.

3 There is a picture _____ the wall.

4 There is a ball _____ the chair.

C 우리말과 일치하도록 빈칸에 알맞은 전치사를 쓰시오.

1 모퉁이에서 왼쪽으로 도세요.
→ Turn left _____ the corner.

2 많은 사람들이 저 건물 안에서 일한다.
→ Many people work _____ that building.

3 그녀는 열쇠를 소파 뒤에서 발견했다.
→ She found her key _____ the sofa.

4 나의 집 옆에 큰 가게가 있다.
→ There is a big store _____ my house.

30초 완성 map

전치사
- 위치
  - ❶
    - _____ the sofa (소파 위에)
    - _____ the tree (나무 아래에)
    - _____ the box (상자 뒤에)
    - _____ the bank _____ the park (은행과 공원 사이에)
    - _____ the basket (바구니 안에)
    - in _____ of the gate (문 앞에)
    - next _____ my seat (내 자리 옆에)
- 장소
  - ❷
    - They are (in / at) home. 그들은 집에 있다.
    - I learned English (in / at) LA. 나는 LA에서 영어를 배웠다.

시간을 나타내는 전치사, 그 밖의 전치사

1 시간을 나타내는 전치사

at	구체적인 시각, 하루의 때	at 10 o'clock at noon	at 4 p.m. at night
on	요일, 날짜, 특정한 날	on Monday on Christmas Day	on September 28 on my birthday
in	연도, 월, 계절, 오전/오후/저녁	in 2017 in summer	in March in the morning / afternoon / evening

The bakery opens **at** 9 o'clock.
The music festival begins **on** Friday.
People get more colds **in** winter.

2 기간을 나타내는 전치사

for + 숫자를 포함한 구체적인 기간	~ 동안	for five hours	for a month
during + 특정 기간을 나타내는 명사(구)		during winter vacation	during the exam

Paul slept **for** *four hours* last night.
We visited five cities **during** *the trip*.

3 수단·도구를 나타내는 전치사

by + 수단	~을 타고, ~을 이용하여	by bus	by taxi	by plane
		by email	by mail	by text message
with + 도구	~을 가지고	with a key	with a knife	with scissors

I'll go to Busan **by** plane.
Ted sent his report **by** email.
Sally ate noodles **with** chopsticks.

비교 point

월 앞에 쓰이는 in vs. on

월 앞에는 전치사 in을 쓰지만 월 뒤에 숫자가 와서 날짜를 나타낼 때는 on을 쓴다.

1 We first met (in / on) October.

2 We first met (in / on) October 13, 2020.

개념 우선 확인 | 옳은 표현 고르기

1 밤에
   ☐ in night
   ☐ at night

2 봄에
   ☐ in spring
   ☐ at spring

3 택시로
   ☐ by taxi
   ☐ with taxi

4 쉬는 시간 동안
   ☐ for the break
   ☐ during the break

A 괄호 안에서 알맞은 것을 고르시오.

1 They first met (in / on) December 24.

2 He usually goes to bed (at / on) 11 o'clock.

3 I fell asleep (during / for) the movie.

4 You have to send your report (by / with) email.

B 〈보기〉에서 알맞은 전치사를 골라 대화를 완성하시오. (단, 한 번씩만 사용할 것)

보기	for	in	on	during

1 A When are you going to go to New York?
   B I'm going to go there _____ April.

2 A When did it happen?
   B It happened _____ August 10, 1939.

3 A When did you take these pictures?
   B I took them _____ winter vacation.

4 A How long did he work last night?
   B He worked _____ two hours.

C 밑줄 친 부분을 어법에 맞게 고쳐 쓰시오.

1 They always have lunch in noon.

2 She cut the chocolate cake by a knife.

3 Please turn off your cell phone in the exam.

4 Jasmin and I are going to meet at Thanksgiving Day.

30초 완성 map

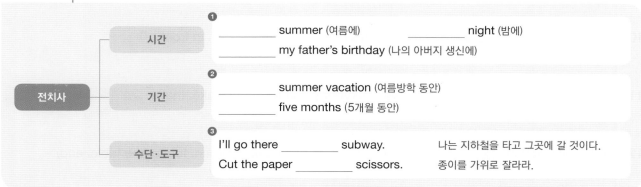

전치사	시간	❶ _____ summer (여름에)　　_____ night (밤에) _____ my father's birthday (나의 아버지 생신에)
	기간	❷ _____ summer vacation (여름방학 동안) _____ five months (5개월 동안)
	수단·도구	❸ I'll go there _____ subway.　나는 지하철을 타고 그곳에 갈 것이다. Cut the paper _____ scissors.　종이를 가위로 잘라라.

서술형 대비 문장 쓰기

Answers p. 24

☐ **빈칸 완성**　괄호 안의 말을 이용하여 빈칸 완성하기

01　이 카메라는 값이 싸고 좋다. (cheap, nice)

→ This camera is _____ .

02　네가 택시를 타면 너는 제시간에 도착할 것이다. (take)

→ You will be on time _____ a taxi.

03　한국에는 아름다운 궁궐들이 많이 있다. (Korea)

→ There are many beautiful palaces _____ .

04　Emily는 항상 아침에 산책을 한다. (the morning)

→ Emily always takes a walk _____ .

✓ **오류 수정**　어법에 맞게 문장 고쳐 쓰기

05　I called Peter, or he didn't answer.

→ I called Peter, _____ .

06　We won the match in December 30, 2021.

→ We won the match _____ .

07　They stayed at the hotel during three days.

→ They stayed _____ .

08　It is dangerous to cut the paper by a knife.

→ It is dangerous _____ .

≡ **배열 영작**　괄호 안의 말을 바르게 배열하기

09　그는 2003년에 이 책을 썼다. (wrote, 2003, in, he, this book)

→ _____

10　그는 그의 차를 그의 집 앞에 세워 두었다. (he, his house, his car, parked, in front of)

→ _____

11　모두가 내가 실수했다는 것을 안다. (knows, everybody, made, I, a mistake, that)

→ _____

12　나는 소파와 탁자 사이에서 그 동전을 찾았다. (I, the sofa, the coin, between, found, the table, and)

→ _____

시험에 꼭 나오는 출제 포인트

출제 포인트 ① and, but, or는 문법적으로 대등한 것을 연결한다!

괄호 안의 말을 알맞은 형태로 바꿔 문장을 완성하시오.

(1) My dog is old but _____. (health)

(2) I enjoy taking pictures and _____ them on my blog. (post)

출제 포인트 ② 접속사의 의미와 쓰임을 파악하자!

우리말과 일치하도록 빈칸에 알맞은 접속사를 쓰시오.

(1) 그녀는 그가 부자인 것을 모른다.
　→ She doesn't know _____ he is rich.

(2) 비가 오고 있어서 우리는 테니스를 치지 않았다.
　→ We didn't play tennis _____ it was raining.

> **고득점 POINT** 접속사 if가 이끄는 조건절의 시제
>
> **우리말과 일치하도록 괄호 안의 말을 이용하여 문장을 완성하시오.**
>
> 눈이 오면 우리는 눈사람을 만들 것이다. (snow)
> → We will make a snowman if it _____.

출제 포인트 ③ 다양한 뜻으로 사용되는 전치사의 쓰임을 구분하자!

빈칸에 공통으로 들어갈 전치사를 쓰시오.

- There is a lamp _____ the desk.
- We ate a lot of food _____ Chuseok.

> **고득점 POINT** 전치사 at, on, in 구분하기
>
> **밑줄 친 부분이 어법상 틀린 것을 모두 고르면?**
>
> ① He lived <u>at</u> Chicago.
> ② There is a ball <u>on</u> the bench.
> ③ We arrived <u>at</u> the airport at noon.
> ④ I usually do my homework <u>in</u> night.
> ⑤ I received chocolate <u>on</u> Valentine's Day.

출제 포인트 ④ 전치사의 의미를 잘 구분하여 사용하자!

우리말과 일치하도록 밑줄 친 부분을 바르게 고쳐 쓰시오.

(1) 도서관 앞에 공원이 있다.
　→ There is a park <u>next to</u> the library.　　　　→ _____

(2) 학교와 은행 사이에 커피숍이 있다.
　→ There is a coffee shop <u>behind</u> the school and the bank.　→ _____

(3) 나는 30분 동안 피아노 연습을 했다.
　→ I practiced the piano <u>during</u> thirty minutes.　　→ _____

01 빈칸에 들어갈 말로 알맞은 것은? |3점|

> Don't sit _____ the floor. It's cold.

① on ② at ③ in
④ under ⑤ behind

[02-03] 두 문장의 의미가 같도록 할 때 빈칸에 알맞은 것을 고르시오. |6점, 각 3점|

02

> He was not careful, so he fell down.
> = He fell down _____ he was not careful.

① if ② and ③ that
④ when ⑤ because

03

> John was standing in front of Danny in the line.
> = Danny was standing _____ John in the line.

① on ② next to
③ under ④ behind
⑤ between

[04-05] 빈칸에 공통으로 들어갈 말로 알맞은 것을 고르시오. |6점, 각 3점|

04

> • I was very sick _____ happy.
> • Nick likes to read comic books, _____ I don't like to read them.

① or ② but ③ when
④ and ⑤ because

05

> • He feels nervous _____ front of many people.
> • There are lots of famous restaurants _____ Paris.

① on ② at ③ in
④ by ⑤ with

06 ①~⑤ 중 접속사 If(if)가 들어갈 위치로 알맞은 곳은? |3점|

> (①) We won't go (②) on a picnic (③) the weather is (④) bad (⑤).

① ② ③ ④ ⑤

07 빈칸에 들어갈 전치사가 나머지와 <u>다른</u> 것은? |4점|

① We can see many roses _____ May.
② She put the pictures _____ the table.
③ Don't make any noise _____ the library.
④ I'm going to travel to Japan _____ August.
⑤ There was a little cat _____ the basket.

08 우리말과 일치하도록 할 때, 빈칸에 들어갈 말이 순서대로 바르게 짝지어진 것은? |3점|

> Ashley와 나는 그 소식을 들었을 때 울었다.
> → Ashley _____ I cried _____ we heard the news.

① or – if ② or – when
③ but – if ④ and – when
⑤ and – because

09 다음 그림을 설명한 문장 중 틀린 것은? |3점|

① There is a cat in the room.
② There is a chair next to the table.
③ There is a clock on the wall.
④ There are two cushions on the sofa.
⑤ There is a book between the lamp and the vase.

10 다음 빈칸에 들어갈 말이 순서대로 바르게 짝지어진 것은? |3점|

• You won't get there on time _____ you don't hurry.
• I hope _____ I can go to my favorite singer's concert.

① if – that　　② if – when
③ that – if　　④ that – when
⑤ that – that

11 밑줄 친 전치사의 쓰임이 틀린 것은? |4점|

① Please cut it with scissors.
② You'll find the store at the corner.
③ Flowers are everywhere in spring.
④ The festival will start in September 17.
⑤ I sat next to the window and looked outside.

12 밑줄 친 부분의 쓰임이 〈보기〉와 다른 것은? |4점|

보기　I was glad when I won a gold medal.

① She was alone when I saw her.
② When he went out, it started snowing.
③ When did she come back from school?
④ What did you do when you were in London?
⑤ What do you want to be when you grow up?

13 (A)~(C)에 들어갈 말이 바르게 짝지어진 것은? |4점|

• She goes to work (A) by / with subway.
• The restaurants didn't open (B) for / during the Chuseok holidays.
• We arrived in New York (C) in / at night.

	(A)	(B)	(C)
①	by	for	in
②	by	during	in
③	by	during	at
④	with	for	in
⑤	with	during	at

14 밑줄 친 부분의 쓰임이 어색한 것은? |4점|

① I know that she is your mom.
② He took a taxi if he got up late.
③ You should get some rest if you're tired.
④ Cathy saw him when she was at the mall.
⑤ Danny was happy because he won the game.

15 밑줄 친 that 중 생략할 수 있는 것은? |4점|

① Who is that tall man?
② Is that your umbrella?
③ I know that is your house.
④ This is mine, and that is yours.
⑤ Do you think that he is honest?

16 대화의 밑줄 친 ⓐ~ⓔ 중 어법상 틀린 부분을 잘못 고친 것은? |5점|

> **A** John, what do you usually do ⓐat your free time?
> **B** I enjoy going hiking and ⓑtake pictures.
> **A** When do you usually go hiking?
> **B** ⓒDuring Sundays.
> **A** How about this Sunday?
> **B** I'm not sure. I'll stay ⓓin home if it ⓔwill snow.

① ⓐ → in   ② ⓑ → to take
③ ⓒ → On   ④ ⓓ → at
⑤ ⓔ → snows

17 빈칸 ⓐ~ⓒ에 들어갈 전치사가 순서대로 바르게 짝지어진 것은? |4점|

> **A** I'm going to stay ___ⓐ___ Australia this summer.
> **B** Wow! How long are you going to stay there?
> **A** ___ⓑ___ two weeks.
> **B** What will you do ___ⓒ___ your trip?
> **A** I will visit some famous places there.

① at – For – during
② at – During – for
③ in – For – during
④ in – During – for
⑤ on – During – during

18 빈칸에 공통으로 들어갈 전치사를 쓰시오. |3점|

> • I left my cell phone _____ my desk.
> • The music festival begins _____ Friday.

19 두 문장을 한 문장으로 나타낼 때, 빈칸에 알맞은 접속사를 쓰시오. |3점|

> I can't visit the museum. I have a lot of work to do today.
>
> → I can't visit the museum _____ I have a lot of work to do today.

20 우리말과 일치하도록 괄호 안의 말을 바르게 배열하시오. |3점|

> 나는 그 책이 지루하다고 생각한다.
> (think, the book, I, boring, is, that)
>
> → _____

21 〈보기〉에서 알맞은 말을 골라 다음 글을 완성하시오. |3점|

보기	in	at	for	during

> Jack is my best friend. He moved to a big city _____ 2015. Today, he is coming to visit me. He will stay here _____ three weeks.

22 그림을 보고, 알맞은 전치사를 사용하여 문장을 완성하시오. |4점, 각 2점|

(1)

→ The dog is _____ _____

_____ the door.

(2)

→ The pharmacy is _____ _____

the bookstore.

23 다음과 같이 줄을 설 때, 네 번째 서 있는 사람의 이름을 쓰시오. |3점|

• Seho is first in line.
• Minho is right behind Seho.
• Sangmin is between Minho and Jiho.
• Jiho is in front of Juwon.

→ _____

24 〈보기〉에서 알맞은 접속사를 골라 주어진 두 문장을 한 문장으로 쓰시오. |6점, 각 3점|

보기 that   because   but   when

(1) I like cold drinks. + Jack likes hot drinks.

→ _____

_____

(2) My mom was cooking. + I came home.

→ _____

_____

25 두 문장을 〈조건〉에 맞게 한 문장으로 쓰시오. |4점|

It will be sunny.
We will go to the beach.

조건 1. 조건을 나타내는 접속사로 문장을 시작할 것
     2. 필요시 형태를 바꿀 것

→ _____

26 그림을 보고, 〈조건〉에 맞게 문장을 완성하시오. |5점|

조건 1. and, but, or 중 하나를 반드시 사용할 것
     2. little food, the refrigerator를 사용할 것

I was really hungry, _____ there was

_____ .

27 다음 지호의 토요일 계획표를 보고, 빈칸에 알맞은 전치사를 써서 문장을 완성하시오. |6점, 각 2점|

9:00-11:00	practice the piano
12:00	have lunch with Mike
4:00	go shopping

(1) Jiho will practice the piano _____ two hours.

(2) Jiho will have lunch with Mike _____ noon.

(3) Jiho will go shopping _____ the afternoon.

1 일반동사의 과거형 규칙 변화

Chapter 02 p. 28

(1) 대부분의 동사: 동사원형+-ed

help	**helped**	돕다	play	**played**	놀다
visit	**visited**	방문하다	want	**wanted**	원하다

(2) -e로 끝나는 동사: 동사원형+-d

arrive	**arrived**	도착하다	bake	**baked**	굽다
believe	**believed**	믿다	decide	**decided**	결정하다
like	**liked**	좋아하다	save	**saved**	아끼다

(3) 「자음+y」로 끝나는 동사: y를 i로 고치고+-ed

carry	**carried**	들고 있다	cry	**cried**	울다
hurry	**hurried**	서두르다	study	**studied**	공부하다
try	**tried**	노력하다	worry	**worried**	걱정하다

(4) 「단모음+단자음」으로 끝나는 동사: 마지막 자음을 한 번 더 쓰고+-ed

clap	**clapped**	박수치다	drop	**dropped**	떨어뜨리다
jog	**jogged**	조깅하다	plan	**planned**	계획하다
shop	**shopped**	쇼핑하다	stop	**stopped**	멈추다

2 일반동사의 과거형 불규칙 변화

Chapter 02 p. 28

(1) 형태가 같은 동사

cut	**cut**	자르다	cost	**cost**	(비용이) 들다
hit	**hit**	치다	hurt	**hurt**	다치다
put	**put**	놓다	read	**read**[red]	읽다
set	**set**	놓다	shut	**shut**	닫다

(2) 모음이 바뀌는 동사

become	**became**	되다	hold	**held**	잡다
begin	**began**	시작하다	know	**knew**	알다
choose	**chose**	선택하다	meet	**met**	만나다

draw	**drew**	그리다		ride	**rode**	타다
drink	**drank**	마시다		rise	**rose**	오르다
drive	**drove**	운전하다		run	**ran**	달리다
fall	**fell**	떨어지다		see	**saw**	보다
sing	**sang**	노래하다		sit	**sat**	앉다
freeze	**froze**	얼다		swim	**swam**	수영하다
get	**got**	얻다		throw	**threw**	던지다
give	**gave**	주다		win	**won**	이기다
grow	**grew**	자라다		write	**wrote**	쓰다

(3) 형태가 완전히 달라지는 동사

break	**broke**	깨뜨리다		lose	**lost**	잃다
bring	**brought**	가져오다		make	**made**	만들다
build	**built**	짓다		mean	**meant**	의미하다
buy	**bought**	사다		pay	**paid**	지불하다
catch	**caught**	잡다		say	**said**	말하다
do	**did**	하다		sell	**sold**	팔다
eat	**ate**	먹다		send	**sent**	보내다
feel	**felt**	느끼다		shake	**shook**	흔들다
fight	**fought**	싸우다		sleep	**slept**	자다
find	**found**	찾다		speak	**spoke**	말하다
fly	**flew**	날다		spend	**spent**	보내다
go	**went**	가다		have	**had**	가지고 있다
stand	**stood**	서다		hear	**heard**	듣다
take	**took**	가지고 가다		hide	**hid**	숨기다
teach	**taught**	가르치다		tell	**told**	말하다
leave	**left**	떠나다		think	**thought**	생각하다
lend	**lent**	빌려주다		understand	**understood**	이해하다
lie	**lay**	눕다		wear	**wore**	입다

부록

3 주의해야 할 명사 복수형 Chapter 03 p. 40

(1) -s, -x, -sh, -ch, -o로 끝나는 명사: 명사+-es

bus	**buses**	버스
box	**boxes**	상자
brush	**brushes**	붓
church	**churches**	교회
potato	**potatoes**	감자

class	**classes**	수업
fox	**foxes**	여우
dish	**dishes**	접시
watch	**watches**	시계
tomato	**tomatoes**	토마토

(2) 「자음+y」로 끝나는 명사: y를 i로 고치고+-es

baby	**babies**	아기
body	**bodies**	신체
candy	**candies**	사탕
party	**parties**	파티

city	**cities**	도시
country	**countries**	나라
diary	**diaries**	일기
story	**stories**	이야기

(3) -f, -fe로 끝나는 명사: f, fe를 v로 고치고+-es

knife	**knives**	칼
life	**lives**	인생
thief	**thieves**	도둑

leaf	**leaves**	나뭇잎
shelf	**shelves**	선반
wolf	**wolves**	늑대

(4) 불규칙 변화

man	**men**	남자
foot	**feet**	발
child	**children**	어린이
person	**people**	사람

woman	**women**	여자
tooth	**teeth**	치아(이빨)
mouse	**mice**	쥐

(5) 형태가 같은 경우

fish	**fish**	물고기
sheep	**sheep**	양

deer	**deer**	사슴

4 주의해야 할 비교급·최상급

(1) 「단모음＋단자음」으로 끝나는 경우: 마지막 자음을 한번 더 쓰고＋-er/-est

big	bigger	biggest	큰
fat	fatter	fattest	뚱뚱한
hot	hotter	hottest	뜨거운
thin	thinner	thinnest	얇은
sad	sadder	saddest	슬픈

(2) 「자음＋y」로 끝나는 경우: y를 i로 고치고＋-er/-est

busy	busier	busiest	바쁜
easy	easier	easiest	쉬운
happy	happier	happiest	행복한
heavy	heavier	heaviest	무거운
noisy	noisier	noisiest	시끄러운
pretty	prettier	prettiest	예쁜
ugly	uglier	ugliest	못난

(3) 3음절 이상, -ous, -ful, -ing 등으로 끝나는 2음절인 경우: more/most＋원급

exciting	more exciting	most exciting	흥미진진한
interesting	more interesting	most interesting	재미있는
popular	more popular	most popular	인기 있는
famous	more famous	most famous	유명한
useful	more useful	most useful	유용한
boring	more boring	most boring	지루한

(4) 불규칙 변화

good	better	best	좋은
well	better	best	잘
bad	worse	worst	나쁜
many	more	most	(수가) 많은
much	more	most	(양이) 많은
little	less	least	적은
far	further	furthest	먼

동아출판 영어 교재 가이드

영역	브랜드	초1~2	초3~4	초5~6	중1	중2	중3	고1	고2	고3
문법	[초·중등] 개념서 그래머 클리어 스타터 중학 영문법 클리어									
	[중등] 문법 문제서 그래머 클라우드 3000제									
	[중등] 실전 문제서 빠르게 통하는 영문법 핵심 1200제									
	[중등] 서술형 영문법 서술형에 더 강해지는 중학 영문법									
	[고등] 시험 영문법 시험에 더 강해지는 고등 영문법									
	[고등] 개념서 Supreme 고등 영문법									
어법	[고등] 기본서 Supreme 수능 어법 기본 실전									
쓰기	[중등] 영작 집중 훈련서 중학 문법+쓰기 클리어									

문법 개념과 내신을 한번에 끝내다

문장 구조 시각화로
핵심 문법 개념 CLEAR!

시험포인트 및 비교포인트로
헷갈리는 문법 CLEAR!

더 확대된 실전테스트로
학교 시험 대비 CLEAR!

Grammar clear

중학 영문법

클리어.

WORKBOOK

Level 1

동아출판

중학 영문법 클리어.

Level 1

WORKBOOK

UNIT 01 be동사의 현재형과 과거형

Answers p. 26

A 어법 선택

괄호 안에서 알맞은 것을 고르시오.

1 I (am / are) from Canada.

2 It (am / is) my favorite song.

3 We (are / is) baseball players.

4 Her bicycle (are / is) very nice.

5 You (was / are) 14 years old.

6 I (am / was) in Australia last month.

7 They (are / were) good friends now.

8 Mark (is / was) late for school yesterday.

9 Susan and Jake (is / are) in the classroom.

10 Your keys (are / were) on the table this morning.

B 빈칸 완성

빈칸에 알맞은 be동사를 〈보기〉에서 골라 쓰시오.

보기	am	are	is	was	were

1 I _____ in Toronto now.

2 My father _____ busy last week.

3 We _____ at the library yesterday.

4 The babies _____ sleepy now.

5 Jim _____ in his room an hour ago.

6 My English teacher _____ angry now.

7 Leo and Amy _____ at the gym now.

8 The song _____ very popular in 2015.

9 Luna and I _____ in the same club last year.

10 The restaurant _____ open last night.

밑줄 친 부분을 어법에 맞게 고쳐 쓰시오.

1 I <u>are</u> a middle school student now. → _____

2 Your baby <u>are</u> happy now. → _____

3 Daniel <u>am</u> my little brother. → _____

4 They <u>are</u> in New York in 2010. → _____

5 The writer <u>is</u> famous five years ago. → _____

6 The twins <u>are</u> very tired last night. → _____

7 My sister <u>is</u> sick last weekend. → _____

8 Katie and I <u>was</u> home yesterday. → _____

9 The dog and the cat <u>is</u> in the park now. → _____

10 The windows <u>is</u> open an hour ago. → _____

D

영작

우리말과 일치하도록 괄호 안의 말을 바르게 배열하시오.

1 우리 집은 매우 작다. (very, small, is)

→ Our house _____ .

2 그 소년들은 영리했다. (smart, were)

→ The boys _____ .

3 나는 오늘 아침에 배가 고팠다. (hungry, was)

→ I _____ this morning.

4 Anna와 Rose는 여기에 있다. (and, Anna, are, Rose)

→ _____ here.

5 많은 사람들이 경기장에 있었다. (were, people, many)

→ _____ in the stadium.

6 그 서점은 지난주에 문을 열었다. (open, the bookstore, was)

→ _____ last week.

7 나의 할머니는 병원에 계신다. (grandmother, my, the hospital, is, in)

→ _____

UNIT 02 be동사의 부정문

Answers p. 26

A 어법 선택

괄호 안에서 알맞은 것을 고르시오.

1 They (aren't / wasn't) my cousins.

2 He (isn't / aren't) a famous cook.

3 (I'm not / I amn't) a good dancer.

4 We (wasn't / weren't) at school yesterday.

5 You (isn't / aren't) late for the party.

6 The girl (wasn't / weren't) ready for the contest.

7 Maya (isn't / aren't) afraid of cats.

8 The story (aren't / isn't) interesting at all.

9 It (wasn't / isn't) in my bag last night.

10 The children (weren't / wasn't) under the tree.

B 빈칸 완성

빈칸에 알맞은 말을 〈보기〉에서 골라 쓰시오.

보기	am not	aren't	isn't	wasn't	weren't

1 I _____ thirsty now.

2 We _____ sad yesterday.

3 The bus _____ full this morning.

4 They _____ at my house last night.

5 The weather _____ cold right now.

6 The camping trip _____ fun last weekend.

7 Jimin and I _____ good at English right now.

8 The movie _____ popular two years ago.

9 My grandparents _____ in Busan now.

10 Your shoes _____ at the door yesterday.

C 어법 수정

밑줄 친 부분이 맞으면 ○, 틀리면 바르게 고쳐 쓰시오.

1 My name <u>is not</u> Lisa. → _____

2 I <u>amn't</u> a high school student. → _____

3 The book <u>not is</u> difficult. → _____

4 They <u>aren't</u> in the garden now. → _____

5 <u>That's not</u> a good idea. → _____

6 These apples <u>isn't</u> delicious. → _____

7 The boxes <u>wasn't</u> there yesterday. → _____

8 Our car <u>aren't</u> old and dirty. → _____

9 He <u>aren't</u> in the office an hour ago. → _____

10 It <u>weren't</u> an interesting question. → _____

D 영작

우리말과 일치하도록 괄호 안의 말을 바르게 배열하시오.

1 James는 가수가 아니다. (is, a, singer, not)

→ James _____ .

2 그 방들은 크지 않다. (are, large, not)

→ The rooms _____ .

3 나는 축구를 잘 못한다. (not, I, good, am)

→ _____ at soccer.

4 그 학생들은 도서관에서 조용하지 않았다. (weren't, the students, quiet)

→ _____ in the library.

5 우리는 지난주에 서울에 없었다. (in Seoul, were, we, not)

→ _____ last week.

6 그녀는 회의에 참석하지 않았다. (she, not, was, present)

→ _____ at the meeting.

7 그들은 그때 초등학생이 아니었다. (weren't, students, elementary school)

→ They _____ at that time.

UNIT 3 be동사의 의문문

Answers p. 26

A
어법 선택

괄호 안에서 알맞은 것을 고르시오.

1 (Are / Is) you a basketball player?

2 (Is / Are) your father an engineer?

3 (Is / Are) his parents proud of him?

4 (Is / Were) your sister ten years old?

5 (Am / Is) I right about this problem?

6 (Is / Are) Ted and Kate your classmates?

7 (Are / Is) the musicians from London?

8 (Is / Was) the music too loud last night?

9 (Was / Were) your daughters at the beach?

10 (Are / Were) Nina and Daniel at the meeting yesterday?

B
문장 완성

괄호 안의 말과 be동사를 이용하여 의문문을 완성하시오.

1 A _____ a good singer? (Michael)

   B Yes, he is.

2 A _____ wrong about that? (I)

   B Yes, you were.

3 A _____ good at French? (you)

   B No, I'm not.

4 A _____ warm? (this room)

   B No, it isn't.

5 A _____ late for the movie? (we)

   B Yes, you are.

6 A _____ for me? (those flowers)

   B No, they weren't.

C
어법 수정

밑줄 친 부분이 맞으면 ○, 틀리면 바르게 고쳐 쓰시오.

1 <u>Am</u> I a good student? → _____

2 <u>Are</u> the teacher from Chicago? → _____

3 <u>Is</u> the weather beautiful yesterday? → _____

4 <u>Are</u> Lisa and Dan in LA last Sunday? → _____

5 <u>Was</u> the eggs in the basket this morning? → _____

6 A <u>Is</u> the movie scary? B Yes, it is. → _____

7 A <u>Was</u> this shirt too small for me? B No, it isn't. → _____

8 A <u>Are</u> they in the building yesterday? B Yes, they were. → _____

9 A <u>Was</u> her favorite music K-pop? B Yes, it was. → _____

10 A <u>Were</u> your friends at your home now? B No, they aren't. → _____

D
영작

우리말과 일치하도록 괄호 안의 말을 바르게 배열하시오.

1 제가 곤경에 처한 겁니까? (I, am)

→ _____ in trouble?

2 그의 눈은 파란색이었습니까? (his eyes, were)

→ _____ blue?

3 이 카메라는 새것인가요? (this, is, camera)

→ _____ a new one?

4 너의 학교가 집에서 멀리 떨어져 있었니? (your school, was, far away)

→ _____ from your house?

5 당신은 지금 부엌에 있나요? (in the kitchen, you, are)

→ _____ now?

6 그림들이 벽에 걸려 있나요? (on the wall, the paintings, are)

→ _____

7 그녀는 그때 행복했나요? (she, was, at that time, happy)

→ _____

UNIT 01 일반동사의 현재형

Answers p. 27

A 어법 선택   괄호 안에서 알맞은 것을 고르시오.

1 Joan (like / likes) mathematics.

2 We (eat / eats) rice every day.

3 This kite (fly / flies) high in the sky.

4 My daughter (play / plays) the violin well.

5 The early bird (catch / catches) the worm.

6 Mark's baby (cry / cries) a lot every night.

7 Minji and I (do / does) yoga after school.

8 Eva (watch / watches) television in her room.

9 David and his family (live / lives) in New York.

10 The twins (want / wants) new bikes for Christmas.

B 빈칸 완성   괄호 안의 동사를 현재형으로 바꿔 빈칸에 쓰시오.

1 He _____ the ball very well. (pass)

2 Mr. Jones _____ our bikes for us. (fix)

3 We _____ toast for breakfast. (have)

4 I _____ to bed around ten o'clock. (go)

5 This animal _____ out at night. (come)

6 Charlie _____ up late on Sundays. (get)

7 My brother and I _____ together. (study)

8 He usually _____ to music in his car. (listen)

9 Anna _____ her grandparents every month. (visit)

10 The new teacher _____ us too many questions. (ask)

밑줄 친 부분을 어법에 맞게 고쳐 쓰시오.

1 I <u>works</u> at this hospital.   → _____

2 The table <u>have</u> four legs.   → _____

3 He <u>know</u> my phone number.   → _____

4 The river <u>run</u> through the city.   → _____

5 She <u>drys</u> her hair with a towel.   → _____

6 Mr. Davis <u>teach</u> science at our school.   → _____

7 The sun <u>gos</u> down late in summer.   → _____

8 Andy and Jane <u>walks</u> to school together.   → _____

9 My brother <u>do</u> the dishes on Saturdays.   → _____

10 We <u>eats</u> lunch in the school cafeteria.   → _____

D
영작

우리말과 일치하도록 괄호 안의 말을 바르게 배열하시오.

1 그는 매일 그림을 그린다. (he, pictures, draws)

→ _____ every day.

2 Jessica는 노래를 매우 잘 부른다. (well, sings, very)

→ Jessica _____.

3 나의 아버지는 너무 빠르게 운전하신다. (my, drives, father)

→ _____ too fast.

4 나는 자주 사람들의 이름을 잊어버린다. (people's, names, forget)

→ I often _____.

5 그녀는 식사 전에 손을 씻는다. (her hands, she, washes)

→ _____ before meals.

6 Jiho는 영어를 매우 열심히 공부한다. (studies, very, hard, English)

→ Jiho _____.

7 그들은 다른 사람들로부터 도움을 원한다. (some help, they, want, from others)

→ _____

UNIT 02 일반동사의 과거형

Answers p. 27

A 어법 선택

괄호 안에서 알맞은 것을 고르시오.

1 I (write / wrote) two letters last week.

2 He (play / played) the guitar yesterday.

3 Ann (do / did) the dishes after breakfast.

4 Kevin (buyed / bought) this computer last year.

5 He (dance / danced) all evening with Rachel.

6 We (maked / made) pineapple pizza for lunch.

7 The man (put / putted) his bag on the bench.

8 I (drinked / drank) a cup of coffee this morning.

9 Bella and Jim (watchd / watched) the show last weekend.

10 She (droped / dropped) her glasses on the floor.

B 빈칸 완성

괄호 안의 동사를 과거형으로 바꿔 빈칸에 쓰시오.

1 I _____ all day long. (cry)

2 She _____ to the door. (run)

3 The kind man _____ us. (help)

4 They _____ their children. (love)

5 The man _____ the room. (leave)

6 He _____ back home early. (come)

7 We _____ home late at night. (arrive)

8 The game _____ one hour ago. (start)

9 I _____ to the movies with Nora. (go)

10 Mia _____ the apple with a knife. (cut)

C
어법 수정
밑줄 친 부분을 어법에 맞게 고쳐 쓰시오.

1 He <u>eated</u> two hamburgers last Sunday. → _____

2 We <u>walkd</u> to the train station yesterday. → _____

3 I <u>seed</u> you at the mall last Friday. → _____

4 Mr. White <u>teached</u> us music two years ago. → _____

5 I <u>tryed</u> the new dress on last night. → _____

6 A storm <u>hitted</u> the country last summer. → _____

7 I <u>haved</u> salad for breakfast this morning. → _____

8 The rain <u>stoped</u> yesterday afternoon. → _____

9 He <u>readed</u> that book a month ago. → _____

10 Grandpa <u>gived</u> us some money last weekend. → _____

D
영작
우리말과 일치하도록 괄호 안의 말을 바르게 배열하시오.

1 Jean과 Kelly는 파티를 계획했다. (a party, planned)

→ Jean and Kelly _____ .

2 그녀의 가족은 새로운 집으로 이사 갔다. (moved, her family)

→ _____ to a new house.

3 나는 엄마를 위해 팬케이크를 만들었다. (I, pancakes, made)

→ _____ for my mother.

4 나는 탁자 아래에서 내 지갑을 찾았다. (found, I, my wallet)

→ _____ under the table.

5 Rachel은 나에게 Fred에 대해 이야기했다. (me, told, Rachel)

→ _____ about Fred.

6 우리는 클래식 음악을 들었다. (to, we, classical music, listened)

→ _____

7 우리는 그 남자로부터 그 이야기를 들었다. (from, we, the story, heard, the man)

→ _____

UNIT 3 일반동사의 부정문과 의문문

Answers p. 27

A 문장 전환

밑줄 친 부분을 부정문의 형태로 바꿔 쓰시오. (단, 줄임말을 사용할 것)

1 They <u>live</u> in a big city. → _____

2 We <u>saw</u> Harry at the party. → _____

3 The shop <u>closes</u> on Sundays. → _____

4 My parents <u>like</u> old movies. → _____

5 He <u>broke</u> the window yesterday. → _____

6 The girl <u>eats</u> vegetables every day. → _____

7 They <u>played</u> soccer on the playground. → _____

8 Chris and Sally <u>know</u> my friend Daniel. → _____

9 Ryan <u>finished</u> his history homework. → _____

10 She <u>put</u> her hands on his shoulders. → _____

B 문장 전환

밑줄 친 부분을 의문문의 형태로 바꿔 쓰시오.

1 <u>You opened</u> the door? → _____

2 <u>Jack's father plays</u> chess? → _____

3 <u>He speaks</u> Spanish very well? → _____

4 <u>They missed</u> the train for Busan? → _____

5 <u>Maya lives</u> with her two sisters? → _____

6 <u>She took</u> a walk three hours ago? → _____

7 <u>I told</u> you about my puppy? → _____

8 <u>We need</u> the new sofa right away? → _____

9 <u>Your friends found</u> your house? → _____

10 <u>You remember</u> my phone number? → _____

C

어법 수정

밑줄 친 부분을 어법에 맞게 고쳐 쓰시오.

1 My cat <u>don't</u> like fish. → _____

2 <u>Do</u> it snow a lot in Korea? → _____

3 He <u>don't</u> live in a small town. → _____

4 Bananas <u>doesn't</u> grow well here. → _____

5 She <u>don't</u> have her own computer. → _____

6 <u>Does</u> he visit his parents last month? → _____

7 Jiyun <u>doesn't</u> go to school yesterday. → _____

8 <u>You do</u> get up at 7 o'clock every morning? → _____

9 <u>Do</u> your mother work at the post office? → _____

10 <u>Do</u> you watch the game on TV yesterday? → _____

D

영작

우리말과 일치하도록 괄호 안의 말을 이용하여 문장을 완성하시오.

1 나는 더 많은 돈이 필요하지 않다. (need)

→ _____ more money.

2 너는 오늘 수업이 있니? (have, class)

→ _____ today?

3 그녀는 록 음악을 좋아하지 않는다. (like)

→ _____ rock music.

4 그는 그 신발을 작년에 샀니? (buy, the shoes)

→ _____ last year?

5 이 버스는 박물관으로 갑니까? (this bus, go)

→ _____ to the museum?

6 너의 오빠는 그 소식을 들었니? (your brother, hear)

→ _____ the news?

7 Fred와 Ted는 어제 테니스를 치지 않았다. (play, tennis)

→ _____ yesterday.

UNIT 01 명사

Answers p. 28

A 어법 선택

괄호 안에서 알맞은 것을 고르시오.

1 My name is (Karen / a Karen).

2 Please pass me the (salt / salts).

3 Do you want some (milk / milks)?

4 Alice really likes (babys / babies).

5 The animal has four (foots / feet).

6 I need two (egg / eggs) for a cake.

7 He fell in (love / a love) with Mary.

8 (A friendship / Friendship) is an important thing.

9 David usually eats (apple / apples) for breakfast.

10 The town is famous for its old (churchs / churches).

B 빈칸 완성

괄호 안의 말을 복수형으로 바꿔 빈칸에 쓰시오.

1 I have only five _____. (dish)

2 She has two _____. (child)

3 There are six _____ in the box. (ball)

4 Three _____ walked along the river. (man)

5 They saw two _____ in the park. (deer)

6 Greg put some _____ in his car. (box)

7 I brush my _____ three times a day. (tooth)

8 Please put the _____ on the table. (knife)

9 My father ate two _____ of pizza. (slice)

10 Olivia drinks three _____ of milk every day. (glass)

| **C** 어법 수정 | 밑줄 친 부분을 어법에 맞게 고쳐 쓰시오. |

1 Mr. Brown has four <u>puppys</u>. → _____

2 I saw three <u>wolfes</u> at the zoo. → _____

3 Can I have two <u>cup of coffee</u>? → _____

4 Big <u>city</u> are always crowded. → _____

5 Did the two <u>woman</u> live here? → _____

6 The <u>leafs</u> of the tree are green. → _____

7 She found <u>a happiness</u> in her life. → _____

8 My sister ate three <u>pieces of cakes</u>. → _____

9 My dad and I like <u>tomatos</u> very much. → _____

10 Put <u>cheeses</u>, salt, and <u>sugars</u> in a pan. → _____

| **D** 영작 | 우리말과 일치하도록 괄호 안의 말을 이용하여 문장을 완성하시오. |

1 그 고양이는 숲에서 쥐 세 마리를 잡았다. (mouse)

→ The cat caught _____ in the woods.

2 두 개의 벤치가 큰 나무 아래에 있다. (bench)

→ _____ are under the big tree.

3 나의 할아버지는 농장에 열 마리의 양을 가지고 계신다. (sheep)

→ My grandfather has _____ on his farm.

4 우리는 도로 위에서 많은 차들을 보았다. (many, car)

→ We saw _____ on the road.

5 그는 밥 두 그릇을 먹었다. (bowl, rice)

→ He ate _____.

6 그녀는 빵 한 조각 위에 버터를 발랐다. (slice, bread)

→ She put butter on _____.

7 나는 벽 위에 있는 세 마리 파리를 봤다. (fly, on the wall)

→ I saw _____.

UNIT 02 관사

Answers p. 28

A 어법 선택

괄호 안에서 알맞은 것을 고르시오.

1 I have (a / an) bicycle.

2 It was (a / an) easy question.

3 Adam sings like (a / an) bird.

4 The bus left (a / an) hour late.

5 We saw (a / an) elephant there.

6 He found (a / an) pencil on his desk.

7 Ann had (a / an) unhappy childhood.

8 They moved into (a / an) new house.

9 He bought (a / an) ticket for the concert.

10 She went to (a / an) university in England.

B 빈칸 완성

빈칸에 알맞은 말을 〈보기〉에서 골라 쓰시오.

보기	a	an	the	× (관사 필요 없음)

1 I have _____ new idea.

2 My grandfather is _____ actor.

3 Let's play _____ soccer after school.

4 Maggie plays _____ violin very well.

5 They have _____ lunch at 12 o'clock.

6 Can you pass me _____ notebook? It's mine.

7 A cat lives in my garden. _____ cat likes me very much.

8 Please turn off _____ heater. It's too hot here.

9 She wrote a history book. _____ book is very popular.

10 My brother goes to _____ bed at 9 every day.

밑줄 친 부분이 맞으면 ○, 틀리면 바르게 고쳐 쓰시오.

1 Mr. Yoon has <u>daughter</u>. → _____

2 Look at <u>a</u> car. It's very fast. → _____

3 He went to the airport <u>by taxi</u>. → _____

4 Ms. Lauren teaches <u>the math</u>. → _____

5 Do you have <u>a</u> email address? → _____

6 Her dad is <u>a</u> fashion designer. → _____

7 Please close <u>a</u> window. It's raining. → _____

8 I played <u>the</u> piano for <u>an</u> hour. → _____

9 My brother has <u>a breakfast</u> every day. → _____

10 We saw a movie. <u>The</u> movie was exciting. → _____

괄호 안의 말을 이용하여 문장을 완성하시오. (필요시 알맞은 관사를 넣을 것)

1 그녀는 멋진 코트 한 벌을 가지고 있다. (nice, coat)

→ She has _____.

2 나는 학교에서 교복을 입는다. (wear, uniform)

→ I _____ at school.

3 너는 야구를 하니? (play, baseball)

→ Do you _____?

4 TV를 꺼 주세요. 너무 시끄러워요. (turn off, TV)

→ Please _____. It is too loud.

5 나는 저녁 식사 전에 첼로를 연주했다. (play, cello)

→ I _____ before dinner.

6 내 여동생은 과학을 매우 좋아한다. (like, science)

→ My sister _____ very much.

7 너는 버스로 학교에 가니? (go, to, school, by, bus)

→ Do you _____?

UNIT 01 인칭대명사, 비인칭 주어

Answers p. 29

A 빈칸 완성

빈칸에 알맞은 인칭대명사를 쓰시오.

1 This is not my coat. The red coat is _____.

2 My uncle has a son. _____ name is Luke.

3 _____ is raining. Bring your umbrella.

4 I saw Emma yesterday. _____ was with Jack.

5 My grandparents live in Gangreung. _____ have a big farm.

6 Did you watch the soccer game? _____ was really exciting.

7 Chris and I had dinner together. _____ had a great time.

8 The supermarket is open on Sundays. _____ is Sunday today.

9 Minji and Sora have two cats. _____ cats are so cute.

10 Tom and Mia are my classmates. I invited _____ to my birthday party.

B 어법 선택

괄호 안에서 알맞은 것을 고르시오.

1 Amy has a dog. (She / Her) dog likes people.

2 I have a laptop. I bought (it / them) last month.

3 Cindy likes my new jacket. I like (her / hers), too.

4 Mike and Ron are (Leo / Leo's) best friends.

5 I remember Kate's birthday. (It / She) is July 13.

6 Can I use your pen? I left (my / mine) at home.

7 The bank closes at 4. (That / It) is already 4 o'clock.

8 I don't like this house. (It's / Its) windows are too small.

9 They saw (me / I) and (me / my) dog at the park.

10 Jeff spilled juice on (his / him) shirt, so (his / he) washed it.

어법 수정 **밑줄 친 부분이 맞으면 ○, 틀리면 바르게 고쳐 쓰시오.**

1 Wash <u>you</u> hands first. → _____

2 The man helped <u>we</u>. → _____

3 The girl lost <u>hers</u> shoes. → _____

4 This phone number is not <u>his</u>. → _____

5 I have a dog. <u>It's</u> tail is short. → _____

6 She didn't invite <u>him</u> to dinner. → _____

7 Did you wait for <u>they</u>? → _____

8 <u>He</u> team won the game. → _____

9 My parents don't understand <u>me</u>. → _____

10 The children didn't do <u>their</u> homework. → _____

D

영작 **우리말과 일치하도록 괄호 안의 말을 이용하여 문장을 완성하시오.**

1 나는 그것들을 집에 두고 왔다. (leave)

→ _____ at home.

2 어제 우리는 늦었다. (late)

→ _____ yesterday.

3 너는 네 열쇠를 책상 위에 두었다. (put, key)

→ _____ on the desk.

4 바깥은 춥다. (cold)

→ _____ outside.

5 Tony와 Tina는 그들의 아이들과 놀았다. (play, with, children)

→ Tony and Tina _____.

6 그녀는 부유하다. (rich)

→ _____

7 그것들은 우리의 책들이다. (book)

→ _____

UNIT 02 지시대명사, 부정대명사, 재귀대명사

Answers p. 29

A 어법 선택

괄호 안에서 알맞은 것을 고르시오.

1 I bought (this / these) T-shirt last year.

2 I hurt (me / myself) in a soccer game.

3 (That / Those) two sisters always fight.

4 She looked at (myself / herself) in the mirror.

5 My desk is old. I need a new (one / it).

6 Did you cut your hair (yourself / itself)?

7 We love (ourself / ourselves) very much.

8 Do you see (this / those) birds in the tree?

9 I want some flowers. I like these yellow (one / ones).

10 (This is / These are) my brother's paper planes.

B 빈칸 완성

빈칸에 알맞은 말을 〈보기〉에서 골라 쓰시오.

보기	this	that	these	those

1 Look at _____ kite in the sky.

2 Look at _____ cute birds on the roof.

3 Ken lives in _____ house over there.

4 Come here and look! _____ flowers are so beautiful.

5 Do you know _____ people over there?

6 Here is a picture of my family. _____ is my sister Jessy.

7 I found three books in this box. Are _____ your books?

8 The bank is in _____ building across the street.

9 I'm reading a newspaper, but I don't understand _____ word here.

밑줄 친 부분이 맞으면 ○, 틀리면 바르게 고쳐 쓰시오.

1 These cake over here is delicious. → _____

2 He cleaned his room myself. → _____

3 Look over there. That children are playing baseball. → _____

4 I introduced me to the others. → _____

5 Jina expresses herself well in English. → _____

6 I lost my colored pencils. I need new one. → _____

7 Whose pen is this? I found it on my desk. → _____

8 The ducks washed themself in the pond. → _____

9 I bought a red cap. I want a green it, too. → _____

10 Kelly herself baked the chocolate cookies. → _____

우리말과 일치하도록 괄호 안의 말을 바르게 배열하시오.

1 나는 이 그림이 좋다. (painting, I, this, like)

→ _____

2 저것은 나의 자동차이다. (my, is, that, car)

→ _____

3 저 신발들은 나의 것이다. (shoes, are, those, mine)

→ _____

4 당신 자신을 믿으세요. (in, believe, yourself)

→ _____

5 그가 이 수학 문제들을 풀었다. (math, these, problems, solved, he)

→ _____

6 내가 그것을 직접 고쳤다. (fixed, I, myself, it)

→ _____

7 이 가방은 크다. 나는 작은 것을 원한다. (want, one, I, a, small)

→ This bag is big. _____

UNIT 01 현재시제, 과거시제

Answers p. 30

A 어법 선택

괄호 안에서 알맞은 것을 고르시오.

1 My father (write / writes) novels.

2 She (leaves / left) two hours ago.

3 I (help / helped) my mom last weekend.

4 The Han River (runs / ran) through Seoul.

5 They (haved / had) dinner together last night.

6 Alfred Nobel (invents / invented) dynamite in 1867.

7 Mr. Smith is rich. He (has / had) a lot of money.

8 Brenda (read / reads) books at home yesterday.

9 The kangaroo always (carries / carried) its baby.

10 My grandparents (live / lived) in New York now.

B 빈칸 완성

괄호 안의 동사를 알맞은 형태로 바꿔 빈칸에 쓰시오.

1 It _____ a lot yesterday. (snow)

2 She _____ on a picnic every Saturday. (go)

3 We_____ in the same class last year. (be)

4 She _____ a new chair last month. (buy)

5 He _____ swimming lessons two years ago. (take)

6 I _____ my glasses last weekend. (break)

7 Sophia _____ a letter to her parents last week. (write)

8 Hurricane Katrina _____ America in 2005. (hit)

9 He _____ up late this morning. (wake)

10 The school bus always _____ at 7:30. (arrive)

C 어법 수정

밑줄 친 부분을 어법에 맞게 고쳐 쓰시오.

1 I <u>do</u> my homework yesterday. → _____

2 The moon <u>went</u> around the earth. → _____

3 This train <u>stop</u> at every station. → _____

4 I <u>meet</u> my aunt last night. → _____

5 The First World War <u>starts</u> in 1914. → _____

6 He <u>comes</u> to Seoul a week ago. → _____

7 Dad <u>get</u> up early every morning. → _____

8 Greg <u>plays</u> football last Saturday. → _____

9 Paris <u>was</u> the capital of France. *capital 수도 → _____

10 She <u>wins</u> the gold medal in 2020. → _____

D 영작

우리말과 일치하도록 괄호 안의 말을 바르게 배열하시오.

1 그녀는 매일 아침 신문을 읽는다. (reads, she, the newspaper)

→ _____ every morning.

2 Lucas는 컴퓨터 게임을 좋아한다. (likes, games, computer)

→ Lucas _____.

3 Columbus는 1492년에 미국을 발견했다. (America, discovered, Columbus)

→ _____ in 1492.

4 나는 어젯밤에 흥미로운 쇼를 봤다. (I, an, watched, show, interesting)

→ _____ last night.

5 지구는 둥글다. (is, the earth, round)

→ _____

6 그녀는 매일 청바지를 입는다. (blue jeans, she, wears, every day)

→ _____

7 그 버스는 정류장으로 갔다. (to, the station, went, the bus)

→ _____

UNIT 02 미래시제

Answers p. 30

A
어법 선택

괄호 안에서 알맞은 것을 고르시오.

1 Jack and I (am going to / are going to) sing five songs.

2 They will (dance / dancing) at the party tonight.

3 Dad is going to (wash / washes) the dishes.

4 Are James and Olivia going (move / to move) to Busan?

5 She (will not change / will change not) her mind.

6 Jack, you (willn't / won't) get there on time.

7 (Is / Will) she going to go shopping tomorrow?

8 (Will the train / The train will) leave at 9 o'clock?

9 They are (go / going to go) on vacation next month.

10 My mom (is not going to / is going not to) cook for us tonight.

B
문장 완성

우리말과 일치하도록 〈보기〉에서 알맞은 동사를 골라 괄호 안의 말을 이용하여 문장을 완성하시오.

보기	open	see	swim	travel	play

1 그 쇼핑몰은 다음 달에 열 것이다. (will)

→ The shopping mall _____ next month.

2 Sarah는 연주회에서 바이올린을 연주할 예정이다. (be going to)

→ Sarah _____ the violin in the concert.

3 우리는 자전거를 타고 전 세계를 여행할 것이다. (will)

→ We _____ around the world by bicycle.

4 내 남동생과 나는 바다에서 수영을 하지 않을 것이다. (be going to)

→ My brother and I _____ in the sea.

5 Mike는 다음 주 월요일에 치과에 갈 것이다. (be going to)

→ Mike _____ a dentist next Monday.

C
어법 수정

밑줄 친 부분을 어법에 맞게 고쳐 쓰시오.

1 She <u>willn't</u> turn on the radio. → _____

2 <u>Are you going stay</u> up late tonight? → _____

3 Will the concert <u>is</u> next month? → _____

4 We are <u>go to</u> start the game soon. → _____

5 I <u>will buying</u> some milk at the supermarket. → _____

6 You <u>will fail not</u> the exam next week. → _____

7 My parents will <u>is</u> back early from work. → _____

8 Eva and Ryan <u>isn't going to play</u> badminton. → _____

9 <u>Will</u> you going to meet him after school? → _____

10 The weather won't <u>to be</u> good this weekend. → _____

D
영작

우리말과 일치하도록 괄호 안의 말을 이용하여 문장을 완성하시오.

1 나는 중학생이 될 것이다. (be going to, be)

→ _____ a middle school student.

2 그녀는 9시쯤 집에 도착할 것이다. (will, arrive, home)

→ _____ around 9.

3 나의 아버지는 내일 자동차를 사용하시지 않을 것이다. (not, be going to, use, my father)

→ _____ his car tomorrow.

4 너는 그에게 편지를 보낼 거니? (will, send, a letter)

→ _____ to him?

5 오늘 오후에 비가 올까요? (be going to, rain, it)

→ _____ this afternoon?

6 너는 곧 일어날 거니? (be going to, get up, soon)

→ _____

7 내가 나중에 그녀에게 전화할게. (will, call, later, her)

→ _____

UNIT 3 현재진행형

Answers p. 30

A 어법 선택 괄호 안에서 알맞은 것을 고르시오.

1 Is your brother (sleep / sleeping)?

2 It (is / be) not snowing a lot now.

3 Is she (reads / reading) a book?

4 Dad (is not washing / is washing not) his car.

5 (Are / Do) they enjoying the party?

6 Bill and Ann (is / are) traveling in Africa.

7 The girl (isn't / doesn't) looking at the painting.

8 (Are / Is) you and your sister going home?

9 (I'm not / I don't) surfing the Internet.

10 We (walking / are walking) down the street.

B 문장 완성 괄호 안의 말을 이용하여 현재진행형 문장을 완성하시오.

1 The baby _____ now. (cry)

2 She _____ over there. (shop)

3 I _____ to you. (not, lie)

4 Mr. Park _____ in the pool. (swim)

5 Listen! My favorite band _____ a song. (play)

6 Chris _____ his bicycle now. (not, ride)

7 Please be quiet. I _____ my homework. (do)

8 He _____ breakfast in bed now. (have)

9 You _____ too fast. Will you slow down? (talk)

10 _____ you _____ Christmas cards now? (make)

밑줄 친 부분을 어법에 맞게 고쳐 쓰시오.

1 I <u>amn't listening</u> to music now. → _____

2 Look! The sun <u>are coming</u> up. → _____

3 Is your dog <u>runing</u> in the yard? → _____

4 He isn't <u>wear</u> a jacket. → _____

5 All the students <u>be</u> taking notes now. → _____

6 Let's turn on the light. It <u>does</u> getting dark. → _____

7 <u>Does</u> your brother playing the piano now? → _____

8 <u>Is</u> the children jumping around? It's too noisy. → _____

9 Look! A woman <u>cleaning</u> the window over there. → _____

10 The cat is <u>sits</u> on the chair. It's so cute. → _____

우리말과 일치하도록 괄호 안의 말을 이용하여 문장을 완성하시오.

1 그 소년들은 공원에서 춤을 추고 있다. (dance)

→ _____ in the park.

2 너는 내 말을 듣고 있니? (listen)

→ _____ to me?

3 그들은 TV를 보고 있지 않다. (watch)

→ _____ TV.

4 Jessica는 지금 햄버거를 먹고 있다. (have)

→ _____ a hamburger now.

5 Mark와 Eric은 잔디에 누워 있나요? (lie)

→ _____ on the grass?

6 그는 그 그림을 벽에 걸고 있지 않다. (put the picture)

→ _____ on the wall.

7 David가 복사를 하고 있나요? (make a copy)

→ _____

UNIT 1 조동사의 개념

Answers p. 31

A 어법 선택 괄호 안에서 알맞은 것을 고르시오.

1 She (can / cans) cook steak.

2 You must (be / are) home by 9.

3 You (take should / should take) the train.

4 Jim (can not / cannot) speak French well.

5 (Can you / You can) visit us next Sunday?

6 Should he (leave / leaves) the party now?

7 The baby (may be not / may not be) hungry.

8 My best friend may (give / gives) me a present.

9 You (should not / not should) tell her my secret.

10 We (don't must / must not) cross the street here.

B 문장 전환 주어진 문장을 괄호 안의 지시대로 바꿔 쓰시오.

1 You must take pictures here. (부정문)

→ You _____ pictures here.

2 I may go home now. (의문문)

→ _____ home now?

3 Katie can swim very fast. (의문문)

→ _____ very fast?

4 You should eat lots of fruit. (부정문)

→ You _____ lots of fruit.

5 He can understand these words. (부정문)

→ He _____ these words.

6 We should finish it by tomorrow. (의문문)

→ _____ it by tomorrow?

C 어법 수정 | 밑줄 친 부분이 맞으면 ○, 틀리면 바르게 고쳐 쓰시오.

1 He <u>musts get</u> home on time. → _____

2 <u>Can you climb</u> the tree? → _____

3 It <u>mayn't rain</u> tomorrow. → _____

4 You <u>should get</u> ready soon. → _____

5 I <u>can not remember</u> his name. → _____

6 Grace <u>can plays</u> the flute well. → _____

7 It <u>may is</u> cold this weekend. → _____

8 You <u>must bring</u> your passport. → _____

9 The image <u>not may be</u> real. → _____

10 <u>Do I should wear</u> my uniform? → _____

D 영작 | 우리말과 일치하도록 괄호 안의 말을 바르게 배열하시오.

1 Ron은 피아노를 칠 수 없다. (cannot, Ron, play)

→ _____ the piano.

2 너는 지금 잠자리에 들어야 한다. (you, to, must, go, bed)

→ _____ now.

3 그녀는 이탈리아에 가지 않을지도 모른다. (may, she, not, go)

→ _____ to Italy.

4 내가 파티에 그를 초대해야 하나요? (I, should, him, invite)

→ _____ to the party?

5 당신은 도서관에서 떠들어서는 안 된다. (not, make, must, you, noise)

→ _____ in the library.

6 당신은 당신의 가방을 가지고 있어야 한다. (keep, your, you, bag, should)

→ _____ with you.

7 너는 체스를 둘 수 있니? (chess, play, can, you)

→ _____

UNIT 02 can, may

Answers p. 31

A
어법 선택

괄호 안에서 알맞은 것을 고르시오.

1 Emma (may go / go may) to university.

2 I (can't / can not) sleep well at night.

3 James (may not / mays not) work here.

4 May I (ask / can ask) you some questions?

5 Take off your shoes. You (can / can't) wear them here.

6 My grandmother (cannot / are not able to) swim.

7 Laura (mayn't / may not) come here next week.

8 He will (can / be able to) come and see you tomorrow.

9 A Can you draw cartoons?   B Yes, I (can / can't).

10 She (is able to / can be able to) run 100 meters in 12 seconds.

B
문장 완성

괄호 안의 말을 이용하여 문장을 완성하시오. (필요시 형태를 바꿀 것)

1 You _____ my pencil. (use, can)

2 I _____ in the sea. (swim, can)

3 You _____ these cookies. (eat, may)

4 My brother _____ a bicycle. (not, can, ride)

5 _____ I _____ here for a moment? (sit, may)

6 Daniel _____ home. (not, may, be)

7 _____ to the concert with you? (I, go, can)

8 The teacher _____ my name. (know, may)

9 He _____ it by tomorrow. (not, can, finish)

10 _____ you _____ the volume? (turn down, can)

밑줄 친 부분을 어법에 맞게 고쳐 쓰시오.

1 You can open the window? → _____

2 May borrow I your cell phone? → _____

3 Mom cannot helps us right now. → _____

4 I am able not to hear very well. → _____

5 He mays not come to the party. → _____

6 We may able to travel to Mars. → _____

7 She will can find a new job soon. → _____

8 I will can't go camping this weekend. → _____

9 Mr. Jones doesn't may be busy today. → _____

10 Do you can speak any foreign languages? → _____

우리말과 일치하도록 괄호 안의 말을 바르게 배열하시오.

1 그는 또 늦을지도 모른다. (be, may, late, he)

→ _____ again.

2 우리는 그 호텔에서 강을 볼 수 있다. (can, the river, we, see)

→ _____ from the hotel.

3 당신은 그것을 믿지 않을지도 모른다. (it, not, may, believe)

→ You _____ .

4 Ted는 곧 그의 고양이를 찾을 수 있을 것이다. (will, find, his cat, be able to)

→ Ted _____ soon.

5 저에게 질문을 하셔도 돼요. (me, can, you, ask)

→ _____ questions.

6 나중에 전화해 줄래? (can, me, you, call)

→ _____ later?

7 사람들은 언젠가 그것을 즐길 수 있게 될 것이다. (will, it, people, enjoy, be able to)

→ _____ someday.

UNIT 3   must, have to, should

Answers p. 31

A 어법 선택   **괄호 안에서 알맞은 것을 고르시오.**

1   This bag (must / will must) be yours.

2   You (don't must / must not) lie.

3   We are late. We (must / has to) hurry.

4   A soldier (should / have to) wear a uniform.

5   She (must not / doesn't) have to make lunch for me.

6   You (must not / don't have) to worry about that.

7   He (will must / will have to) stay here until Sunday.

8   It's late. You (will must / should) call your mother.

9   My sister and I (didn't must / didn't have to) clean our room.

10   A baseball player (has to / don't have to) do lots of training.

B 문장 완성   **괄호 안의 말을 이용하여 문장을 완성하시오. (필요시 형태를 바꿀 것)**

1   He _____ every day. (exercise, must)

2   I _____ more vegetables. (eat, should)

3   Sue _____ early every day. (get up, have to)

4   We _____ on the grass. (not, must, sit)

5   He _____ to work on Fridays. (not, have to, go)

6   You _____ in the building. (not, smoke, must)

7   He _____ a doctor yesterday. (see, have to)

8   You _____ a bath every day. (not, have to, take)

9   Parents _____ their children alone. (not, should, leave)

10   I don't know. You _____ the teacher. (have to, will, ask)

C 어법 수정 　밑줄 친 부분을 어법에 맞게 고쳐 쓰시오.

1　She <u>musts finish</u> her homework.　→ _____

2　Jack <u>don't have to</u> run to school.　→ _____

3　He will <u>has to</u> study hard for the exam.　→ _____

4　My brother <u>have to</u> do the dishes every evening.　→ _____

5　It <u>must is</u> a very busy day for you.　→ _____

6　It's a secret. You <u>must don't</u> tell anyone.　→ _____

7　You will <u>must</u> pay for your lessons next month.　→ _____

8　You <u>don't should</u> play games after 9 p.m.　→ _____

9　I <u>have to</u> buy an umbrella yesterday. It rained a lot.　→ _____

10　There is no school today. I <u>have not to</u> get up early.　→ _____

D 영작 　우리말과 일치하도록 괄호 안의 말을 바르게 배열하시오.

1　우리는 계단에서 뛰어서는 안 된다. (should, run, we, not)

→ _____ on the stairs.

2　우리는 매일 자외선 차단제를 발라야 한다. (sunscreen, we, put on, should)

→ _____ every day.

3　나는 7시까지 집에 돌아와야 할 것이다. (come back, will, home, have to)

→ I _____ by 7.

4　여기서는 빨리 운전하면 안 된다. (not, must, fast, drive)

→ You _____ here.

5　David는 그 버스를 탈 필요가 없다. (doesn't, the bus, take, have to)

→ David _____ .

6　당신은 Jackson 씨임이 틀림없군요. (be, must, Mr. Jackson, you)

→ _____

7　그녀는 한국어를 배워야 했다. (Korean, she, learn, had to)

→ _____

UNIT 01 to부정사의 명사적 용법

Answers p. 32

A 개념 확인

밑줄 친 부분이 문장에서 어떤 역할을 하는지 ✔ 표시하시오.   주어: ㈜ 목적어: ㉥ 보어: ㉦

1   We decided to take a taxi.   ㈜ ㉥ ㉦

2   His plan is to return home.   ㈜ ㉥ ㉦

3   It is fun to speak English.   ㈜ ㉥ ㉦

4   He wants to cook for me.   ㈜ ㉥ ㉦

5   My goal is to write a novel.   ㈜ ㉥ ㉦

6   Elsa likes to spend time alone.   ㈜ ㉥ ㉦

7   It is important to believe in yourself.   ㈜ ㉥ ㉦

8   I hope to be a great musician.   ㈜ ㉥ ㉦

9   My dream is to travel around the world.   ㈜ ㉥ ㉦

10   My grandmother learned to use a computer.   ㈜ ㉥ ㉦

B 어법 선택

괄호 안에서 알맞은 것을 고르시오.

1   His goal is (win / to win) first prize.

2   She hopes (see / to see) him again.

3   It's important to (make / making) good friends.

4   He wants (solve / to solve) the problem.

5   My dream is (be / to be) a zookeeper.

6   We tried (to not eat / not to eat) fast food.

7   It is difficult (learn / to learn) a foreign language.

8   I chose (wear / to wear) my school uniform.

9   He expected (to pass / passing) the test.

10   It is a good idea (takes / to take) notes in class.

밑줄 친 부분에 유의하여 해석을 완성하시오.

1 Do you <u>want to play baseball</u>? 당신은 _____?

2 We agreed <u>to work together</u>. 우리는 _____ 동의했다.

3 I decided <u>not to leave today</u>. 나는 _____ 결정했다.

4 My goal was <u>to be a designer</u>. 나의 목표는 _____ 이었다.

5 I expected <u>to go with him</u>. 나는 _____ 기대했다.

6 It is dangerous <u>to swim in the sea</u>. _____ 위험하다.

밑줄 친 부분을 어법에 맞게 고쳐 쓰시오.

1 They plan <u>moving</u> to New York. → _____

2 Her plan is <u>build</u> her own house. → _____

3 To read books <u>are</u> good for you. → _____

4 <u>That</u> was easy to find your house. → _____

5 You have to promise <u>to don't laugh</u>. → _____

6 Sean and Ted are planning <u>traveling</u> to Turkey. → _____

우리말과 일치하도록 괄호 안의 말을 바르게 배열하시오.

1 나는 훌륭한 예술가가 되기를 바란다. (become, a good artist, to)

→ I hope _____.

2 그의 목표는 올림픽 금메달을 따는 것이다. (to, an, win, Olympic gold medal)

→ His goal is _____.

3 나는 오늘 테니스 연습을 하고 싶지 않다. (today, to, tennis, practice)

→ I don't want _____.

4 나는 요즘 승마를 배우고 있다. (these days, ride, to, a horse)

→ I'm learning _____.

5 우리의 국가적 영웅들을 기억하는 것은 중요하다. (remember, to, national heroes, our)

→ It is important _____.

UNIT 02 to부정사의 형용사적 용법과 부사적 용법

Answers p. 32

A 개념 확인

괄호 안에서 밑줄 친 to부정사의 의미로 알맞은 것을 고르시오.

1 I'm happy to meet you. (너를 만날 / 너를 만나서)

2 I have no time to wait. (기다릴 / 기다리기 위해)

3 We worked hard to help them. (그들을 도와서 / 그들을 돕기 위해)

4 Jason has lots of work to finish. (끝낼 / 끝내기 위해)

5 She listens to music to relax. (긴장을 풀기 위해 / 긴장을 푸는 것을)

6 He grew up to be a doctor. (의사가 될 / 의사가 되었다)

7 They left early to catch the train. (기차를 잡아탈 / 기차를 잡아타기 위해)

8 Do you have a dress to wear tonight? (오늘 밤에 입을 / 오늘 밤에 입기 위해)

9 He was sad to hear the news. (그 소식을 들어서 / 그 소식을 듣기 위해)

10 I went to the bookstore to buy some books. (책을 몇 권 사기 위해 / 책을 몇 권 살)

B 빈칸 완성

〈보기〉에서 알맞은 말을 골라 to부정사로 바꿔 빈칸에 쓰시오.

보기	study	turn on	help	park

1 I need somebody _____ me.

2 We found a place _____ our car.

3 He went to Paris _____ art history.

4 Press this button _____ the computer.

보기	write	wash	be	catch

5 Use soap _____ your hands.

6 He has some letters _____ .

7 She had to run _____ the bus.

8 My grandmother lived _____ 90 years old.

C 해석 완성

밑줄 친 부분에 유의하여 해석을 완성하시오.

1 She has homework <u>to do</u>.
그녀는 _____ 숙제가 있다.

2 We are glad <u>to see you again</u>.
우리는 _____ 기쁘다.

3 They came here <u>to look for gold</u>.
그들은 _____ 여기에 왔다.

4 He went to the park <u>to take pictures</u>.
그는 _____ 공원에 갔다.

5 I have enough money <u>to buy the cap</u>.
나는 _____ 충분한 돈이 있다.

D 어법 수정

밑줄 친 부분이 맞으면 ○, 틀리면 바르게 고쳐 쓰시오.

1 I called him to <u>said</u> goodbye.
→ _____

2 He didn't have a chance <u>visit</u> his parents.
→ _____

3 Ted was surprised <u>to find</u> a dog in his bed.
→ _____

4 We went to the bakery to <u>bought</u> some bread.
→ _____

5 She grew up to <u>being</u> a famous musician.
→ _____

E 영작

우리말과 일치하도록 괄호 안의 말을 바르게 배열하시오.

1 그는 책을 읽기 위해 전등을 켰다. (read, to, a book)

→ He turned on the light _____.

2 문을 열기 위해 이 열쇠를 사용해라. (to, the door, open)

→ Use this key _____.

3 이곳에는 볼 것이 아무것도 없다. (to, nothing, see, here)

→ There's _____.

4 그녀는 자라서 사진작가가 되었다. (to, a photographer, be)

→ She grew up _____.

5 나는 내 친구를 공항에서 만나서 기뻤다. (at, to, my friend, the airport, meet)

→ I was happy _____.

6 엄마는 나에게 영화 보러 갈 돈을 주셨다. (some money, to, the movies, go, to)

→ Mom gave me _____.

UNIT 3 동명사

Answers p. 32

A 개념 확인

밑줄 친 부분이 문장에서 어떤 역할을 하는지 ✔ 표시하시오.

주어: ㉧ 목적어: ㉤ 보어: ㉫

1 My job is <u>drawing pictures</u>. ㉧ ㉤ ㉫

2 <u>Swimming</u> is difficult for me. ㉧ ㉤ ㉫

3 I finished <u>cleaning my room</u>. ㉧ ㉤ ㉫

4 His hobby is <u>taking bike trips</u>. ㉧ ㉤ ㉫

5 We enjoyed <u>playing tennis together</u>. ㉧ ㉤ ㉫

6 <u>Walking in the rain</u> can be exciting. ㉧ ㉤ ㉫

7 My favorite exercise is <u>jogging in the morning</u>. ㉧ ㉤ ㉫

8 Do you mind <u>closing the door</u>? ㉧ ㉤ ㉫

9 <u>Helping other people</u> is important. ㉧ ㉤ ㉫

10 Could you please stop <u>making noise</u>? ㉧ ㉤ ㉫

B 빈칸 완성

괄호 안에 주어진 말을 동명사로 바꿔 빈칸에 쓰시오.

1 _____ English is not easy. (learn)

2 Please stop _____ in class. (talk)

3 He finished _____ the novel. (read)

4 She enjoys _____ in winter. (ski)

5 I'll go _____ this weekend. (shop)

6 You should avoid _____ at night. (eat)

7 _____ in this weather is not safe. (drive)

8 My hobby is _____ to music. (listen)

9 My father quit _____ last year. (smoke)

10 How about _____ at the bus stop? (meet)

밑줄 친 부분이 맞으면 ○, 틀리면 바르게 고쳐 쓰시오.

1 His job is <u>write</u> novels. → _____

2 I finished <u>to paint</u> the wall. → _____

3 She gave up <u>eat</u> chocolate. → _____

4 <u>Swim</u> is his favorite activity. → _____

5 She practices <u>to sing</u> by herself. → _____

6 Watching movies <u>are</u> my hobby. → _____

7 The baby didn't stop <u>cry</u>. → _____

8 Rachel went <u>fishing</u> last weekend. → _____

9 I don't feel like <u>to talk</u> about it now. → _____

10 He avoided <u>answering</u> my question. → _____

우리말과 일치하도록 괄호 안의 말을 바르게 배열하시오.

1 나는 숙제를 하느라 바쁘다. (doing, busy, homework, my)

→ I'm _____ .

2 저는 창문을 여는 것을 개의치 않습니다. (mind, the window, opening)

→ I don't _____ .

3 나의 취미는 야구 경기를 보는 것이다. (watching, games, baseball, is)

→ My hobby _____ .

4 너는 가족과 함께 하이킹하는 것을 즐기니? (hiking, family, with, your, enjoy)

→ Do you _____ ?

5 이 책을 다 읽는 것은 쉽지 않았다. (this book, reading, finish)

→ It wasn't easy to _____ .

6 너의 오래된 휴대전화를 파는 게 어때? (your, selling, cell phone, old)

→ What about _____ ?

7 너는 나쁜 일에 대해 생각하는 것을 멈춰야 한다. (about, bad things, thinking, stop)

→ You must _____ .

UNIT 01

who, whom, whose, what, which

Answers p. 33

A 어법 선택

괄호 안에서 알맞은 것을 고르시오.

1   (What / Who) sent you the letter?

2   (Who / Whose) does Jack like?

3   (Whom / Whose) cell phone is this?

4   (Who / Whom) broke the window?

5   (Who / Whose) are you waiting for?

6   (Who / What) did Dan forget to do?

7   (Whose / Who) name should I write?

8   (Who / What) happened to your brother?

9   (Which / Who) train goes to Busan?

10   (What color / Whose color) is your backpack?

B 대화 완성

의문문에 알맞은 대답을 골라 선으로 연결하시오.

1   Who likes apples?   · ⓐ They are my sister's.

2   Whose shoes are they?   · ⓑ Some milk.

3   What did they buy at the store?   · ⓒ Jason does.

4   Who does Paul love?   · ⓐ Red.

5   What did you see last night?   · ⓑ He loves Rachel.

6   Which color do you like better, blue or red? ·   · ⓒ A superhero movie.

7   Whose car is this?   · ⓐ Baseball.

8   Who cleans the bathroom?   · ⓑ It's mine.

9   What is your favorite sport?   · ⓒ My father does.

밑줄 친 부분을 어법에 맞게 고쳐 쓰시오.

1 Who idea is this? → _____

2 What you did say? → _____

3 Who did tell you that? → _____

4 Whose do you want to meet? → _____

5 What you are looking for? → _____

6 Who pen will you borrow? → _____

7 Who does want to eat pizza? → _____

8 Whose books are he carrying? → _____

9 Who you did call to fix your bicycle? → _____

10 Whom do you like better, chicken or beef? → _____

D

영작

우리말과 일치하도록 괄호 안의 말을 바르게 배열하시오.

1 이것과 저것 중 어떤 방이 더 큰가요? (larger, room, which, is)

→ _____, this one or that one?

2 그 남자는 그녀에게 무엇을 이야기하고 있는가? (is, what, telling, the man)

→ _____ her?

3 누가 너에게 이 코트를 사 주었니? (this coat, who, bought)

→ _____ for you?

4 누가 이 책을 썼나요? (wrote, this book, who)

→ _____

5 너는 누구의 노트북을 빌렸니? (did, whose, borrow, laptop, you)

→ _____

6 그 아이스크림은 무슨 맛인가요? (flavor, what, the ice cream, is)

→ _____

7 당신은 어느 동아리에 가입하고 싶습니까? (club, join, do, want, you, which, to)

→ _____

where, when, why, how

Answers p. 33

A 어법 선택

괄호 안에서 알맞은 것을 고르시오.

1 A (Where / When) does she live? B She lives near here.

2 A (How / When) did he arrive? B An hour ago.

3 A (Why / How) did you go there? B To meet my friend.

4 A (When / How) do you feel? B I feel great.

5 A (Where / When) did you get it? B At a gift shop.

6 A (When / Why) is the bus late? B Because of a traffic jam.

B 빈칸 완성

빈칸에 알맞은 말을 〈보기〉에서 골라 쓰시오.

| 보기 | How old | How tall | How often | How far |
| | How long | How many | How much | |

1 A _____ is Amy?

   B She is 150 centimeters tall.

2 A _____ is your dog?

   B Three years old.

3 A _____ will you stay in this town?

   B For four days.

4 A _____ sisters do you have?

   B Two.

5 A _____ does he come here?

   B Twice a week.

6 A _____ is the concert ticket?

   B It's 50 dollars.

7 A _____ is the supermarket from here?

   B It's a five-minute walk from here.

밑줄 친 부분을 어법에 맞게 고쳐 쓰시오.

1 A <u>What old</u> is your younger sister? B Twelve. → _____

2 A <u>When often</u> does the bus come? B Every hour.

→ _____

3 A <u>How much</u> people are waiting in line? B Fifty. → _____

4 A <u>When</u> can I find the post office? B You can find one on the corner.

→ _____

5 A <u>Why</u> do you spend your free time? B I usually read books.

→ _____

6 A <u>When</u> does he get up so early? B Because he jogs in the morning.

→ _____

7 A <u>How many</u> coffee does she drink? B Two cups a day.

→ _____

우리말과 일치하도록 괄호 안의 말을 바르게 배열하시오.

1 당신은 어디에서 왔습니까? (from, where, you, are)

→ _____

2 우리는 언제 게임을 할 수 있나요? (we, games, when, play, can)

→ _____

3 당신은 왜 나에게 거짓말을 했습니까? (to me, did, lie, why, you)

→ _____

4 그 건물은 얼마나 높습니까? (the building, tall, is, how)

→ _____

5 영화가 언제 시작하나요? (when, start, does, the movie)

→ _____

6 당신은 얼마나 많은 우유를 마십니까? (do, how much, drink, you, milk)

→ _____

7 당신은 얼마나 많은 입장권을 원합니까? (tickets, you, how many, do, want)

→ _____

UNIT 01 명령문, Let's ~, There is/are ~

Answers p. 34

A
어법 선택

괄호 안에서 알맞은 것을 고르시오.

1 Let's (go / goes) home together.

2 Jim, (cleans / clean) your room now.

3 (Be / Do) careful with the glass.

4 There (is / are) a bird in the tree.

5 (Be not / Don't be) nervous.

6 (Not / Don't) close the window.

7 Let's (not / don't) go swimming.

8 (Turn / Turning) left at the corner.

9 (Is / Are) there four cups on the table?

10 It's too expensive. (Buy not / Don't buy) it.

B
문장 완성

우리말과 일치하도록 괄호 안의 말을 이용하여 문장을 완성하시오.

1 Jack을 초대하자. (invite)

→ _____ Jack.

2 이 펜을 Alice에게 줘. (give)

→ _____ this pen to Alice.

3 이 근처에는 세 개의 은행이 있다. (there, bank)

→ _____ near here.

4 그 버스를 타지 말자. (not, take)

→ _____ the bus.

5 피아노 연주를 멈추지 마라. (stop)

→ _____ playing the piano.

6 그 병에는 우유가 조금 있었다. (there, some milk)

→ _____ in the bottle.

밑줄 친 부분을 어법에 맞게 고쳐 쓰시오.

1 Please <u>being</u> quiet.　　　　　　　　　　　→ _____

2 Let's <u>plays</u> basketball.　　　　　　　　　→ _____

3 <u>Takes</u> your umbrella.　　　　　　　　　　→ _____

4 <u>Watch not</u> too much TV.　　　　　　　　→ _____

5 There <u>are</u> someone at the door.　　　　→ _____

6 Let's <u>going</u> to see a movie.　　　　　　→ _____

7 <u>Is</u> there any apples in the basket?　　→ _____

8 There <u>was</u> only five people on the bus.　→ _____

9 Let's <u>tell not</u> her about our problems.　→ _____

10 There is <u>big houses</u> near the beach.　→ _____

우리말과 일치하도록 괄호 안의 말을 바르게 배열하시오.

1 식사 후에 이를 닦으시오. (teeth, your, brush)

→ _____ after meals.

2 동물원에 많은 사람들이 있었다. (many, were, there, people)

→ _____ at the zoo.

3 여기에서 사진을 찍지 마시오. (do, photos, take, not)

→ _____ here.

4 그 마을에 어린 소년이 한 명 있었다. (little, a, was, boy, there)

→ _____ in the village.

5 극장 안에 빈 자리가 있습니까? (any, there, empty seats, are)

→ _____ in the theater?

6 Ted를 기다리자. (wait, let's, Ted, for)

→ _____

7 소음을 만들지 말자. (not, make, let's, noise)

→ _____

UNIT 2 감탄문, 부가의문문

Answers p. 34

A
어법 선택

괄호 안에서 알맞은 것을 고르시오.

1 (What / How) fast he runs!

2 (What / How) a beautiful flower it is!

3 You did your best, (didn't / aren't) you?

4 Alice can't use chopsticks, (does / can) she?

5 It snowed a lot in Seoul, (didn't / wasn't) it?

6 What (lovely people / a lovely people) they are!

7 The movie was exciting, (weren't / wasn't) it?

8 They went out to eat yesterday, (did / didn't) they?

9 Mike gets up early in the morning, (doesn't / don't) he?

10 Annie is not going to work with them, (is / isn't) she?

B
문장 완성

괄호 안의 말을 이용하여 감탄문을 완성하시오.

1 You are very clever. (how)

→ _____ you are!

2 It is a very interesting story. (what)

→ _____ it is!

3 The boy is very polite. (how)

→ _____ the boy is!

4 That is a very dangerous road. (what)

→ _____ that is!

5 They are very beautiful stars. (what)

→ _____ they are!

밑줄 친 부분이 맞으면 ○, 틀리면 바르게 고쳐 쓰시오.

1 What <u>cute dog</u> it is! → _____

2 She's not late, <u>does she</u>? → _____

3 <u>How a handsome</u> he is! → _____

4 You're doing well, <u>weren't you</u>? → _____

5 What a good student <u>is she</u>! → _____

6 You don't want to stay here, <u>will you</u>? → _____

7 He turned off the light, <u>didn't he</u>? → _____

8 What <u>a great doctors</u> she is! → _____

9 You played tennis with Alex, <u>don't you</u>? → _____

10 Her uncle can cook very well, <u>can't he</u>? → _____

우리말과 일치하도록 괄호 안의 말을 바르게 배열하시오.

1 Daniel은 콘서트를 열 거야, 그렇지 않니? (isn't, a concert, he, hold)

→ Daniel is going to _____ ?

2 그것은 정말 쉬운 질문이구나! (it, an, is, what, question, easy)

→ _____

3 너 잠을 잘 못 잤구나, 그렇지? (you, well, didn't, you, sleep, did)

→ _____

4 날씨가 정말 춥구나! (the, cold, is, weather, how)

→ _____

5 너의 부모님은 수영을 못하시지, 그렇지? (can't, swim, they, can, your parents)

→ _____

6 이것은 참 멋진 그림이구나! (is, this, picture, a, what, nice)

→ _____

7 Bella는 Justin을 좋아해, 그렇지 않니? (she, Bella, doesn't, likes, Justin)

→ _____

UNIT 01 목적어가 두 개 있는 문장

Answers p. 35

A 어법 선택

괄호 안에서 알맞은 것을 고르시오.

1 Mr. Kim taught (math us / us math).

2 My sister gave her shoes (me / to me).

3 He made pancakes (to / for) his children.

4 Dad bought (me a computer / a computer me).

5 He showed (me to his blog / his blog to me).

6 Daniel sent a postcard (Monica / to Monica).

7 She told the news (to / for) a lot of people.

8 I bought some flowers (to / for) my grandparents.

9 They wrote (their parents / to their parents) long letters.

10 Stella sent her boyfriend (a text message / to a text message).

B 문장 완성

우리말과 일치하도록 괄호 안의 말을 이용하여 문장을 완성하시오. (필요시 단어를 추가할 것)

1 그녀는 우리에게 피자를 요리해 줬다. (us, cook)

→ She _____ pizza _____ .

2 나의 조부모님께서 나에게 새 자전거를 사 주셨다. (me, buy)

→ My grandparents _____ a new bicycle.

3 우리 선생님은 가끔 우리에게 흥미로운 이야기들을 해 주신다. (us, tell)

→ Our teacher sometimes _____ interesting stories.

4 네가 Mark에게 편지를 보냈니? (Mark, send)

→ Did you _____ a letter _____ ?

5 집에 오는 길에 달걀 좀 사다 줘. (me, get)

→ Please _____ some eggs on your way home.

6 Simon은 여동생에게 샌드위치를 만들어 주었다. (his sister, make)

→ Simon _____ sandwiches _____ .

C 어법 수정

밑줄 친 부분이 맞으면 ○, 틀리면 바르게 고쳐 쓰시오.

1 I will give to you a call later. → _____

2 I showed them famous paintings. → _____

3 My father bought a puppy to me. → _____

4 My brother told the news to me. → _____

5 David made for her a paper flower. → _____

6 When did you send it to Lucy? → _____

7 They got for him many presents. → _____

8 He cooked spaghetti his brother. → _____

9 She will ask to you some questions. → _____

10 Mr. Lee taught their the history of Korea. → _____

D 영작

우리말과 일치하도록 괄호 안의 말을 바르게 배열하시오.

1 그는 나에게 자신의 비밀을 말해 주었다. (his, me, told, secret)

→ He _____.

2 내가 너에게 아침을 만들어 줄게. (you, will, breakfast, make)

→ I _____.

3 Daisy는 나에게 소고기 수프를 요리해 주었다. (beef soup, for, cooked, me)

→ Daisy _____.

4 그 친절한 여성이 우리에게 길을 알려줬다. (us, showed, the way)

→ The kind lady _____.

5 Greg는 나에게 내 우산을 가져다 주었다. (for, me, got, my umbrella)

→ Greg _____.

6 당신은 언제 나에게 당신의 책을 빌려줄 건가요? (me, book, lend, your)

→ When will you _____?

7 그는 나에게 아무것도 묻지 않았다. (ask, me, didn't, anything, he)

→ _____

보어가 있는 문장

Answers p. 35

A
어법 선택

괄호 안에서 알맞은 것을 고르시오.

1 She looks (sad / sadly).

2 I feel (sick / like sick) today.

3 The steak smells (good / well).

4 Do you still feel (hungry / hungrily)?

5 He looks like (tired / a doctor).

6 That sounds (interesting / interestingly).

7 Dad's pasta tasted (salt / salty).

8 This scarf keeps me (warm / warmly).

9 This music always makes me (happy / happiness).

10 The picture made Van Gogh (famous / famously).

B
빈칸 완성

〈보기〉에서 동사를 골라 빈칸에 알맞은 형태로 바꿔 쓰시오.

보기	look	feel	keep	sound

1 A What do you think of this dress?

   B It _____ good on you.

2 A How about going out for Mexican food tonight?

   B That _____ like a good idea.

3 A Can you recommend a good way to exercise?

   B Yoga can _____ you healthy.

4 A You look down. What's wrong?

   B I _____ really tired these days. I can't sleep at night.

밑줄 친 부분이 맞으면 ○, 틀리면 바르게 고쳐 쓰시오.

1 They felt <u>proudly</u>. → _____

2 That sounds <u>lovely</u>. → _____

3 This pizza smells <u>badly</u>. → _____

4 The actor looks <u>young</u>. → _____

5 This song made <u>her</u> a superstar. → _____

6 She <u>sounds a bird</u>. → _____

7 The villagers looked very <u>friendly</u>. → _____

8 The watermelon tasted <u>like fresh</u>. → _____

9 Why did you name <u>Bolt your dog</u>? → _____

10 My little brother made me <u>angrily</u>. → _____

우리말과 일치하도록 괄호 안의 말을 바르게 배열하시오.

1 그 아이디어는 완벽하게 들렸다. (sounded, the idea, perfect)

→ _____

2 공기가 상쾌한 냄새가 난다. (fresh, smells, the air)

→ _____

3 그녀의 부모님은 그녀를 아기라고 부른다. (call, a baby, her parents, her)

→ _____

4 그는 왜 심각해 보이니? (does, serious, why, look, he)

→ _____

5 이 영화는 그녀를 백만장자로 만들었다. (this film, a millionaire, her, made)

→ _____

6 너는 손을 깨끗이 유지해야 한다. (your hands, clean, you, keep, should)

→ _____

7 그 대회는 그 피아니스트를 유명하게 만들었다. (the contest, famous, the pianist, made)

→ _____

UNIT 01 형용사

Answers p. 36

A
어법 선택

괄호 안에서 알맞은 것을 고르시오.

1 I have (a little / a few) problems.

2 Would you like (some / any) milk?

3 She bought (a few / a little) potatoes.

4 They didn't buy (any / some) clothes.

5 There was (few / little) water in the bottle.

6 He wants (something special / special something).

7 Ken has (much / a lot of) friends, doesn't he?

8 She spends too (much / many) money on books.

9 There isn't (new anything / anything new) on the menu.

10 There were (few / little) children in the playground.

B
빈칸 완성

우리말과 일치하도록 빈칸에 알맞은 말을 〈보기〉에서 골라 쓰시오.

보기	any	some	much	many	a few	few	little

1 커피 마실래?

→ Do you want _____ coffee?

2 나는 수미에게서 책 몇 권을 빌렸다.

→ I borrowed _____ books from Sumi.

3 지난겨울에는 눈이 많이 오지 않았다.

→ We didn't have _____ snow last winter.

4 너는 남자형제나 여자형제가 있니?

→ Do you have _____ brothers or sisters?

5 해변에는 사람이 거의 없었다.

→ There were _____ people at the beach.

밑줄 친 부분이 맞으면 ○, 틀리면 바르게 고쳐 쓰시오.

1 I ate a cake delicious. → _____

2 She bought much oranges. → _____

3 Do you have some ideas? → _____

4 Put a few salt in the soup. → _____

5 There are lots of places to visit in Seoul. → _____

6 He doesn't have any money. → _____

7 We want to meet new someone. → _____

8 There is a lot of food on the table. → _____

9 I have few time to play with my friends. → _____

10 Maya drinks some coffee every morning. → _____

우리말과 일치하도록 괄호 안의 말을 바르게 배열하시오.

1 나는 뭔가 다른 것을 찾고 있다. (different, looking for, something)

→ I'm _____.

2 사람들이 너무 많은 물을 낭비한다. (much, waste, so, water)

→ People_____.

3 나는 몇 분 후에 돌아올 것이다. (be, a few, back, minutes, in)

→ I'll _____.

4 거리에 사람이 거의 없다. (people, there, few, are)

→ _____ on the street.

5 많은 책을 읽는 것은 당신에게 좋다. (reading, books, is, lots of, good)

→ _____ for you.

6 제게 간식 사 먹을 돈을 좀 주세요. (some, for, give, a snack, me, money)

→ Please _____.

7 나는 약간의 설탕이 필요하다. (sugar, I, a little, need)

→ _____

UNIT 2 부사

Answers p. 36

A
어법 선택

괄호 안에서 알맞은 것을 고르시오.

1 This is a (slow / slowly) train.

2 It is raining (heavy / heavily).

3 The dog is running (fast / fastly).

4 David is a (quick / quickly) walker.

5 We found his house (easy / easily).

6 I tried (hard / hardly) to pass the exam.

7 She speaks English (perfect / perfectly).

8 He (always has / has always) dinner at 7.

9 I'm so sleepy. I can (hard / hardly) keep my eyes open.

10 Jessica arrived (late / lately), so we missed our train.

B
문장 완성

괄호 안의 말을 알맞은 위치에 넣어 문장을 다시 쓰시오.

1 He walks to school. (usually)

→ _____

2 We should leave our house. (early)

→ _____

3 Ron was tired after work. (really)

→ _____

4 He wears glasses in class. (always)

→ _____

5 He rides a skateboard well. (very)

→ _____

6 I will lose my smartphone again. (never)

→ _____

C	밑줄 친 부분이 맞으면 ○, 틀리면 바르게 고쳐 쓰시오.

어법 수정

1 Mark swims <u>fastly</u>. → _____

2 I got up <u>early</u> this morning. → _____

3 I <u>never will</u> do that again. → _____

4 The car was very <u>expensively</u>. → _____

5 He came home <u>lately</u> last night. → _____

6 George and his wife lived <u>happyly</u>. → _____

7 Turtles can live <u>a long very time</u>. → _____

8 My sister washed the cups <u>careful</u>. → _____

9 We <u>sometimes talk</u> about baseball games. → _____

10 Ann studied <u>hardly</u>, so she got a good grade. → _____

D	우리말과 일치하도록 괄호 안의 말을 바르게 배열하시오.

영작

1 천천히 정확하게 말씀해 주세요. (slowly, and, speak, clearly)

→ Please _____ .

2 Mia는 종종 자신의 일에 대해 이야기한다. (Mia, talks, often)

→ _____ about her work.

3 그들은 새로운 것을 쉽게 배운다. (new, easily, things)

→ They learn _____ .

4 John은 최근에 매우 피곤해 보인다. (lately, looks, tired, very)

→ John _____ .

5 나의 남동생은 가끔 나에게 이상한 질문을 한다. (sometimes, my brother, asks, me)

→ _____ strange questions.

6 너는 왜 그렇게 빨리 먹니? (fast, do, why, so, you, eat)

→ _____

7 우리는 그 시험을 위해 열심히 공부했다. (the test, we, hard, for, studied)

→ _____

Answers p. 36

UNIT 3 비교

A
어법 선택

괄호 안에서 알맞은 것을 고르시오.

1 He is (strong / stronger) than Peter.

2 You are (shorter / shortest) than my sister.

3 This is the (best / goodest) room in the hotel.

4 My new car is (faster / the faster) than my old one.

5 Ted is (funniest / the funniest) boy in my class.

6 The sun is (brighter / brightest) than the moon.

7 His brother works (harder / hardest) than he does.

8 Alex is (younger / the youngest) in his family.

9 This is the (longer / longest) river in the world.

10 That flower is (beautifuler / more beautiful) than this one.

B
빈칸 완성

괄호 안의 단어를 비교급이나 최상급으로 바꿔 빈칸에 쓰시오.

1 Your soup is _____ than mine. (hot)

2 Ann is _____ girl in her class. (smart)

3 Today is _____ day of the year. (cold)

4 She is _____ than her husband. (young)

5 It is _____ program these days. (popular)

6 His car is _____ than mine. (comfortable)

7 My ice cream melted _____ than yours did. (quickly)

8 Mt. Everest is _____ mountain in the world. (high)

9 My suitcase was _____ of them all. (heavy)

10 This black shirt is _____ than that red one. (expensive)

밑줄 친 부분을 어법에 맞게 고쳐 쓰시오.

1 Her voice is <u>loud</u> than mine. → _____

2 I got up earlier <u>of</u> my mother did. → _____

3 Jack drives <u>carefully</u> than I do. → _____

4 My bike is cheaper than <u>you</u>. → _____

5 Alice is <u>oldest</u> of the three girls. → _____

6 July was <u>the hotest</u> month of the year. → _____

7 He is <u>the more</u> famous writer in Korea. → _____

8 You can do it <u>more well</u> than anyone does. → _____

9 This is <u>the baddest</u> restaurant in town. → _____

10 The days are <u>the shortest</u> than the nights during winter. → _____

우리말과 일치하도록 괄호 안의 말을 바르게 배열하시오.

1 어제 날씨보다 오늘 날씨가 더 좋다. (yesterday's, better, than)

→ Today's weather is _____ .

2 내 신발이 너의 것보다 더 비싸다. (yours, expensive, more, than)

→ My shoes are _____ .

3 토론토는 캐나다에서 가장 큰 도시이다. (in, biggest, the, city, Canada)

→ Toronto is _____ .

4 Jim은 우리 반에서 가장 잘생긴 소년이다. (most, in, my, handsome, the, boy, class)

→ Jim is _____ .

5 이것이 세 개 중에 가장 좋은 스마트폰이다. (of, smartphone, best, the, the three)

→ This is _____ .

6 야구가 축구보다 더 재미있다. (soccer, more, than, interesting, is, baseball)

→ _____

7 그것은 올해 최악의 영화이다. (the year, worst, of, that, is, movie, the)

→ _____

UNIT 1 접속사

Answers p. 37

A 어법 선택

괄호 안에서 알맞은 것을 고르시오.

1 She invited Julie (and / but) Harry.

2 Can you speak English (or / but) French?

3 We hope (if / that) you have a great time.

4 He was poor (that / when) he was young.

5 This dress is ugly (or / but) expensive.

6 Please call me (when / because) you are ready.

7 I went home (that / because) the movie was boring.

8 I think (that / because) I should get some rest.

9 We will stay home if it (rains / will rain) tomorrow.

10 Leo can't go with us (that / because) he is too busy.

B 빈칸 완성

빈칸에 알맞은 말을 〈보기〉에서 골라 쓰시오.

보기	and	but	or

1 He is tall _____ strong.

2 Which is bigger, an elephant _____ a cow?

3 I like her, _____ she doesn't like me.

보기	that	because	if

4 I hope _____ you will win the match.

5 I will buy you a doll _____ I find a cute one.

6 She cleaned her room _____ it was too dirty.

〈보기〉에서 알맞은 말을 골라 문장을 완성하시오.

| 보기 | it was cold | they weren't home | my sister bought a card |
| | she got up early | we missed the bus | he has time tomorrow |

1 She was tired, but _____.

2 Jacob will visit me if _____.

3 I put on my gloves because _____.

4 Fortunately, the fire started when _____.

5 I made a cake for my mother, and _____.

6 We were late because _____.

우리말과 일치하도록 괄호 안의 말을 바르게 배열하시오.

1 나는 네가 그것을 할 수 있다고 믿어. (that, it, can, you, do)

→ I believe _____.

2 당신이 도움이 필요하다면 내가 도울게요. (you, if, help, need)

→ I'll help you _____.

3 나는 네가 시험에 통과했다는 것을 들었다. (the exam, that, passed, you)

→ I heard _____.

4 그는 빨리 달렸지만 경주에서 이기지 못했다. (but, didn't, he, the race, win)

→ He ran fast, _____.

5 그녀는 이탈리아에 있을 때 나에게 편지를 썼다. (she, when, in Italy, was)

→ She wrote a letter to me _____.

6 너는 나와 같이 가도 되고 여기서 기다려도 된다. (come, wait, or, here, with me)

→ You can _____.

7 집에 음식이 없어서 우리는 슈퍼마켓에 갔다. (at home, there, because, no, was, food)

→ We went to the supermarket _____.

UNIT 02 위치·장소를 나타내는 전치사

Answers p. 37

A 어법 선택

괄호 안에서 알맞은 것을 고르시오.

1 My sister sat (on / behind) the floor.

2 What letter is (between / behind) A and C?

3 Andy is (between / in front of) his car.

4 I was standing (at / behind) a tall woman.

5 The box is (between / next to) the basket.

6 There are many cars (in / under) the bridge.

7 What time did you arrive (on / at) the airport?

8 The picture is hanging (on / behind) the wall.

9 There is a famous restaurant (at / in) this building.

10 There are many beautiful places (in / at) Paris.

B 빈칸 완성

빈칸에 알맞은 말을 〈보기〉에서 골라 쓰시오.

보기	in	on	at	under

1 Get off _____ the next stop.

2 The boy is hiding _____ the table.

3 The music room is _____ the third floor.

4 We saw a famous musical _____ New York.

보기	behind	front	next	between

5 There is a tall tree in _____ of the café.

6 What is _____ the bank and the library?

7 There is a big bear _____ the hunter.

8 The police station is _____ to the museum.

밑줄 친 부분을 어법에 맞게 고쳐 쓰시오.

1 He is studying <u>at</u> his room. → _____

2 The car is <u>behind of</u> the house. → _____

3 Please put the spoons <u>in</u> the table. → _____

4 Please turn right <u>in</u> the corner. → _____

5 There were no students <u>on</u> the classroom. → _____

6 I waited for Lisa <u>under</u> the bus stop. → _____

7 You can find a bank <u>next</u> the supermarket. → _____

8 We had a great time <u>on</u> Spain last summer. → _____

9 Let's meet at 9 <u>in front</u> the theater. → _____

10 Our cat sleeps between my father <u>or</u> my mother. → _____

우리말과 일치하도록 괄호 안의 말을 바르게 배열하시오.

1 나는 지하철역에서 Jack을 만났다. (subway station, at, the)

→ I met Jack _____.

2 그들은 나무 아래에서 휴식을 취했다. (under, took, the tree, a break)

→ They _____.

3 방 안에 침대가 있다. (the room, is, a bed, in)

→ There _____.

4 주차장은 건물 뒤에 있다. (is, the building, behind)

→ The parking lot _____.

5 James는 Ann과 Ted 사이에 앉아 있다. (and, between, Ann, Ted)

→ James is sitting _____.

6 펜 두 개가 책상 위에 있다. (on, two, the desk, pens, are)

→ _____

7 너의 자전거는 정문 앞에 있다. (is, your bicycle, the gate, in front of)

→ _____

UNIT 3 시간을 나타내는 전치사, 그 밖의 전치사

Answers p. 37

A 어법 선택

괄호 안에서 알맞은 것을 고르시오.

1 I'll be home (on / in) Sunday.

2 They bought this house (at / in) 2010.

3 Did you come here (by / with) bus?

4 We usually have lunch (on / at) noon.

5 The class starts (on / in) September 1.

6 He cut the watermelon (by / with) a knife.

7 The mountain is beautiful (at / in) autumn.

8 I lived in London (for / during) three years.

9 She likes listening to music (in / on) the morning.

10 There was a heavy snowfall (for / during) the night. *snowfall 강설 (눈이 오는 것)

B 빈칸 완성

빈칸에 알맞은 말을 〈보기〉에서 골라 쓰시오.

보기	at	on	in

1 The concert ends _____ 9:30.

2 I came to Korea _____ 2002.

3 He sent me a card _____ my birthday.

보기	during	for	by	with

4 They went to the airport _____ taxi.

5 I play tennis _____ an hour every day.

6 Kelly can't eat rice _____ chopsticks.

7 She lost her bag _____ the trip.

C 어법 수정

밑줄 친 부분이 맞으면 ○, 틀리면 바르게 고쳐 쓰시오.

1 He went to Japan on plane. → _____

2 We have a lot of rain in summer. → _____

3 This street is very dark in night. → _____

4 Amy's birthday is in December 4. → _____

5 He entered middle school on 2022. → _____

6 Emily cut her hair with scissors. → _____

7 David arrived in Las Vegas in Monday. → _____

8 The first train leaves on 7 every day. → _____

9 I practiced swimming during two hours. → _____

10 Do you get presents in Children's Day? → _____

D 영작

우리말과 일치하도록 괄호 안의 말을 바르게 배열하시오.

1 나는 Jason을 30분 동안 기다렸다. (for, waited, 30 minutes, for Jason)

→ I _____.

2 Eric은 자신의 보고서를 이메일로 보냈다. (by, report, email, his, sent)

→ Eric _____.

3 그녀는 휴가 동안에 뉴욕을 방문했다. (visited, during, New York, her vacation)

→ She _____.

4 이 펜으로 당신의 이름을 써주세요. (write, this pen, your name, with)

→ Please _____.

5 기차로 한 시간 정도 걸린다. (an hour, about, train, by)

→ It takes _____.

6 그는 수요일마다 바이올린 레슨을 받는다. (a violin lesson, Wednesdays, takes, on)

→ He _____.

7 그 슈퍼마켓은 오후 10시에 닫는다. (at, closes, the supermarket, 10 p.m.)

→ _____

중학 영문법

클리어.

Level 1

WORKBOOK